Adobe
Photoshop CC
and Lightroom CC
for Photographers

Second Edition

CLASSROOM IN A BOOK®
The official training workbook from Adobe

RC Concepcion

Adobe® Photoshop® CC and Lightroom® CC for Photographers Classroom in a Book®, Second Edition

Adobe Press is an imprint of Pearson Education, Inc. For the latest on Adobe Press books, go to www.adobepress. com. To report errors, please send a note to errata@peachpit.com. For information regarding permissions, request forms, and the appropriate contacts within the Pearson Education Global Rights & Permissions department, please visit www.pearsoned.com/permissions/.

Cover Illustration: Christopher Wilson Photography

ISBN-13:   978-0-13-549507-0

ISBN-10:   0-13-549507-5

WHERE ARE THE LESSON FILES?

Purchase of this Classroom in a Book in any format gives you access to the lesson files you'll need to complete the exercises in the book.

You'll find the files you need on your **Account** page at peachpit.com on the **Registered Products** tab.

1 Go to www.peachpit.com/register.

2 Sign in or create a new account.

3 Enter the ISBN: **9780135495070**.

4 Answer the questions as proof of purchase.

5 The lesson files can be accessed through the Registered Products tab on your Account page.

6 Click the Access Bonus Content link below the title of your product to proceed to the download page. Click the lesson file links to download them to your computer.

CONTENTS

2   ORGANIZING YOUR PHOTOS INTO LIGHTROOM COLLECTIONS

3   USING LIGHTROOM'S DEVELOP MODULE FOR GLOBAL ADJUSTMENTS

**4 USING LIGHTROOM'S DEVELOP MODULE FOR LOCAL
AND CREATIVE ADJUSTMENTS**

5 FIXING COMMON PHOTOGRAPHY PROBLEMS

6 LIGHTROOM–PHOTOSHOP ROUNDTRIP WORKFLOW

7 LIGHTROOM TO PHOTOSHOP FOR SELECTING AND MASKING

8 LIGHTROOM TO PHOTOSHOP FOR RETOUCHING

9 LIGHTROOM TO PHOTOSHOP FOR SPECIAL EFFECTS

10 LIGHTROOM TO PHOTOSHOP FOR COMBINING PHOTOS

11 EXPORTING AND SHOWING OFF YOUR WORK

GETTING STARTED

An infinite amount of stuff that has nothing to do with pressing the shutter button goes into the making of a picture. Truth be told, in photography, you will find yourself involved with so many things, before and after the click of the shutter, that it often feels like the pictures themselves are the smallest part of the process. You will spend countless hours and a lot of hard-earned money to make the very best picture—or several hundred of them—in search of the perfect one.

Key parts of the before and after processes often are relegated to the unsexy bin of education yet are the most important. For example, if you take 100 pictures just to get one perfect shot, what are you supposed to do with the other 99? If you do this step over and over, how do you make room for all of your future pictures on your relatively small computer? Even more pressing, how can you take the perfect moment that you captured and make sure that every bit of oomph is wrung out of that file and that you put your best foot forward?

That is exactly what this book aims to teach you—finally.

With your Adobe Creative Cloud subscription, you have access to the most important programs in a photographer's arsenal: Adobe Photoshop CC and Adobe Photoshop Lightroom CC. My goal is to share with you how these programs fit into your day-to-day life as a photographer. I'll share with you exactly where each program shines, and give you the workflow steps you need to make sure you're never lost and never wasting time at the computer.

The goal is to make this easy enough to do quickly, and get you back out there making pictures.

About Classroom in a Book

Adobe Photoshop CC and Lightroom CC for Photographers Classroom in a Book® is part of the official training series for Adobe graphics and publishing software, developed with the support of Adobe product experts. The lessons are designed to let you learn at your own pace. If you're new to Lightroom or Photoshop, you'll learn the fundamental concepts and features you'll need in order to work with these programs together. If you've been using Lightroom or Photoshop for a while, you'll find that Classroom in a Book teaches advanced features too, focusing on tips and techniques for using the latest versions of the applications together.

Although each lesson provides step-by-step instructions for creating a specific project, there's plenty of room for exploration and experimentation. Each lesson concludes with review questions highlighting important concepts from that lesson. You can follow the book from start to finish, or do only the lessons that match your interests and needs. That said, the "Getting Started" material is a *must* read.

Windows vs. macOS instructions

In most cases, Lightroom and Photoshop perform identically in both Windows and macOS. Minor differences exist between the two versions, mostly due to platform-specific issues out of the control of the programs. Most of these are simply differences in keyboard shortcuts, how dialog boxes are displayed, and how buttons are named. In most cases, screen shots were made in the macOS versions of Lightroom and Photoshop and may appear different from your own screen.

Where specific commands differ, they are noted within the text. Windows commands are listed first, followed by the macOS equivalent, such as Ctrl+C/ Command+C.

Prerequisites

Before jumping into the lessons in this book, make sure you have a working knowledge of your computer and its operating system. Also make sure that your system is set up correctly and that you've installed the required software and hardware, because the software must be purchased separately from this book.

You need to install Lightroom CC, Photoshop CC, and the latest version of Adobe Camera Raw for Photoshop CC. You're welcome to follow along with versions of the programs as far back as Adobe Photoshop Lightroom 4 and Adobe Photoshop CS6, but in that case, some exercises in the book will not work as written. For system requirements and support, visit helpx.adobe.com/photoshop.html and helpx.adobe.com/lightroom.html.

This book was crafted specifically for using Lightroom CC and Photoshop CC together for photographers. Although it includes enough information to get you up and running in both programs, it's not a comprehensive manual. When you're ready to dive further into each program, pick up *Adobe Photoshop Lightroom Classic CC Classroom in a Book* and *Adobe Photoshop CC Classroom in a Book*.

Online content

Your purchase of this Classroom in a Book includes online materials provided by way of your Account page on peachpit.com. These include:

Lesson Files

To work through the projects in this book, you will need to download the lesson files from peachpit.com. You can download the files for individual lessons, or it may be possible to download them all in a single file.

Web Edition

The Web Edition is an online interactive version of the book, providing an enhanced learning experience. Your Web Edition can be accessed from any device with a connection to the Internet, and it contains:

- The complete text of the book
- Hours of instructional video keyed to the text
- Interactive quizzes

In addition, the Web Edition may be updated when Adobe adds significant feature updates between major Creative Cloud releases. To accommodate the changes, sections of the online book may be updated or new sections may be added.

Accessing the Lesson Files and Web Edition

If you purchased an eBook from peachpit.com or adobepress.com, your Web Edition will automatically appear under the Digital Purchases tab on your Account page. Click the Launch link to access the product. Continue reading to learn how to register your product to get access to the lesson files. If you purchased an eBook from a different vendor or you bought a print book, you must register your purchase on peachpit.com in order to access the online content:

1 Go to www.peachpit.com/register.

2 Sign in or create a new account.

3 Enter the ISBN: 9780135495070.

4 Answer the questions as proof of purchase.

5 The Web Edition will appear under the Digital Purchases tab on your Account page. Click the Launch link to access the product.

The Lesson Files can be accessed through the Registered Products tab on your Account page. Click the Access Bonus Content link below the title of your product to proceed to the download page. Click the lesson file links to download them to your computer.

6   Create a new folder inside the Users/username/Documents folder on your computer, and then name the new folder **LPCIB**.

7   If you downloaded the entire Lessons folder, drag that Lessons folder into the
LPCIB folder you created in step 6. Alternatively, if you downloaded folders for
one or more individual lessons, first create a Lessons folder inside your LPCIB
folder, then drag the individual lesson folder(s) into your LPCIB/Lessons folder.

8   Keep the lesson files on your computer until you've completed all the exercises.

The downloadable sample images are practice files, provided for your personal use
in these lessons. It is illegal to use them commercially or to publish or distribute
them in any way without written permission from Adobe Systems Inc. *and* the
individual photographers who took the pictures.

Installing Lightroom and Photoshop

Before you begin using *Adobe Photoshop CC and Lightroom CC for Photographers
Classroom in a Book*, make sure that your system is set up correctly.

The Photoshop software and the Lightroom software are not included with this
book; you must purchase the software separately. You can buy them together
through the Adobe Creative Cloud Photography plan or with a Creative Cloud
complete membership, which also includes Adobe InDesign CC and more. As of
this writing, you can purchase the Photography plan for as little as $19.99 a month,
and students can get *all* of the applications for $19.99. Visit www.adobe.com/
creativecloud/photography.html for more information.

Why use both Lightroom and Photoshop?

Once you make your pictures, you will need to showcase the very best ones, without
showing those that didn't make the cut. You'll have to make sure that each of your
pictures contains information for people to contact you should they wish. For some
images, you'll also need to add artistic effects, design elements, and text. Finally,
you will need to take these creations and share them with others online. Lightroom
is the program that will help you keep all of your information in place; Photoshop
will be responsible for specialized tasks that really cannot be done anywhere else.

How Lightroom and Photoshop differ

While Lightroom and Photoshop are both programs that provide photo editing
capabilities, Lightroom's ability to keep you organized really stands out. Lightroom
was designed to handle a photographer's *entire* post-capture workflow, including
downloading content from your memory card to your hard drive, assessing, culling,

rating, tagging, organizing, searching, editing, sharing, and outputting your pictures for various uses, including in print templates, books, slideshows, and web galleries. Photoshop, on the other hand, was designed for a single task: editing images. It does this phenomenally well, and fundamentally differently from Lightroom.

When you open an image in Photoshop, it is made of a series of colored dots, or pixels. Until recently, Photoshop's greatest skill was manipulating these pixels through the use of filters, fills, and special effects. But it had an Achilles' heel.

You see, Photoshop is a destructive editor—your ability to reverse any amount of pushing and pulling of these pixels was limited by a finite number of undos. Close and save the document at a moment when you weren't satisfied with the picture, and when you reopened it, that edited picture was your starting point. If you undersaturated a color, there was no way to get that color back. Further, any edits that you made to a picture could only be done one image at a time.

Photoshop has a way to counteract this by using different types of layers—elements (or whole pictures) that are stacked on top of one another, like layers in a sandwich. While layers offer increased creativity and control, they also add to the overall complexity of the image, and the file size just gets bigger and bigger.

Note: You can think of layers as the ingredients on this delicious (not real) burger. The burger composite is made up of many layers (different toppings, the patty, and the bread); you see a single image. The Layers panel, on the right, shows you an exploded view. In fact, while the burger shows you a top-to-bottom construction, the french fries are actually *behind* the burger image. In this screen capture, you can see that the picture is not only a construction of a series of images, but also a bird's-eye view of a series of elements arranged on a page.

With the advent of Smart Objects, Smart Filters, vector shapes, text, and frames, it is hard to argue that Photoshop is solely a pixel-editing tool. While these additions certainly make Photoshop push past its pixel past, its magic moments are still in those little dots—something you just cannot do anywhere else.

So if Photoshop is the program that you use when you absolutely need to take care of a specific task, where does that leave Lightroom? I think of Lightroom as an amazing organizational program that happens to let you develop and share your pictures. Its biggest strength lies in how it organizes images, and how it helps you get to your very best shots.

Here's an analogy that I think helps explain what Lightroom does in terms of organization: Imagine you are sitting at home when someone knocks on the door and presents you with a box of pictures. They ask you to store the pictures for safekeeping, so you take the box into your home and place it on top of your desk in the living room. In order to remember where you placed those pictures, you pull out a notebook and write down that they are in a box on the desk in the living room.

There's another knock at the door, and another box of pictures appears. You take these pictures and place them inside one of the drawers in your bedroom. You want to remember where they are, so you write it down in your notebook. More boxes of pictures appear, and you continue to place them in different areas of your house, writing down the location of each box of pictures in your notebook. That notebook becomes the central record of where the boxes of pictures are stored in your home.

Now, imagine that you're bored one day while at home, and you take the pictures that are in the box on top of the desk in the living room, and place them in a particular order. You want to make a note of this change, so you write down in your notebook that the pictures on top of the desk in the living room have been organized in a specific fashion.

The notebook you've been using serves as the master record of the location of each box of pictures inside your home, as well as a record of all the changes you've made to each picture. That notebook is your Lightroom catalog—it's a digital notebook that keeps track of where your images are and what you have done to them.

Lightroom doesn't store your images; it stores *information* about your images in the *catalog*. This catalog includes a ton of information about each image (or video), including where the file lives on your drives; the camera settings at capture; any descriptions, keywords, ratings, and so on, that you apply in Lightroom's Library module; and a running list of *every* edit you ever make in Lightroom's Develop module. This essentially gives you unlimited sequential undos forever.

Note: If you're using Lightroom CC on a mobile device, you're editing previews of the images referenced by the Lightroom catalog on your computer.

Although your edits are reflected in the image preview in Lightroom, they're applied only when you export a *copy* of the image—Lightroom never lays a hand on your original photographs, making it a true nondestructive editor. The catalog lets you work on multiple images at a time through the use of synchronization and virtual copies (we'll cover that a little later). You can also use Lightroom to create print templates, photo books, slideshows, and web galleries, and you can include your Photoshop documents in those projects.

As you can see in this illustration, your Lightroom experience comprises many pieces and parts: your images (wherever they live), the Lightroom application, the catalog, and a folder of presets.

We'll dig into the specifics of using both programs later in this book, but the concepts introduced here form a firm foundation for everything else you'll learn. Now let's take a look at which program you should use for which specific tasks.

Where Lightroom excels

Lightroom's database nature enables it to shine at many essential organizational chores. It's also a powerful editor: you can use it to apply edits to an entire photo or to certain parts of it, you can sync or copy edits between photos, and you can easily output those photos in myriad ways. Here's a short list of when to use Lightroom over Photoshop:

- Photo and video management

  Lightroom's Library module is the perfect place to assess, compare, rate, and cull your images, as well as to apply descriptive keywords and other markers, such as colored labels and flags. As you'll learn in Lesson 2, "Organizing Your Photos into Lightroom Collections," the Library module also has several filters you can use to view a subset of your images, and you can easily organize images into what are called *collections*.

- Raw processing

  You can edit many file formats in Lightroom's Develop module (TIFF, PSD, JPEG, PNG), but it excels at processing and translating raw files, the unprocessed sensor data that some cameras—and even some smartphones—can record.

Note: Raw isn't an acronym, so there's no need to write it in all caps even though many people and software companies do.

Raw vs. JPEG

You may not realize it, but when you shoot in JPEG format, your camera processes the image by applying the settings buried deep within your camera's menu, such as noise reduction, sharpening, color and contrast boosting, color space, and some compression to save space on the memory card. Although you can edit a JPEG in both Lightroom and Photoshop, the changes your camera made when converting the sensor data into the JPEG are baked into the file and cannot be undone. (The same thing happens with a TIFF, and since it can produce dramatically larger file sizes than raw format, it's now rarely used as a capture format.)

None of that permanent in-camera processing happens with raw files, which is one reason why a JPEG and a raw file of exactly the same image probably won't look the same when you view them on your computer. Another reason is that raw files contain a wider range of colors and tones than JPEGs (*tones* refers to luminosity information that you can think of as brightness values). For the mathematically curious, 4 trillion colors and tones can theoretically be saved into a 14-bit-per-channel raw file, whereas a maximum of 16 million colors can be saved into a standard 8-bit-per-channel JPEG. (Raw files can be 12-, 14-, or 16-bit, depending on the camera.)

So, using raw data in applications that can interpret it—say, Camera Raw, Photoshop, Lightroom, and so on—gives you far more editing flexibility because you have more data to work with and you can process that data however you want. Raw files also let you change the color of light, called *white balance*, captured in the scene. With a JPEG, the white balance is baked into the file, so all you can really do is shift the colors by fiddling with your image editor's Temperature and Tint sliders. As you can see here, Lightroom's white balance menu has far more options for a raw file (left) than it does for a JPEG (right).

Lightroom automatically maintains the large range of colors (called *color space*) and high bit depth that a raw file includes. That's why you want to do as much processing to a raw file in Lightroom as you can and only pass the file over to Photoshop when you need to do something that Lightroom can't.

> **Note:** *Color space* refers to the range of colors available to work with. Raw processors use ProPhoto RGB, the largest color space to date (see the sidebar "Choosing a color space" in Lesson 6, "Lightroom–Photoshop Roundtrip Workflow," for more). *Bit depth* refers to how many colors the image itself can contain. For example, JPEGs are 8-bit images that can contain 256 different colors and tones in each of the three color channels: red, green, and blue. Raw images, on the other hand, can be 12-, 14-, or 16-bit, and the latter would contain a whopping 65,536 different colors and tones in each channel.

Photoshop's raw processor, Adobe Camera Raw, uses the same underlying engine as Lightroom, essential for times when you need to hand the file from Lightroom into Photoshop.

- Global photo adjustments

Common global photo adjustments—cropping, straightening, fixing perspective and lens distortion, sharpening, adjusting tone and color, reducing noise, and adding edge vignettes—are incredibly easy to perform in Lightroom. Most of the controls are slider-based, highly discoverable, and logically arranged. You'll learn how to use these controls in Lesson 3, "Using Lightroom's Develop Module for Global Adjustments."

- Local adjustments

Even Lightroom's local adjustment tools—those that affect certain parts of the image rather than the whole thing, including the Adjustment Brush, Graduated Filter, and Radial Filter—use sliders, although these changes occur only in areas marked with a tool or painted with a brush on the image. These local tools make it easy to fix overexposed skies, add extra sharpening to specific areas, emphasize and de-emphasize portions of a picture, and more. There's an entire lesson dedicated to common problems and how to fix them in Lightroom—Lesson 4, "Using Lightroom's Develop Module for Local and Creative Adjustments."

Lightroom's Spot Removal tool can be set to either Healing (blends with the surrounding pixels) or Cloning (copies pixels with no blending) mode, meaning you can click or drag to remove blemishes, wrinkles, stray hairs, power lines, smudges, sensor spots—anything that's fairly small. You even get opacity control so that you can dial back the strength of the change.

> **Note:** Sensor spots are spots in your image caused by dust specks on the camera's sensor.

- HDR and panorama stitching

Lightroom offers a merge feature for combining multiple exposures into a single high dynamic range (HDR) image, as well as for stitching multiple images into a panorama. Once the images are combined or stitched, you can adjust tone and color using the global or local adjustment tools described earlier.

- Processing multiple photos

    Lightroom was built for high-volume photographers: You can use it to synchro-nize changes across an unlimited number of photos or you can copy and paste edits instead. You can sync or copy/paste both global *and* local adjustments—the latter is great for removing sensor spots from a slew of images. And you get to choose exactly which edits are synced or copied/pasted.

    You can also save a preset for almost anything you do in Lightroom, which can dramatically speed up your workflow. Presets can be applied during the import process, manually whenever you want, or when you export images. Preset opportunities include, but are not limited to: adding copyright information; file-naming schemes; any settings in the Develop module; settings for all local adjustment tools; template customizations for books, slideshows, prints, and web projects; identity plates (the branding at the upper left of the interface); watermarks; exporting specific sizes and file formats; and uploading online.

- Sharing, resizing, outputting, and watermarking

    If you regularly prepare images for other destinations—say, to feature on your website, to email, to submit to a stock service or a photo contest, or to post on Facebook or Flickr—you can automate the process using Lightroom export presets (they're called *publish services*).

    You even have the option to take a select number of images from a photo shoot, organize them into a collection, and share that collection online. Further, people you share the collection with can rate and provide feedback on the images, giv-ing you a way to connect to clients and friends.

- Create pro-level photo books, slideshows, and prints

    Lightroom includes several ways for you to show off your best work, whether it's for use in your own portfolio or to sell to a client. The books, slideshows, and print templates are highly customizable. You'll learn how to create some of these projects later in the book.

Is Lightroom better at everything than Photoshop? No. In the next section, you'll learn when to send the image over to Photoshop to take your images further.

Where Photoshop excels

Photoshop is the gold standard in creative editing and precise corrections. While Lightroom can be a great solution for developing your pictures, the following sce-narios outline where Photoshop would be a better tool to take the image further:

Note: *Compositing* means to combine two or more images into a single image.

- Combining photographs

    Lightroom has the capacity to make HDR images and panoramas with relative ease. What it cannot do is combine multiple images artistically into one final product. To do that, you need to rely on Photoshop's ability to use layers. This is especially true if you want to create a collage, add texture effects, or perform any photo compositing. In fact, some of the most common photographic problems (fixing glare, compositing expressions from different shots, creating group photos from individual images) are beyond the scope of Lightroom. They can be done quite easily in Photoshop.

Also, while Lightroom does great work with HDR images and panoramas, it requires a trip into Photoshop to use tools like the Adaptive Wide Angle filter, Perspective Warp, and Puppet Warp to really finish the images off.

- Making precise selections and targeted adjustments

Lightroom took great leaps forward with the local adjustment tools, but any work that needs to be done at a granular level needs to be done down to the pixel in Photoshop. You can even take this detail work further through the use of *selections*. The most recent versions of Photoshop take the tedius process of selecting a portion of an image (like a person) and make it quick using artificial intelligence, turning a process that took minutes into one that takes seconds. Once you've made a selection, you can hide elements in a picture using a *layer mask*, giving you even more control over what is highlighted and what is not.

Selecting and masking are crucial when you want to swap out a background in a portrait, substitute a dull sky for a more exciting one, create a transparent background in a commercial product shot, or change the tone or color of a selected area. You'll learn how to do these things in Lesson 7, "Lightroom to Photoshop for Selecting and Masking."

- High-end portrait retouching, alterations, and photo restoration

While Lightroom can give you quick ways to retouch an image, Photoshop makes quick work of things like skin retouching, photo restoration, and alterations. Photoshop's Liquify filter has been redesigned to take a lot of the guesswork out of retouching, letting you get results faster. Some of these techniques are covered in Lesson 8, "Lightroom to Photoshop for Retouching."

- Removing and repositioning objects

Lightroom's Content-Aware features can remove small items, but Photoshop's Content-Aware technologies are at the core of its pixel-pushing magic, letting you remove bigger objects or reposition them in a photo. Photoshop intelligently analyzes the surrounding pixels, or another area that you designate, in order to make the removal or repositioning as realistic as possible. From Content-Aware Fill to Content-Aware Scale, healing, and moving, it's best to save yourself time and jump right into Photoshop for these problems.

- Filling in the corners of a photo after straightening or perspective correction

Lightroom includes a powerful Crop tool that can straighten an image, and the Transform panel's Upright feature can correct perspective problems in a snap.

However, both of these fixes can result in empty corners, which may cause you to crop the image more aggressively than you want. Photoshop can use its Content-Aware technologies to fill in those blank areas, both in the Crop tool or through Fill commands.

- Text, design, illustration, 3D, and video work

  If you are a designer, you'll need Photoshop to add any design elements to your image, as Lightroom doesn't have these features. Text, shapes, and patterns are all vital to graphic designers, and can only be found inside Photoshop.

  You can start with a photograph, export the image into Photoshop, add any design flair you need, and save the finished copy right back into Lightroom for later use. We}ll explore some of these techniques in Lesson 9, "Lightroom to Photoshop for Special Effects."

- Special effects

  Photoshop includes a wide variety of filters and layer styles, giving you an incredibly creative arsenal to express yourself with. From simple blurs to using advanced relighting, oil painting, and more, all of this can be done relatively quickly in Photoshop.

The next few sections explain how to access the exercise files included with this book, as well as how to create a Lightroom catalog.

Creating a Lightroom catalog for use with this book

As you learned in "How Lightroom and Photoshop differ," a Lightroom catalog is a database that stores information about the photographs and video clips you import. Some photographers use a single catalog for all their Lightroom photographs, and some use several. I recommend you keep all your images in one catalog.

Let's go back to the notebook analogy. Imagine I asked you to find a picture from your summer vacation to Mexico. If the image is in your home, you have to remember which notebook contains the location of your vacation images before you can find the location of the picture itself. If you forgot that you had a notebook that included vacation images, that image could very well be lost forever.

This is the same in a Lightroom catalog. You don't have the option to search across Lightroom catalogs, so you would be stuck in the exact same scenario—trying to remember which catalog contains the information you need. Or you can search just one catalog a lot more quickly.

This begs the question, how big can a catalog get? While there is no practical limit to the size of the catalog, I can safely attest that I have operated with a catalog of more than 700,000 images without a problem. Remember, the catalog does not actually contain your images. Think of this as a really large digital notebook, keeping a record of where your images are and what you've done to them.

While the Lightroom catalog keeps a record of the location of your images, it also keeps previews of the thumbnails for the images in your library. These can take up a bit of space, depending on your preferences, but we'll tackle how to mitigate that in a later lesson.

A final note: while your images can live on multiple hard drives, I recommend that you keep your Lightroom catalog on your computer.

For the purposes of following along with this book, and to help you understand concepts as we build them out, we'll make a separate catalog. Here's how:

1 Launch Lightroom.

    When you first launch Lightroom, an empty Lightroom catalog is created in Users/*username*/Pictures/Lightroom. If you're using Lightroom CC, the default catalog filename is Lightroom Catalog.lrcat. If you don't see the name of the current catalog at the top of Lightroom and you want to, press Shift+F several times to cycle to Normal screen mode.

2 Choose File > New Catalog in the menu bar at the top of the Library module.

3 In the dialog box that appears, navigate to the LPCIB folder in your Documents folder (Users/*username*/Documents/LPCIB), and then enter **LPCIB Catalog** as the name of the new catalog.

4 Click Create. If you see a Back Up Catalog message, click the button labeled Skip This Time.

    This opens your new, empty LPCIB catalog. Under the hood, you've created, inside your Documents/LPCIB folder, an LPCIB Catalog folder that contains the database and image preview files for your new LPCIB catalog.

● **Note:** The Back Up Catalog message refers to backing up your Lightroom catalog only, not your images or presets. It is making a copy of your notebook.

You'll import the lesson files into this LPCIB catalog, lesson by lesson, starting in the Lesson 1 section "Importing photos from a hard drive." That section contains a detailed explanation of the import process you'll use throughout this book and when you're working with your own photos. It walks you through the process of importing files from a hard drive into Lightroom, using the Lesson 1 files as an example.

In subsequent lessons (2 through 11), you'll import the lesson files by following the short instructions in the section "Preparing for this lesson," which you'll find at the beginning of each lesson. If at any time you want more information about how to import lesson files, review the section "Importing photos from a hard drive" in Lesson 1.

Getting help

Help is available from several sources, each one useful to you in different circumstances.

● **Note:** If you've downloaded the Help PDFs, you don't need to be connected to the Internet to view Help in Lightroom or Photoshop. However, with an active Internet connection, you can access the most up-to-date information.

Help in the applications

The complete user documentation for Lightroom and Photoshop is available from the Help menu in each program. This content displays in your default web browser. This documentation provides quick access to summarized information on common tasks and concepts, and can be especially useful if you are new to Lightroom or if you are not connected to the Internet. The first time you enter any of the Lightroom modules, you'll see module-specific tips that will help you get started by identifying the components of the Lightroom workspace and stepping you through the workflow. You can dismiss the tips if you wish by clicking the Close button (x) in the upper-right corner of the floating tips window. Select Turn Off Tips at the lower left to disable the tips for all of the Lightroom modules. You can call up the module tips at any time by choosing Help > *Module name* Tips. In the Lightroom Help menu, you can also access a list of keyboard shortcuts applicable to the current module.

Help on the web

You can access the most comprehensive and up-to-date documentation on Lightroom and Photoshop via your default web browser. Point your browser to helpx.adobe.com/lightroom.html or helpx.adobe.com/photoshop.html.

Help PDFs

Download PDF help documents, optimized for printing, at helpx.adobe.com/pdf/lightroom_reference.pdf or helpx.adobe.com/pdf/photoshop_reference.pdf.

Additional resources

Adobe Photoshop CC and Lightroom CC for Photographers Classroom in a Book is not meant to replace the documentation that comes with either program or to be a comprehensive reference for every feature. Only the commands and options used in the lessons are explained in this book. For comprehensive information about program features and tutorials, please refer to these resources:

Adobe Photoshop Lightroom CC Learn & Support: You can search and browse Lightroom help and support content from Adobe at helpx.adobe.com/lightroom.html.

Adobe Photoshop CC Learn & Support: You can search and browse Photoshop help and support content from Adobe at helpx.adobe.com/photoshop.html.

Adobe Forums: You can tap into peer-to-peer discussions, questions, and answers on Adobe products at forums.adobe.com.

Adobe Creative Cloud Tutorials: Visit helpx.adobe.com/creative-cloud/learn/ tutorials.html for inspiration, key techniques, cross-product workflows, and updates on new features.

Resources for educators: A treasure trove of information for instructors who teach classes on Adobe software is offered at www.adobe.com/education and edex.adobe.com. Find solutions for education at all levels, including free curricula that use an integrated approach to teaching Adobe software and that can be used to prepare for the Adobe Certified Associate exams.

Your author's websites: aboutrc.com and firstshotschool.com contain photography, Photoshop, and Lightroom tips, links to several books, and educational videos.

Also check out these useful links:

Adobe Photoshop Lightroom CC product home page:

www.adobe.com/products/photoshop-lightroom.html

Adobe Photoshop CC product home page:

www.adobe.com/products/photoshop.html

Adobe Authorized Training Centers

Adobe Authorized Training Centers offer instructor-led courses and training on Adobe products, employing only Adobe Certified Instructors. A directory of AATCs is available at partners.adobe.com.

1 IMPORTING AND MANAGING PHOTOS IN LIGHTROOM

Lesson overview

This lesson covers everything you need to know to start using Adobe Photoshop Lightroom CC's Library module (if you're already familiar with the program, this lesson has practical and useful information for you, too). You'll decide where to store your photos and walk through the process of importing them into a catalog. You'll learn what the Library module's panels do and how to customize your experience.

In this lesson, you'll learn how to:

- Choose where and in what folder structure to store your photos.

- Import photos into a Lightroom catalog from your memory card or a folder on your hard drive.

- Use the Library module's various panels.

- Customize what you see in the Library module.

- Add a copyright to your photos.

- Use the Library module to view, compare, and rename photos.

 This lesson will take about 2 hours to complete. Please log in to your account on peachpit.com to download the files for this lesson, or go to the "Getting Started" section at the beginning of this book and follow the instructions under "Accessing the lesson files and Web Edition." Store the files on your computer in a convenient location. Your Account page is also where you'll find any updates to the lessons or to the lesson files. Look on the Lesson & Update Files tab to access the most current content.

Lightroom's Library module makes it easy to import and view your image collection.

Preparing for this lesson

Before diving into the content of this lesson, make sure you do the following:

1 Follow the instructions in "Getting Started" at the beginning of this book to create an LPCIB folder on your computer and then download the lesson files into that folder. If the Lesson 1 files are not already on your computer, download the Lesson 01 folder from your Account page at peachpit.com to Users/*username*/Documents/LPCIB/Lessons.

2 Create a new Lightroom catalog named **LPCIB**, as described in "Creating a Lightroom catalog for use with this book" in "Getting Started."

3 Open the LPCIB catalog by choosing File > Open Catalog or by choosing File > Open Recent > LPCIB Catalog.

You'll learn how to add the Lesson 1 files to your new Lightroom catalog later in this lesson. The next section focuses on how to store your photos.

Storing your photographs (you need a plan)

● **Note:** To create a complete Lightroom backup, you must back up your photos, your Lightroom catalog, and the Lightroom Presets folder.

Lightroom is a database that stores information about your images. It doesn't store the images themselves, so your photos can live anywhere. In fact, I recommend that you store your images in a place other than your computer's hard drive.

I think of this as the beauty and plague of what we do. We make pictures, and they take up space. As we get better, we are inspired to make more pictures, and they take up space even faster. In no time at all, we find ourselves with a stack of hard drives and no idea where any images live.

Rather than filling up your computer's hard drive and having to consider where to move your growing photo library, it's important to have a game plan for this as soon as possible. Many skip this part of the process to get to developing images. That is the sexier part of this book, but I'll leave you with this: I'm blessed to work with amazing photographers all over the world. Of the thousands that I've trained, written for, or helped in a seminar, fewer than 10 percent ask me for tips about using the Develop module. The majority of them have 10 hard drives, a ton of images scattered everywhere, and no idea how to make sense of it all.

I currently have more than 300,000 images in my Lightroom catalog, but still have more than 250 GB of free space on my laptop's 1-TB hard drive. How is that possible? My images are stored on a combination of the computer hard drive, an external drive, and a network-attached storage drive, or NAS. An NAS is basically a really big, expandable hard drive. Instead of plugging this hard drive into your computer via a USB cable, you plug it into your network. No computer is required!

There is a benefit to keeping as much free space as possible on your computer from a performance point of view. The free space on the computer's hard drive is used constantly by running applications (especially Photoshop), so the more free space it has, the zippier the programs will run—double bonus!

Although I recommend keeping your actual photos on external hard drives, because a Lightroom catalog is fairly small in file size (remember, it is only a database file), it's common to keep that on your computer's internal drive.

While this section does get a little specific in its recommendations for storing and organizing your photos, I guarantee you it's not hard. After a couple of imports, you will find it incredibly easy. And I guarantee you will thank me for it. Just stick with it.

⬤ **Note:** This book focuses on photos, but much of what you'll learn here also applies to video— you can import and manage video clips in Lightroom's Library module, too. Although you can perform rudimentary video edits in Lightroom, you can do far more to video in Photoshop. For more on working with video in Lightroom and Photoshop, check out *Adobe Photoshop Lightroom Classic CC Classroom in a Book (2018 release),* by John Evans and Katrin Straub, and *Adobe Photoshop CC Classroom in a Book (2018 release),* by Andrew Faulkner and Conrad Chavez, as well as your author's books, *The Enthusiast's Guide to Lightroom* and *The Enthusiast's Guide to Photoshop.*

Folders store; they do not organize

To keep a handle on your growing library, you need to store your pictures in folders. Coming up with a solid strategy for naming and organizing your folders can pay big dividends later on in your photography adventures.

During the import process, Lightroom records the location of your folders in the Folders panel of the Library module. Once you tell Lightroom about your folder structure, resist the urge to make any changes to your folders—especially outside of Lightroom. If you edit folder names or move photos between folders using your computer's operating system—essentially, behind Lightroom's back—it won't know where your photos are.

Going back to the house analogy in "Getting Started," it would be like walking into the house where your images are in specific boxes in specific rooms, moving one of the boxes, and never writing it down in the notebook. Chaos would ensue.

There are times when you will need to use the Folders panel to change the location of a folder or photo, but try to limit this to moving images to a larger drive or an NAS drive *only*.

If you already have an effective folder structure for your photos, you can continue to use it. If you have an okay folder structure, but have hundreds of folders already made, don't fret. Keep the existing folders as you have them, solemnly swear that you've been changed after this conversation, and go with this new strategy.

Here are some tips to make building a folder structure easy:

- Work in Windows Explorer or macOS Finder to build and populate your folder structure. This is far simpler than doing it in Lightroom using the Folders panel, especially if it involves moving thousands of files.

- Keep in mind that you need a coherent set of folders and subfolders that will accommodate your existing photos, as well as the ones you'll add in the future. In other words, your system needs to be scalable.

- If there are photos on a memory card that you haven't yet copied to your hard drive, use your operating system to copy them into your new folder structure before telling Lightroom about them.

- I set up a folder for each year that I have made pictures. Inside each year folder, I make subfolders for all the events or places I shot that year. Every event folder name starts with the year, then the month and date the images were shot. My folder names are always lowercase and include a descriptive word or short phrase about the shoot. To add a space in a folder name, use an underscore (_). For example, a folder for images I took at the State Fair on January 25, 2019 would be named 2019_jan_25_state_fair.

● **Note:** Some Lightroom users prefer to maintain multiple catalogs to separate personal and professional images. If you're an experienced Lightroom jockey, that may work well for you. However, because Lightroom's search features work on one catalog at a time, you may find it easier to maintain a single catalog instead of several.

Creating and populating your folder structure is critical if you want to have a well-organized photo collection in Lightroom. The next two sections cover how to tell Lightroom about your new folder structure.

Importing photos into a Lightroom catalog

Before you can work with photos in Lightroom, you have to tell Lightroom they exist. This is done through the import process. This is where you record the location of your images into your digital notebook.

The term *import* is necessary but misleading, because your photos don't reside inside Lightroom. If you peek at the terminology used at the top of Lightroom's Import window, you get a much better idea of what's really happening to your photos. Your choices are:

- Copy As DNG and Copy: Both options copy pictures from one place to another, most likely from your camera's memory card onto a hard drive. (For more information, see the sidebar "Understanding Copy As DNG.") Lightroom also creates a database record for each photo and builds a nice preview of it so that you can scroll quickly through them in Lightroom's Library module.

- Add: This option tells Lightroom to add a record and a preview to the catalog for each image while leaving the photos wherever they currently exist on your hard drive (internal or external).

- Move: Similar to Add, this option prompts Lightroom to add a record and preview of the image to the catalog; however, it also moves photos from one place on your drive to another.

Importing photos from a memory card

If you would like to follow along with me through this process, I recommend that you place a memory card in your camera and go take 20 pictures. It doesn't really matter what you take pictures of; the important part is that you have 20 pictures on the card that you can import into your computer.

⬤ **Note:** For more than you ever wanted to know about using Lightroom's Import window, including steps for copying photos from a memory card to a hard drive, pick up a copy of *Adobe Photoshop Lightroom Classic CC Classroom in a Book (2018 release)* by John Evans and Katrin Straub.

Once you connect the memory card to your computer, the Lightroom Import window appears. The import window is separated into three discrete sections: where your images are being imported from, how you would like them handled, and where you would like them stored. Let's walk through importing them:

1 The left side of the Import window shows you the location of your memory card, as well as other folders on your computer that you can import images from. If you inserted a memory card, it should be selected by default here. Leave Eject After Import selected, as it makes sure that you can safely remove the card once the import is complete.

2 The center preview area shows you all the images on the memory card. At the top of the window, choose Copy or Copy As DNG, the two most popular options when importing images from a camera or card reader.

3 All the image thumbnails in the grid in the center preview area are automatically selected, letting you know that they are ready for import. At the bottom of the preview area, you have the options Uncheck All and Check All. Uncheck All allows you to select only a series of images to import.

▶ **Tip:** When you're satisfied that all your photos have been copied from the memory card to your hard drive, return the memory card to your camera, and use the camera controls to erase or reformat it.

If you select Uncheck All, click the first image in the series and then Shift-click the last image in the series to highlight all the images between the two (a contiguous selection). Holding down the Ctrl/Command key as you click lets you highlight multiple images that aren't contiguous.

Although the images are highlighted, they are not selected for import. To select them for import, select the check box at the upper left of one of the highlighted thumbnails, which selects the check boxes for all the highlighted thumbnails.

For a larger view of an image, double-click its thumbnail to bring it up in Loupe view (or press the E key). To return to the grid of images, click the Grid view icon at the bottom left of the preview area or press the G key.

To adjust the size of the thumbnails in Grid view, drag the Thumbnails slider at the lower right of the preview area or press the plus sign (+) and minus sign (−) keys on your keyboard.

4   At the upper right of the window, you'll decide where to save the images you are importing. Lightroom wants to import pictures into your Pictures folder by default. Instead, click the location in the upper right of the window and choose Other Destination from the menu. In the dialog box that appears, choose the year folder in your new setup and create a new event or place folder by clicking New Folder in the dialog box. Click Select Folder/Choose to close it.

5   There are a number of options in the File Handling panel, below the location. Let's start at the top:

   •   Choose Minimal from the Build Previews menu for now. The "What the Build Previews options mean" sidebar explains each preview you can use when working with your images.

   •   We'll talk about Smart Previews later on, so for now, unselect Build Smart Previews.

   •   Select the Do Not Import Suspected Duplicates option, as it prevents you from adding images to your Lightroom catalog that you have already imported. This is especially handy if you shot another series with your memory card, and forgot to format it after importing those images.

   •   While backing up your images to a secondary location sounds like a good option, leave Make A Second Copy To unselected for now.

   •   Collections are a great way to organize your folders, and we'll definitely use them in Lightroom (we'll learn more about them in Lessson 2). For now, leave Add To Collection unselected, as well.

Understanding Copy As DNG

One of the choices in Lightroom's Import window is Copy As DNG. DNG stands for *digital negative*, and it's Adobe's attempt at standardizing an *open* format for raw files. (Samsung uses it as the factory setting for its cameras, too.) One benefit to this format over a *closed* proprietary raw format—say, Canon's CR2 or Nikon's NEF—is that your edits and metadata can be stored inside the original file, instead of in a separate XMP file (also referred to as a sidecar file). Another benefit of DNG is that Lightroom uses it for *Smart Previews*, which let you sync your desktop catalog with your mobile device for editing in Lightroom CC.

Converting proprietary raw formats, or JPEGs for that matter, into DNG is optional, though it's great for archival purposes since it stores all your edits and metadata, too. It takes a while, so if you're going to do it, wait until you've culled your image collection. You can do it at any time in Lightroom's Library module by selecting some photos and choosing Library > Convert Photos To DNG. You can also download the free Adobe DNG Converter to convert files from proprietary raw formats to DNG en masse.

Renaming files and folders during import

In the previous lesson, we talked about the importance of naming your folders to better organize your photos and I gave you an example of how to name them. Here are some tips for renaming your files:

- As with your folders, start the name of every file with the year, then add a month and date.

- Use lowercase when naming your files, and add a descriptive word about the shoot after the date.

- Again, if you need to add a space to your filenames, use an underscore (_) instead of a space.

- At the end of the filename, add C1, C2, C3, and so on, for card 1, card 2, card 3. This helps when you have a shoot that spans multiple cards.

For example, if I want to import images that I took at the state fair on January 25, 2019, my folder would be named 2019_jan_25_state_fair. If I only shot one card during that shoot, the filename would be 2019_jan_25_state_fair_c1_ with a sequential file number at the end. Is the filename long? Yes. Does it give you all the information about the shoot? Absolutely.

Here's the practical reason for adding the C1 to your filenames: Every now and then, during a Lightroom import, you will run into a file that looks like the one here. While it may make for an intereting art project, it's actually something a lot more sinister. It is a corrupt picture, a quick sign that the card you are using may not be as reliable as you think. Memory cards, like everything else, can fail over time and you cannot afford to lose an important shoot because of it. If you are importing from multiple cards, how do you tell which one is the bad one?

As soon as I purchase a memory card, I make it a point to label it using those C numbers. Then, I add that C number to the filename. The moment I see a potential problem with an image, I can look at the name and know exactly which card failed, so I can take that card out of rotation...and give it to a friend. Kidding! A simple addition of C1 or C2 to your filenames can go a long way to helping you troubleshoot. Anal? Yes. Vital? Absolutely.

Let's add this information in the import dialog:

1 In the File Renaming panel, select the Rename Files option and choose Custom Name - Sequence in the Template menu. Type your naming convention in the Custom Text box (I entered **2019_jan_25_state_fair_c1**), and Lightroom will take care of adding the -1 , -2, and so on, to each of the images.

2 In the Destination panel, select the Into Subfolder option and type the name of the folder in the text box (I entered **2019_jan_25_state_fair**). To eliminate excessive folder creation, choose Into One Folder from the Organize menu.

Once this is complete, click the Import button in the lower right, and you're off!

Importing photos from a hard drive

While the previous process works great for importing new photos you shoot or for individuals starting from scratch, most photographers already have folders of images on their hard drives that they now want to add to their Lightroom catalog. Here's how to do that:

1 Open your new Lightroom catalog, and click the Import button at the lower left.

Since this catalog is empty, it automatically opens the Library module in Grid view (where Lightroom displays your images as a grid of thumbnails). When you add more photos in the future, make sure you're in the Library module by clicking the word *Library* in the upper right, and then click the Import button, choose File > Import Photos And Videos, or press Shift+Ctrl+I/ Shift+Command+I.

Adding copyright during import

One step you can take to help protect your photos is to embed copyright and contact information into the metadata of each file. Sadly, this won't keep anyone from stealing your image, but they may think twice about taking it if they find a name attached to it.

The Metadata menu in the Apply During Import window offers the perfect opportunity to add that information to all the photos you're importing. Since the lesson files used in this book were taken by someone else, there's no need to do it; however, it's important for you to set up your own copyright preset for use in the future.

The next time you import your own photos, choose New from the Metadata menu in the Import window. In the resulting dialog box, scroll to the IPTC Copyright area. In the copyright field, enter a copyright symbol by pressing Alt+0169 on a numeric keypad (Windows)—or pressing Option+G (macOS)—followed by the copyright year and your name. In the Copyright Status menu, choose Copyrighted. You can add Rights Usage terms (**All Rights Reserved** was added here) and, if you have a website with more copyright information, the URL to that website. Scroll to the IPTC Creator area, enter any identifying information you wish to include, give your preset a name at the top, and then click Create to save it as a preset.

To apply this copyright preset to photos as you import them, simply choose it from the Metadata menu. You can also apply a metadata preset later by selecting some thumbnails and then using the Library module's Metadata panel.

2 In the Import window that appears, use the Source panel in the upper left to navigate to where the photos live. Click the name of any folder to expand it so you can see its contents. Locate the lesson files, which should be in Users/*username*/Documents/LPCIB/Lessons, and then pick the Lesson 01 folder.

Thumbnail previews of the photos in the Lesson 01 folder appear in the middle of the Import window. If they don't, select the Include Subfolders option at the top of the Source panel.

3 In the workflow bar at the top of the Import window, make sure Add is selected (it should be, by default). As you learned in the previous section, this tells Lightroom to *add* information about these photos to the catalog, but to leave the photos in the folders and on the drives where they currently reside.

▶ **Tip:** When you're importing your own photos, it may be tempting to deselect the bad ones. As you'll learn later in this lesson, it's quicker to import them all and then assess and cull them in the Library module, especially if you take a lot of pictures!

4 The check box at the upper left of each thumbnail selects that photo to be added to your catalog. For this lesson, leave all the check boxes selected so that Lightroom adds all the files.

5 In the File Handling panel at the upper right, choose Minimal from the Build Previews menu (if the panel is collapsed, click its header to expand it). This menu determines the size of the previews displayed in the middle of the Library module. For more information on preview sizes, see the sidebar "What the Build Previews options mean."

6 For the purposes of this lesson, leave the other options in the File Handling panel unselected.

● **Note:** The Keywords field and the Develop Settings menu in the Import window's Apply During Import panel are useful only for keywords and develop settings that apply globally to all the photos you're currently importing. You can add keywords and apply Develop module presets that are specific to individual photos later in the Library module.

What the Build Previews options mean

- Minimal and Embedded & Sidecar: These options make use of previews embedded in the original photographs. These relatively small previews are used to quickly display initial thumbnails in the Library module. The Minimal option uses the small, non-color-managed JPEG preview embedded in a file by your camera during capture. The Embedded & Sidecar option looks for and uses any larger preview that may be embedded in the file. If you're importing lots of photos and you want the import process to be as fast as possible, choose Minimal. Later on, when you've got more time, you can have Lightroom generate larger previews for selected photos by going into the Library module and choosing either Library > Previews > Build 1:1 Previews or Library > Previews > Build Standard-Sized Previews.

- Standard: This option can speed your browsing in the Library module, without slowing down the import process as much as the 1:1 option discussed next. It builds standard-sized previews during import that are useful for viewing photos in Loupe view in the Library module. The size of a standard-sized preview is governed by an option in Catalog Settings—for Windows, choose Edit > Catalog Settings; for macOS, choose Lightroom > Catalog Settings. On the File Handling tab, click the Standard Preview Size menu. There you can choose a size up to 2880 pixels on the long edge. Ideally, choose a standard preview size that is equal to or slightly larger than the screen resolution of your monitor.

- 1:1: This option builds additional previews that are the same size as the original photographs. 1:1 previews are useful for zooming in to check sharpness and noise in the Library module. If you choose to have Lightroom build these previews upon import, you won't have to wait for a 1:1 preview to generate when you zoom in to an image in the Library module. However, 1:1 previews take the longest time to import and are the largest in file size in the Previews.lrdata catalog file. You can manage the size issue either by selecting thumbnails in the Library module and choosing Library > Previews > Discard 1:1 previews, or by choosing to discard 1:1 previews automatically after a particular number of days in preferences. In Windows, choose Edit > Catalog Settings and click the File Handling tab; for macOS, choose Lightroom > Catalog Settings and click the File Handling tab. Lightroom will rebuild the 1:1 previews when you ask for them by zooming in.

7 Click the Import button at the lower right of the Import window. Lightroom adds the photos to your catalog with the settings you specified and closes the Import window.

Back in the Library module, bars in the upper-left corner show Lightroom's progress as it adds the photos to your catalog and builds previews of them. Once finished, Lightroom activates the Previous Import collection in the Catalog panel near the top of the left-side panels, and you see image thumbnails in the center preview area, as well as in the Filmstrip panel at the bottom.

In the next section, you'll learn your way around Lightroom's Library module.

Using the Library module

You'll spend a lot of time in Lightroom's Library module. Its various panels and tools will help you make short work of managing, assessing, and organizing your photos. In the following sections, you'll learn what the panels do, how to select images, and how to customize what you're viewing in a variety of ways.

Meeting the panels

Each Lightroom module includes a column of panels on the left and right, and a customizable preview area in the middle with a row of tools underneath. In the Library module, you get source panels on the left and information panels on the right.

The panel at the bottom is the Filmstrip, and it displays your image previews horizontally. It's useful for selecting images whenever you're not viewing them as a grid of thumbnails, and for working with specific images in Lightroom's other modules.

> **Tip:** You can collapse (or expand) any panel by clicking its name. To expand or collapse the Filmstrip, click the triangle that appears beneath it at the bottom of the workspace.

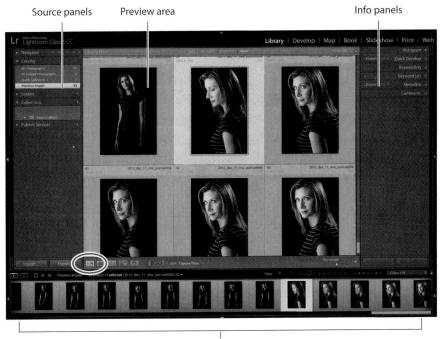

Source panels   Preview area   Info panels

Filmstrip

By default, the Library module opens in Grid view, which is indicated by the icon circled in the toolbar below the preview area. The selected collection in the Catalog panel on the left indicates which images you're currently viewing.

Source panels

The primary function of the panels on the left side of the Library module is to determine what is shown in the preview area. Here's what they do:

- Navigator: This panel lets you control zoom level and which area of the photo is displayed in the preview area.

  - The Fit option fits the currently selected photo within the preview area so you can see the whole thing.

  - The Fill option shows as much of the photo as can fit the largest dimension of the preview area.

  - 1:1 shows the photo at 100% size.

  - The ratio menu on the right has other frequently used zoom levels. With the Navigator set to Fit, you see a white border around the image in the Navigator panel. Once you zoom in (say, using Fill or 1:1), the rectangle reduces in size to indicate the part of the photo you're currently viewing in the preview area. To see another area of the photo, click within the rectangle (the cursor turns into a crosshair), and drag it to the area you want to see zoomed.

▶ **Tip:** Lightroom remembers your most recently used zoom levels and lets you cycle between them using the Spacebar on your keyboard. For example, to quickly switch between Fit and 1:1, click once on Fit, and then click once on 1:1. Now tap the Spacebar to switch between those two choices.

Note: When you designate a collection as the target collection, you can add images to it by pressing B on your keyboard, which is quicker than manually dragging thumbnails into it. You'll learn how to create a target collection in Lesson 2, "Organizing Your Photos into Lightroom Collections."

- Catalog: This panel gives you quick access to certain images in your catalog.

  - All Photographs shows you previews of every image in your catalog.

  - Quick Collection shows you the images in a temporary collection (album) you have selected images for, or the collection you've designated as the target collection (say, the collection you're currently populating).

  - Previous Import shows your most recent additions to your catalog.

- Folders: This panel displays your hard drives and folder system. Click any folder to see all the photos it contains; click the triangle next to the folder name to see any subfolders. The Folders panel doesn't display all the folders on your computer; it shows only the ones you've told Lightroom about, using the import process (at this point, that's the Lesson 01 folder inside the Lessons folder, which is inside the LPCIB folder).

By default you won't see parent folders; you only see folders you've told Lightroom about. To reveal a parent folder, as shown on the previous page, right-click a folder and choose Show Parent Folder from the menu.

Tip: The number to the right of a folder or other source in the left column of the Library module is the total number of items it contains.

⦿ **Note:** If you're new to Lightroom, be very careful with the Folders panel because the changes you make physically affect the folder structure and the images on your hard drive.

Once you tell Lightroom about your folder structure, you shouldn't use your computer's operating system to rename or move folders and photos around inside of it.

▶ **Tip:** If your files do get unlinked in Lightroom, you can relocate them by choosing Library > Find All Missing Photos.

- Collections: Think of Lightroom collections as albums. Using collections is a great way to organize and access your keepers. You'll learn more about how to use collections in the next lesson.

▶ **Tip:** If you're tempted to create tons of folders and subfolders to fully organize your photos, don't. You'll be better served by using Lightroom's collections (albums) to organize them instead.

- Publish Services: You'll use this panel to create presets for exporting a *copy* of your photo with your Lightroom edits applied. You can use it to export photos to a hard drive or to upload them online to sites such as Facebook, Flickr, and so on. As you'll learn in Lesson 11, "Exporting and Showing Off Your Work," you can use these presets to change file formats, rename, resize, attach metadata, and even watermark your photos.

Information panels

The panels on the right side of the Library module are where you'll go to get information about, or to add information to, items you've added to your Lightroom catalog. These panels include:

- Histogram: A histogram is a collection of bar graphs representing the dark and light tones contained in each color channel of each pixel in your photo. Dark values are shown on the left side of the histogram, and bright tones are shown on the right side. The width of the histogram represents the full tonal range of the photo, from the darkest shadows (black) to the lightest highlights (white).

  The taller the bar graph, the more pixels you have at that particular brightness level in that color channel. The shorter the graph, the fewer pixels you have at that particular brightness level in that color channel.

▶ **Tip:** Another way to think of a histogram is to imagine that your photo is a mosaic and its individual tiles have been separated into same-color stacks. The taller the stack, the more tiles you have of that particular color.

This image has a darker tonal range—you can see a spike in the shadows due to the black background and black in the model's blouse.

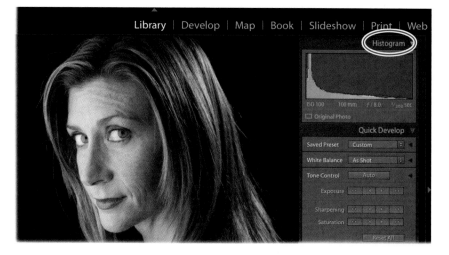

- Quick Develop: You'll do most of your processing in Lightroom's Develop module, but you can do quick fixes in the Library module using the Quick Develop panel. The adjustments you make in this panel are unique because they're *relative* rather than absolute. For example, if you select three photo thumbnails and then click the Exposure button with the left-pointing triangle, the exposure of each photo decreases by a third of a stop relative to the current exposure value of that photo. This means each photo could end up with a different exposure value. In contrast, if you adjust the exposure of one photo in the Develop module and then sync that change with two other photos, all three photos would end up with the exact same exposure value.

▶ **Tip:** The Quick Develop panel also includes a Saved Preset menu that you can use to apply any presets you've made in the Develop module to one or more photos. This is a quick alternative to going into the Develop module only to apply a preset you've made.

- Keywording, Keyword List: These two panels are related to keywords, which are descriptive tags you can apply to images in order to find them more easily later on. The Keywording panel is useful for adding and applying keywords to selected photos all in one step; it's also useful for seeing which keywords have been applied to selected photos. The Keyword List panel shows you a list of all the keywords that exist in your catalog; it's useful for creating and organizing keywords. We'll talk more about keywords in Lesson 2.

- Metadata: This panel shows you a host of information about the selected photos, including filename, caption, copyright, dimensions, camera settings, and so on. You can use this panel to fill in any missing information or to change certain information.

● **Note:** Don't bother changing filenames using the Metadata panel; you'll learn how to change filenames en masse later in this lesson, in the section "Renaming your photos."

- Comments: This panel lets you view comments that others have made to a photo you've shared online. The topic of sharing photo collections is beyond the scope of this book, although you can learn more about it by visiting https://helpx.adobe.com/lightroom/how-to/share-photo-gallery.html.

Now that you know your way around the Library module's various panels, you're ready to tackle customizing how the Library module looks.

Customizing your view

As you can see, panels take up quite a bit of room, but you can give your image previews more screen real estate in several ways. For example, you can:

- Hide a column of panels by clicking the triangle inside the thin black border outside that column. Click the triangle again to reveal the panels. (Technically, you can click anywhere within that border to hide or show panels, although the triangle is an easy target.)

  Once you click to hide a column of panels, they show again whenever you move your cursor near them, and then they hide when you mouse away from them. If this constant panel showing and hiding drives you insane (and it probably will), right-click within the outer border and choose Manual from the menu that appears, as shown on the next page. That way, the panels stay hidden until you click within the outside border again.

▶ **Tip:** The customization options in this section are shown using the Library module, but they work in any module you're in.

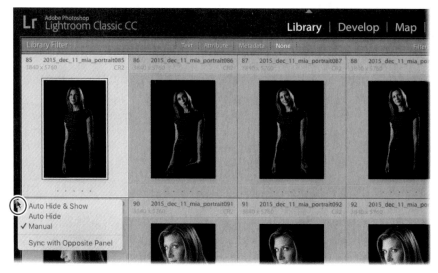

- Hide all the panels on the left and right sides of the workspace by pressing Tab. To show them, press Tab again.

- Hide all panels and toolbars by pressing Shift+Tab, as shown below. To show them again, press Shift+Tab again.

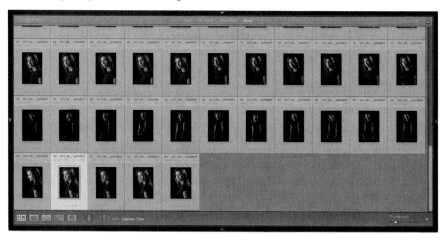

▶ **Tip:** To return quickly to the Library module Grid view, press G on your keyboard. This is the most often used keyboard shortcut in all of Lightroom!

- Dim or hide everything around the image previews with Lights Out mode. For Lights Dim mode, press L on your keyboard and everything outside the image previews is dimmed (including panels, other open apps, and your computer's desktop). Press L a second time for Lights Out mode and everything except your previews turns black, as shown here in Loupe view. Press L again to return to normal view. These views also can be chosen from the Window > Lights Out menu. It's a great way to focus on image previews when you're assessing or comparing them.

- Enlarge a preview to fill your screen by pressing F on your keyboard to enter Full Screen mode. To exit it, press F again. Press Shift+F to cycle through a variety of other screen modes, or access them by choosing Window > Screen Mode.

- Another handy way to manage panels is to use Solo mode. In this mode, only one panel is expanded at a time; the rest remain collapsed. When you click another panel, the one that was open collapses and the new one expands. To enable Solo mode, right-click any panel's name and choose Solo Mode from the resulting menu. This keeps you from having to scroll through a slew of open panels to find the one you want to use.

● **Note:** Once you activate Solo mode, the solid gray panel triangles are filled with dots, as shown below on the right.

You can customize how your image previews are displayed, too. Straight from the factory, the Library module uses Grid view, which displays resizable thumbnails

▶ **Tip:** To change the size of the thumbnail previews, use the Thumbnails slider beneath the previews. Better yet, use a keyboard shortcut: press the minus sign (–) on your keyboard to decrease size or the plus sign (+) to increase size.

Tip: If you don't see the toolbar at the bottom of the Library module's preview area, press T on your keyboard to summon it.

in a grid. (In the Library module toolbar, the grid icon is active and shown in light gray.) The Library module toolbar also houses the following options:

- Loupe view: This option enlarges the selected thumbnail so that it fits within the preview area, however large the preview area currently is. You can trigger it by clicking the Loupe icon (it looks like a darker gray rectangle inside a lighter gray one), by pressing E on your keyboard, or by double-clicking the image.

  Tip: Once you're viewing a photo at 100%, you can drag to move around the photo onscreen (your cursor turns into a tiny hand).

- Compare view: For a side-by-side comparison of one image with another—say, to determine which one is the sharpest—use this option. Ctrl-click/Command-click to select two thumbnails, and then click the Compare icon (the one with the X and Y) or press C on your keyboard. Press the Spacebar to enter Loupe mode, click within the image on the left (called the *select* photo), and then drag to pan around and examine details (your cursor turns into a hand). As you reposition one photo, the other one (called the *candidate*) matches its position. The select photo is marked in the Filmstrip by a white diamond in the upper-right corner of its thumbnail. The candidate is marked by a black diamond.

When you find the image you like the best, mark it as a pick by clicking the tiny flag icon at the image's lower left (you'll learn more about this in Lesson 2, in the section "Applying flag markers in Lightroom"). To exit Compare view, click its icon again or press G to return to Grid view.

Tip: If the candidate looks better than the select, promote the candidate to select by clicking it, and then pressing the Up Arrow key on your keyboard, which moves it to the left position. Lightroom grabs the next image in the Filmstrip panel and displays it on the right as the candidate so that you can repeat the process. This is a great way to find the best photo of a bunch, especially if you shoot in burst mode.

Select   Candidate

The art of selecting thumbnail previews

When you want to select a thumbnail in order to work with it, make a habit of clicking the gray frame surrounding the photo rather than clicking directly atop the photo itself. Why? Because in Lightroom, you can select multiple images, but only one of them can be "most selected," and that's the image that's affected by whatever adjustment you make next (say, using the Library module's Quick Develop panel or any of the adjustments in the Develop module).

Yes, it sounds crazy, but this behavior is intended to keep you from accidentally adjusting a slew of photos if you didn't mean to (perhaps you didn't realize you had multiple photos selected). The only way to understand this (admittedly) confusing concept is to try it yourself using these steps:

1   In Grid view in the Library module, click anywhere on the first thumbnail preview to select it. Now Ctrl-click/Command-click anywhere on the next two thumbnail previews to select them too. (Alternatively, you can Shift-click the third thumbnail to also select the one in between.) If you look closely, you'll see that the first thumbnail is highlighted in a slightly brighter tone than the other two. This brighter tone indicates that it's the most selected thumbnail (shown here at the top).

2   Click directly on the image in the second selected thumbnail.

You might expect step 2 to leave only the second preview selected, deselecting the two other previews, because that's the common behavior in other applications. However, that's not what happened. In this case, clicking directly on the image in the second preview switched the most selected status from the first to the second thumbnail (shown here in the middle).

3   Press Ctrl+D/Command+D to deselect all the thumbnails.

4   Repeat step 1 to select three thumbnails in Grid view again.

5   Now click the gray frame, rather than the image, in the second selected thumbnail.

The result is different than it was in step 2. Clicking the frame, rather than the image, in the second preview left only the second preview selected and deselected the other two previews (shown here in the bottom strip).

This "most selected" business affects the Filmstrip too. The takeaway here is that routinely clicking the frame, rather than the image, in a thumbnail will allow you to avoid being surprised by the less common behavior you saw in step 2. Aren't you glad you bought this book?

- Survey view: This option lets you compare multiple images side by side. To use it, select three or more thumbnails, and then either click the Survey icon (it has three tiny rectangles inside it with three dots) or press N on your keyboard.

To remove a photo from the selection, move your cursor over it and click the X that appears in its lower corner, or click the photo and press the forward slash (/) key on your keyboard. You can also drag to rearrange photos in the preview area while surveying them. When you find the photo you like best, move your cursor over it, and mark it as a pick by clicking the tiny flag icon that appears below its lower-left corner. To exit Survey view, click its icon again or press G to return to Grid view.

The Library module toolbar also has a Sort menu you can use to change the order of your thumbnails. By default, it's set to Capture Time so that thumbnails appear in chronological order, although you can change it to parameters such as Added Order, Edit Time, Edit Count, and a slew of other options, including Rating, File Name, Aspect Ratio, and so on.

Renaming your photos

● **Note:** If you're using Lightroom's Import window to copy photos from your memory card onto a hard drive, you can use the File Renaming panel to rename them then.

Another common task you'll perform in the Library module, if you didn't do it when you imported them, is renaming your photos. Doing so makes them searchable and thus easier to find in the future (after all, the cryptic names your camera gives them aren't exactly helpful).

Although you could use the Library module's Metadata panel to (painstakingly) rename photos one by one (by clicking in the File Name box and typing a new name), there's a quicker method. Here's how to rename photos en masse immediately after adding them to your Lightroom catalog:

1 When Lightroom finishes importing your photos, take a peek at the Catalog panel on the left, and make sure Previous Import is selected.

2 Select all of those photos by pressing Ctrl+A/Command+A or by choosing Edit > Select All.

3 Choose Library > Rename Photos. In the resulting dialog box, pick a naming scheme. Custom Name – Sequence is a good one because it gives you the opportunity to enter something descriptive into the Custom Text box, like an event or place name, and it automatically adds a sequential number after the name. In this case, enter **2016_dec_11_mia_headshot** as your custom text.

4 Enter a starting number into the Start Number box, or let it roll with 1. At the bottom of the dialog box, Lightroom shows you what your naming scheme looks like.

5 Click OK, and Lightroom renames the selected photos in one fell swoop. If you look at the upper left of the interface, you'll see a progress bar.

6 Deselect the images by pressing Ctrl+D/Command+D or by choosing Edit > Select None.

Now that you have a good command of importing your files into Lightroom, we need to focus on how to get the very best images from your shoot into one location. To do that, we need to gain an understanding of how to mark images in Lightroom and how to add select groups of images to collections. So, the next lesson teaches you a simple strategy for assessing and culling your photos.

Tip: If you ask Lightroom to do something that takes a few moments (say, renaming thousands of images), you don't have to wait until it's finished to do something else.

Review questions

1 How do you select only a single series of photos from your memory card to copy to your hard drive and add to your Lightroom catalog?

2 When you select a folder in the Folders panel, which previews will you see in the grid in the center of the Library module?

3 You'll often use the keyboard shortcuts for Grid view and Loupe view in the Library module. What are those shortcuts?

4 How do you collapse all the panels and bars in the Library module for maximum viewing space?

5 How do you enter Lights Dim mode, and then Lights Out mode?

6 How do you compare two photos side by side?

7 What is the easiest way to rename a bunch of photos?

Review answers

1 In the Import window, click Uncheck All. Click the first photo you want to import, then Shift-click the last photo to highlight everything in between, and select the check box at the upper left of any one of the highlighted images to select them all.

2 When you select a folder in the Folders panel, by default you'll see previews of all items in that folder and in any subfolders it contains.

3 Press G on the keyboard to switch to Grid view (thumbnail-sized previews). Press E on the keyboard to switch to Loupe view (the larger view of a photograph).

4 Press Shift+Tab to collapse all the panels and bars in the Library module.

5 Press L to enter Lights Dim mode, and press L again to enter Lights Out mode.

6 Ctrl-click/Command-click two photos, then press C to enter Compare view and the Spacebar to enter Loupe mode. Then, drag around your image.

7 By using the Library > Rename Photos command, you can easily rename a bunch of photos.

2 ORGANIZING YOUR PHOTOS INTO LIGHTROOM COLLECTIONS

Lesson overview

This lesson covers how to sort through your images to separate the ones that are keepers (that you will print, share, or put in your portfolio) and ones you can discard or review later. You'll start by going through a specific workflow for culling images using flags in Adobe Photoshp Lightroom, and walk through the process of sorting those images into discrete collections. From there, you'll learn how to set up a hierarchical structure using collection sets.

In this lesson, you'll learn how to:

- Employ color labels in your image.

- Use a star system to rank your images.

- Filter images based on flags, colors, or other metadata.

- Set up smart collections for specialized tasks.

- Set up a target collection for quick organization.

- Share and get feedback about your published online collections.

 This lesson will take about 2 hours to complete. Please log in to your account on peachpit.com to download the files for this lesson, or go to the "Getting Started" section at the beginning of this book and follow the instructions under "Accessing the lesson files and Web Edition." Store the files on your computer in a convenient location. Your Account page is also where you'll find any updates to the lessons or to the lesson files. Look on the Lesson & Update Files tab to access the most current content.

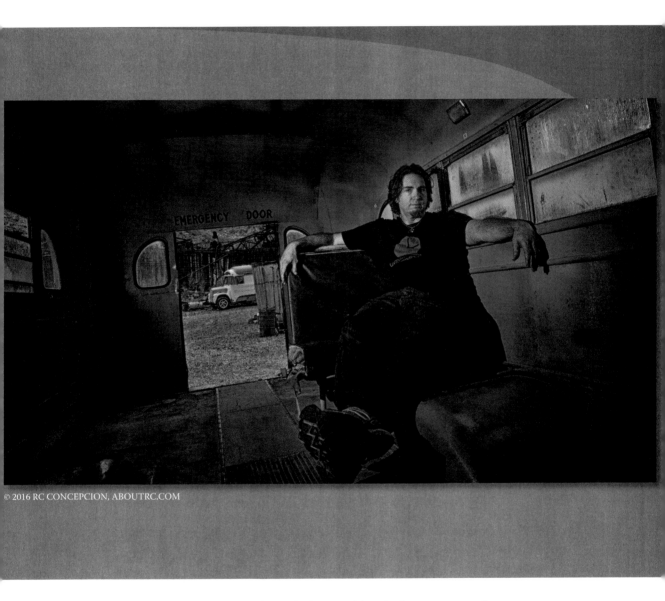

Lightroom's Library module makes it easy to assess and manage your ever-growing image catalog.

Preparing for this lesson

Before diving into the content of this lesson, make sure you do the following:

1 Follow the instructions in the "Getting Started" section at the beginning of this book for setting up an LPCIB folder on your computer, downloading the lesson files to that folder, and creating an LPCIB catalog in Lightroom.

2 Download the Lesson 02 folder from your Account page at peachpit.com to *username*/Documents/LPCIB/Lessons.

3 Launch Lightroom, and open the LPCIB catalog you created by choosing File > Open Catalog and navigating to it. Alternatively, you can choose File > Open Recent > LPCIB Catalog.

4 Add the Lesson 2 files to the LPCIB catalog using the steps in the Lesson 1 section "Importing photos from a hard drive."

Iterative culling: My workflow

The single most tedious task after a photo shoot is sorting bad pictures from good so that you can come up with a plan for editing. This process is known as *culling* and is one of the most important steps you can do in Lightroom.

I spend a lot of time talking to people around the world about their use of Lightroom, and this seems to be the part of the process people struggle with the most. To fix that, I want to share the technique I use when working with my photos. This is something I learned a long time ago, back in my days as a high school teacher, and I call it the "iterative edit."

If you have to take a timed test of multiple choice questions, the best strategy for completing it is to go through the test as fast as you can, answering all the questions that you know you have correct. When you get to a question that you do not know the answer to, the strategy is to skip it. By doing this, you can quickly complete the answers you do know, leaving you more time to work on the ones you don't and allowing you to pick up context clues from your completed anwers.

Now, let's apply this idea to our photography. If a shoot contains 200 pictures, there is a good chance that a large number of those pictures are either really good or really bad. By "bad" I mean things like: out of focus, the eyes are closed in a portrait, or you cut off someone's head. These are things that we immediately know are problems, and we would never spend any time working on these images. Conversely, with the good pictures, we're not trying to pick the very best picture out of the very best series. We're looking for pictures that are okay: it's exposed, it's composed, it has the subject. Ranking them is something we'll do later.

Adding flag markers in Lightroom

Let's begin by going into the Lesson 01 folder in the Library module's Folders panel in Lightroom. This shows a grid of images that we can start culling. As we learned in the previous lesson, we can get rid of the panels on all four sides by pressing Shift-Tab. We can also black out the interface by pressing the L key twice to go into Lights Out mode. This will get rid of all of the distractions in the Lightroom interface that take us away from doing the job at hand—culling.

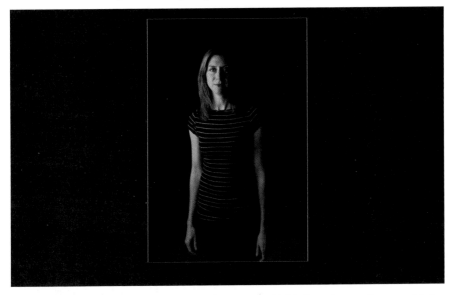

You have a couple of options with this first image. If this is a picture that you think is worth keeping, press P on the keyboard to mark it as a pick. If you believe this picture is completely off, press X to mark it as rejected.

If you have to think for more than half a second about whether this picture is effective, press the Right Arrow key on the keyboard to skip the picture and go on to the next one. Remember your qualifications for bad and good. Do not spend more than a second thinking through these pictures. The goal is to get rid of the pictures that you know will not work.

If you click one of the flags and the picture doesn't advance, choose Photo > Auto Advance. Should you mistakenly flag one of the pictures, press the Left Arrow key to go back to the picture in question, and then press the U key. Pressing U unflags the picture.

Once you finish this process, you should have your pictures sorted into three different types of images: those that you know won't work (the bad images), those that you want to consider for ranking, and those that you have not gone through yet. Lightroom has a way to filter all of these pictures: the Library Filter bar at the top of the center preview area. The Library Filter bar has the following options to help you find specific images:

- Text mode allows you to filter your Lightroom catalog for specfic words. These words can be in the filename, title, caption, or any of the metadata embedded in the image.

- Attribute mode lets you filter out images based on flag status, star rating, color label, or virtual copy status, as shown below.

- Metadata mode lets you sort your images using a host of different metadata items Lightroom has compiled from your images. This is an extremely powerful way of filtering, but outside the scope of this book.

Click the Attribute tab, then select one of the Flag options (pick, unflagged, or rejected) to see only those specific images appear in the preview area. The filter icons are not exclusive—you don't have to select only Reject flags or Pick flags. If you click both in the Attribute filter, Lightroom shows you both sets of images in Grid view.

At the top right of the Filmstrip panel, there are similar Filter options (if you don't see the flag icons next to the Filter menu, choose Flagged from the menu). At the top left of the Filmstrip panel, you see the number of images in that folder or collection that contain a specific flag.

At this point, the images that are the most important part of the process are the unflagged ones. Click the Unflagged Photos Only icon, hide the panels (press Shift-Tab), go into Lights Out mode (press L twice), and repeat the culling process until nothing appears in the preview area.

You will notice that this second iteration of culling goes much faster than the first one. The best thing about this part of the process is that you now have seen the shoot in its entirety, and can make better judgements as to which pictures stay and which pictures go. The only part you'll find disconcerting is the end—when you get to a completely black screen. Don't worry; just turn the lights back on (press L) and bring back the panels (Shift-Tab). You'll notice the screen was black because there were no more unflagged images. Click the Unflagged Photos Only icon again to bring back all your photos, and your cull is complete!

What is a collection?

As your Lightroom library gets bigger and bigger, you'll need to have key images in your catalog accessible for various purposes. As mentioned, prior to Lightroom, photographers who wanted to share a group of images, like a portfolio of portraits, often placed copies of those pictures in a folder to share. As different needs arose, they had to create other folders and store more copies of the same pictures in them. Each folder had a specific need and contained copies of pictures that also lived in other folders. Keeping track of the copies, and the space they occupy, makes this solution untenable. This is where collections save the day.

If you're familiar with iTunes, you can think of Lightroom's collections as playlists for your pictures. You purchase one song and own one physical copy of a song, but that song can live in an unlimited number of playlists. The same holds true for pictures and collections in Lightroom.

On the left side of the Library module, you have a Collections panel. Click the plus sign (+) in the panel header, choose Create Collection, and give the collection a name. From there, you can add images from

Note: Some Lightroom users prefer to maintain multiple catalogs to separate personal and professional images. If you're an experienced Lightroom jockey, that may work well for you. However, because Lightroom's search features work on one catalog at a time, you may find it easier to maintain a single catalog.

throughout your catalog to the collection, no matter what folder they live in, and you can add as many collections as you need for organization.

Every collection that you create in Lightroom can hold images from any folder you have imported into your catalog. It doesn't matter if the images live on your hard drive, an external drive, or a network-attached storage drive. The Lightroom catalog (your digital notebook) notes that you have one physical file but would like to have a reference to that file in multiple collections. The collections serve as a way to look at disparate parts of your photographic life without having to change your folders or make copies of your photos to live in different folders. This is an extremely powerful feature and one that your photographic life will revolve around.

In an effort to show you this concept in its simplest form, I'll share with you a series of photos of my daughter, Sabine, and my wife, Jennifer.

Creating collections from folders of images

Let's experiment with creating collections and adding images to them with the files that we've imported for Lesson 2.

1   Go to the Folders panel in the Library module and click the little triangle to the left of the Lesson 02 folder. Inside that folder, you'll see a series of folders that we'll make into collections.

2   Right-click one of the folders that contains the word *Sabine* in the name, and select Create Collection "*folder name*" from the menu.

3   Repeat this with the other folders that have the word *Sabine* in the name, making collections for each of them. When you're done, you should have a total of eight collections.

4   Click the plus sign (+) on the right side of the Collections panel's header, and create two additional collections: **Best Christmas Moments** and **Cute Sabine Pictures**, as you see here on the right.

While it might seem repetitive to have collections that are named exactly like your folders, there are a couple of really powerful things happening under the hood here. First, unlike in a folder, you can drag the images around within the preview area and sort them into whatever order you like.

Second, you have the option to add images from any of those Sabine collections to the Best Christmas Moments or Cute Sabine Pictures collections. It doesn't matter where those images live or what folders they are in, you can simply drag any of them into a new collection if you'd like. The catalog (your digital notebook) will still reference that one physical file.

To show you the third important part about collections, click the thumbnail of the first picture in the 2008_oct_31_sabine_pumpkin collection and drag it into the Best Christmas Moments or Cute Sabine Pictures collection.

Although we haven't covered developing a picture yet, let's make a quick change to this photo. On the right side of the Library module, open the Quick Develop panel's Tone Control section. Under Exposure, click the double left arrow three times. This should darken the image by three stops. You will see the change in the image in this collection immediately.

The awesome part about this is that the thumbnails of this image in the other two collections also will change to reflect the darker picture. You don't have to remember where the physical picture lives; Lightroom automatically makes that change across all instances of the image by referencing that one physical file.

Before we go any further, let's create collections for the rest of the folders in the Lesson 02 folder (all of the folders with the word *Jenn* in them). You should then have a total of 15 collections.

Creating collection sets

It's easy to see that our list of collections could get a little unwieldy. With so many Sabine collections, it would be hard to scroll and visually see where my work images are versus my family images. That said, there is a common element that runs through all of these collections of Sabine: my daughter, Sabine.

Click the plus sign (+) on the right side of the Collections panel's header, and select Create Collection Set. In the Create Collection Set dialog, create a set called **Sabine Images**, and make sure the Inside A Collection Set check box in the Location area is unselected. Once the collection set is created, drag all of the Sabine collections into the Sabine Images collection set.

The result is a much cleaner look to the Collections panel. If you want to see the pictures inside all the Sabine collections, just click the Sabine Images collection set. If you want to see pictures from one of the individual collections, click that individual collection. But we can take this a step further.

The Jenn collections also could benefit from that type of grouping. Create a collection set called **Jenn Images**, and again, make sure the Inside A Collection Set check box is unselected. Then, drag all the Jenn collections inside the Jenn Images collection set. This makes our collections even cleaner.

But we can take this level of organization further. Another great benefit of the collection set is that it holds not only collections but other collection sets as well.

Looking at the collections that you have here, are there any other common elements that we can group around? Jenn and Sabine are my family. We could theoretically create a collection set called Family Images and place both the Sabine Images and Jenn Images collection sets in it.

Then, should we want to see all the family images, we could click the Family Images collection set. If we want to see a series of Jenn images, we can click the Jenn Images collection set. If we want to see Sabine images, we can click the Sabine Images collection set. To see individual events, we can click the individual collections to drill down further. In other words, a place for everything, and everything in its place.

Sample organizational sets

Now that we know that our collections can be used to see a subset of pictures across our catalog and that collection sets can let us organize all of those views, let's put it into other workflows that make sense.

Let's say I work doing people photography, and I get an assignment to make a series of pictures of my friend Latanya Henry. In that shoot, I would have several groups of pictures—picked images to go over, rejected images, images that I want to edit further, images to take into a slideshow, and so on. If I made a collection for each group, what would happen if I got hired again to make another series of pictures for Latanya? Would I just create "Latanya Picked Images Number 2" and name the other collections in the same manner? That would be too messy.

Instead, what if we made a collection set for Latanya Henry? Then, when I import the first shoot with Latanya, I would make a collection set for that specific shoot. Inside it, I would place all the collections that are related to that shoot.

The next time I shoot with Latanya, I would create a collection set for that second shoot, and repeat the process. Not only does this allow you to see only what you want to see, but it also lets you separate out individual images for the other functions in Lightroom, such as books or slideshows. You can have a collection for each function.

On the next page are a series of sample suggestions that you can use to organize your photography work. If you are a wedding photographer, you can use collection sets on a per couple basis, with a collection set for each wedding. Inside each wedding, you can separate production work (shots from multiple cameras) and the finished work, using collections to sort out the various pieces of the wedding.

If you are a commercial photographer who does multi-day shoots, you can make a collection set for the entire job, organize the days into individual collection sets, and filter out the best shots into a "Best of" collection. If you are a landscape photographer, the organization would be similar to that of a commercial shoot, but instead of jobs, you can sort by locations.

These samples are provided as ideas to get you going, not as hard-and-fast rules for your photography work. The point is that you should take a moment to plan how you want to organize your Lightroom catalog using collections and collection sets. Once you do, it's up to you to stick to that format. It's a little time-consuming at first, but it pays great dividends later on as your catalog gets larger.

What is a smart collection?

Smart collections are collections that you can build based on predefined criteria. Click the plus sign (+) on the right side of the Collections panel's header, and choose Create Smart Collection from the menu.

In the Create Smart Collection dialog box, you can pick from a ton of different criteria to use to pull images into your smart collection. Below the Match menu, the left side shows you the criterion chosen, the center section gives you comparison options, and the right side gives you the restrictions for each criterion. Click the plus sign (+) at the upper right of the rules field to add another criterion (you can have as many as you like).

Once the smart collection has been created, you will see it in the Collections panel with a number of images in it. The number of images in a collection increases or decreases as you flag images across your entire catalog. In this example, I created a smart collection that will keep track of images that I mark as rejected. As I flag my images, no matter where in the catalog the rejected ones live, Lightroom will keep a running tally of them inside this smart collection.

I recommend that you drill down into that column on the left during your smart collection creation. You'll find a ton of parameters that you can immediately put to use in sorting your photographic work.

What is the Quick Collection?

There may be times when you don't necessarily need to create a collection, but would like to temporarily organize a set of images into a group. Rather than creating and deleting a regular collection, moving images around, or exporting images unecessarily, you can use the Quick Collection. The Quick Collection does not live in the Collections panel and is available to you only by clicking Quick Collection in the Catalog panel or pressing Ctrl+B/Command+B.

Add images to the Quick Collection as you move about the Library module by selecting an image and pressing the B key. Or, in Grid view, click the small Quick Collection circle in the upper right of any thumbnail; it turns gray to show you that the photo has been added to the Quick Collection.

What is a target collection?

A target collection takes all the ease of adding images to the Quick Collection and, following the same process, assigns the images to one of the regular collections you've created. To use this feature, right-click a collection you've already created and choose Set As Target Collection (you'll see a plus sign [+] appear to the right

of your collection
name). Now, every
time you press the
B key, the selected
image will be added
to the target collec-
tion you specified,
and not to the Quick
Collection. To turn
the target collection
off, right-click it in

the Collections panel and choose Set Target Collection from the menu again. Then,
the images will go back to being added to the Quick Collection.

Sharing your collections online

Another benefit of having your images in collections is that you can share the collections online. Previously, if you needed to get feeeback on a shoot from someone
else (a client, family members, friends), you would have to export images from the
collection and import them into a third-party website.

In Lightroom Classic CC (desktop), you can automatically sync a collection with
Lightroom CC (mobile) by selecting the Sync With Lightroom CC option in the
Create Collection dialog box. If you forget or decide to sync it later, simply click the
lightning bolt icon to the left of the collection name, and Lightroom will generate
the files and automatically create an album in Lightroom CC and a private website
you can view by loggin in at lightroom.adobe.com. You can make the gallery public
by clicking the Make Public button in the upper-right corner of the preview area.

After you click Make Public, Lightroom creates a URL that you can share with
others (to the left of the button you clicked to make the website public, once you

have made it public). In this online version of Lightroom, all flags, star ratings, color labels, and other metadata settings will appear with the images (as you can see in Grid view below).

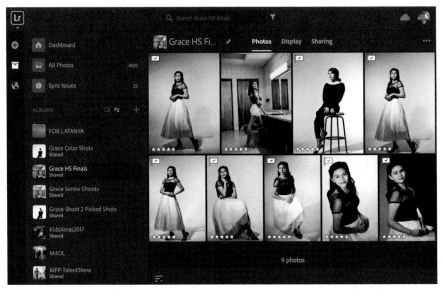

After clicking a thumbnail, you are taken to Loupe view, where you can click the

Show Info icon to see the photo's metadata or the Show Activity icon to leave a comment or read other viewers' comments. Those comments are automatically saved to the cloud and then synced back to your computer for you to review in the Comments panel (which appears below the Metadata panel once a collection is made public).

Adding star ratings and color labels

Rating your images is pretty simple. Pressing the numbers 1–5 will add one to five stars to any images you have selected. To remove any of the star ratings, just select the image and press the number 0.

In addition to pressing 1–5 for star ratings, pressing the numbers 6, 7, 8, and 9 on your keyboard will add the red, yellow, green, and blue colors labels, respectively. There is one color left—purple—that can only be accessed through the Photo > Set

Color Label menu. To remove the color from an individual picture, just select the photo and press the number for the associated color again, and the color is gone.

Now that you know how to add star ratings and colors to your pictures, let's talk about how best to use them. Once your pick and rejected flags have been assigned, you can use star ratings to rank your pictures in a "good, better, best" scenario.

The star rating system also can be useful for flagging images for specific tasks or categories. Your portfolio shots can be your 5-star shots, while images that go into a slideshow can be your 4-star shots. Or, in a wedding shoot, images of the groom's family can be your 3-star shots, while images of the bride's family can be your 2-star shots.

I like to use colors for files that I am going to work on in Photoshop, files that are ready for printing, and final edits of files. Any red-labeled images in my catalog are images that need some work in Photoshop. The green-labeled images are ready for printing. Any purple-labeled images are final copies of images that need no additional editing. I use purple for final images, as it's the only color that I cannot accidentally select with a number key. The colors also make it very easy to spot images in Grid view that need to be worked on.

Adding keywords

Adding keywords is an extremely powerful way to keep track of photos by subject matter in your Lightroom catalog. Think of them as search terms, like the ones you use to find something on the web. Keywords don't take up much space—they're text added to the photo's metadata—so you can apply as many keywords to a photo as you want.

For the best results, make your keywords descriptive of the subject matter, such as "desert," "headshot," "dune," "falcon," and so on. Avoid adding keywords that you've included in the photo's filename, because Lightroom's search capability extends to filenames, too.

You'll develop your own list of keywords as you go, but to get you started, use the following steps to add keywords to the exercise files:

1　In the Library module, go to the Folders panel, scroll down in the Lesson 02 folder, and find the 2016_dec_5_latanya_dubai folder. Right-click the folder and choose Create Collection *"folder name."*

2　In the collections panel, click your new collection and select a series of images from it (click the first photo you want to select, then Shift-click the last image to select all the images in between).

3　In the Keyword List panel on the right, click the plus sign (+) on the left side of the panel's header. In the dialog box that appears, enter **Dune** in the Keyword Name field, and then enter **Sand** and **Desert** in the Synonyms field (use a comma to separate the synonyms). Select the Add To Selected Photos option, leave the three export options selected, and then click Create.

Your new "Dune" keyword appears in the Keyword List panel, and Lightroom adds it to the selected photos. A general keyword like this also can serve as a category in which to nest more specific keywords (say, "Sand" and "Arabian").

4　Now, select all the portrait images and repeat step 3, creating the keyword **Falconry** and applying it to your selected photos.

> **Tip:** To create nested keywords, select an existing keyword in the Keyword List panel and then click the plus sign (+) to add another keyword. To see nested keywords, click the triangle to the left of a keyword in the Keyword List panel to expand your keyword hierarchies. You can also type a keyword into the search field at the top of the Keyword List panel to reveal it in the panel.

5 To see all the photos in your Lightroom catalog that have a specific keyword, move your pointer over the number to the right of that keyword in the Keyword List panel and click the arrow that appears to the number's right.

When you click the arrow to the right of a keyword (circled), Lightroom automatically switches your source to All Photographs in the Catalog panel. Once you apply a keyword to a photo, a tiny tag icon appears in its lower-right corner.

Other ways to apply (and delete) keywords

As you may imagine, there are additional ways to apply keywords. For example, you can:

- Drag and drop the keyword from the Keyword List panel onto one or multiple selected thumbnail previews.

- Drag and drop one or more thumbnails onto a keyword in the Keyword List panel.

- Select one or more thumbnails, and in the Keyword List panel, select the check box that appears to the left of a keyword. To remove a keyword from a photo, do the same thing but deselect the check box that appears to its left.

- Use the Keywording panel (it's above the Keyword List panel). If you go this route, you can create and apply keywords in the same step. To do this, select some thumbnails and then click within the box labeled "Click here to add keywords." Enter a new keyword. If you want to create and apply more than one keyword to the selected photos, use a comma between each keyword. For example, you may enter **Dune, Desert** and then press Enter/Return on your keyboard to create and apply both keywords.

To delete a keyword from your list, use the Keyword List panel (not the Keywording panel). Click the keyword and then click the minus sign (−) on the left side of the panel's header. In the warning dialog that appears, click Delete.

Alternatively, right-click the keyword, and from the menu that appears, click Delete. In the warning dialog, click Delete. (In fact, the aforementioned menu offers several useful options for managing your keywords. For example, you can edit them, remove a keyword from the selected photo, or delete the keyword altogether.)

Either way, the keyword is removed from your keyword list and from any photos you applied it to.

Review questions

1 What's the simplest way to assess and cull recently imported photos?

2 Name three reasons it is important to use collections.

3 What is a smart collection?

4 What is the Quick Collection?

5 How do you share a collection online publicly?

6 How do you add a 5-star rating to a photo?

7 How do you create a new keyword in the Keyword List panel?

Review answers

1 Use the Pick and Reject flags to assess and cull imported photos.

2 First, you can drag images in a collection into any order you want. Second, you can add a photo to as many collections as you want without making a new copy of the photo (saving you disk space). Third, any Develop changes you make to the image will be reflected in each collection it is in.

3 A smart collection is a self-populating album based on criteria that you set.

4 The Quick Collection is a temporary collection that lives in the Catalog panel.

5 Click the lightning bolt icon to the left of the collection name in the Collections panel, then click the Make Public button at the upper right of the preview area.

6 Press the number 5 on your keyboard.

7 Click the plus sign (+) on the left side of the Keyword List panel's header.

3 USING LIGHTROOM'S DEVELOP MODULE FOR GLOBAL ADJUSTMENTS

Lesson overview

Adobe Photoshop Lightroom CC excels at correcting the tone and color of your photos. In this context, *tone* refers to the Exposure, Contrast, Highlights, Shadows, Whites, and Blacks sliders in the Develop module's Basic panel. You'll apply these changes to the entire photo, which is referred to as making *global* adjustments.

In this lesson you'll learn how to:

- Find your way around the Develop module workspace.

- Undo any adjustments you've made.

- Use profiles to re-create camera tone or develop artistic effects.

- Master a typical workflow for adjusting tone and color.

- Reduce noise and sharpen photos.

- Sync changes made to one photo with many.

- Save Develop module settings as defaults and create presets.

 This lesson will take 1 to 2 hours to complete. Please log in to your account on peachpit.com to download the files for this lesson, or go to the "Getting Started" section at the beginning of this book and follow the instructions under "Accessing the lesson files and Web Edition." Store the files on your computer in a convenient location. Your Account page is also where you'll find any updates to the lessons or to the lesson files. Look on the Lesson & Update Files tab to access the most current content.

©2017 RAFAEL CONCEPCION, ABOUTRC.COM

The intuitive controls in Lightroom's Develop module let you easily adjust composition, tone, and color to bring out the best in your photos.

Preparing for this lesson

To get the most out of this lesson, be sure you do the following:

1 Follow the instructions in the "Getting Started" section at the beginning of this book for setting up an LPCIB folder on your computer, downloading the lesson files to that LPCIB folder, and creating an LPCIB catalog in Lightroom.

2 Download the Lesson 03 folder from your Account page at peachpit.com to *username*/Documents/LPCIB/Lessons.

3 Launch Lightroom, and open the LPCIB catalog you created in "Getting Started" by choosing File > Open Catalog and navigating to the LPCIB Catalog. Alternatively, you can choose File > Open Recent > LPCIB Catalog.

4 Add the Lesson 3 files to the LPCIB catalog using the steps in the Lesson 1 section "Importing photos from a hard drive."

5 In the Library module's Folders panel, select Lesson 03.

6 Create a collection called **Develop Module Practice** and place the images from the Lesson 03 folder in that collection.

7 Choose File Name from the Sort menu beneath the center preview area.

Now that your files are in order, you're ready to learn how to use the Develop module workspace to perform global adjustments.

Using the Develop module

The Develop module looks and behaves a lot like the Library module. To get to it, click Develop at the top of the workspace or press D on your keyboard. Lightroom presents you with a column of panels on the left and right. A toolbar and the Filmstrip panel appear at the bottom; click any photo in the Filmstrip to see it in the preview area in the middle. You can expand, collapse, and hide panels (see the section "Meeting the panels" in Lesson 1) in the Develop module just as you can in the Library module, and zooming in to and repositioning a photo onscreen works the same way as described in the Lesson 1 section "Customizing your view."

You'll learn more about using each panel as you progress through this lesson, although the ones on the left are for previewing, applying presets, saving versions, and undoing changes you've made to a photo. The ones on the right let you apply global and local adjustments, so that's where you'll spend the majority of your time. The toolbar below the preview area lets you see before and after views, and a Reference view, and has a menu for adding viewing choices and sorting actions, like a zoom slider or flagging icons. The Filmstrip at the bottom lets you select the image(s) you want to work on.

Although you can select more than one image in the Filmstrip, Lightroom displays the most selected one in the preview area (see the Lesson 1 sidebar "The art of selecting thumbnail previews"). To see a before and after version of the image while you're working on it in the Develop module, press the Backslash key (\) to temporarily view the original version of an image.

▶ **Tip:** Putting your panels in Solo mode is especially helpful in the Develop module, because it allows you to have only one panel open at a time and keeps you from doing so much scrolling. To activate it, right-click any panel's header and choose Solo Mode from the menu. The catch? You will have to do that for each module.

▶ **Tip:** You can show and hide the toolbar below the preview area in any module by pressing T on your keyboard.

▶ **Tip:** The Develop module includes a new Reference view, which allows you to develop an image while comparing it to a second "reference" image in the preview area.

▶ **Tip:** To access other photos without switching to the Library module, click the triangle to the right of the file name, directly above the Filmstrip panel, and pick another source of images from the menu.

Reference View   Before/After views   Click to access other sources of images

Developing your pictures

▶ **Tip:** You can turn each panel's adjustments off and on using the small gray switch that appears at the panel's upper left. This is handy for assessing changes made in a single panel. You can also reset any slider to its default value by double-clicking the text label to the slider's left. The Basic panel doesn't have a switch, although you can press Backslash (\) on your keyboard to see the original, unadjusted photo.

When shooting in raw, you will have an incredible amount of control in recovering details and correcting tone and color to enhance the appearance of your images. Unlike Photoshop, Lightroom is a nondestructive editor (see the "Getting Started" section "How Lightroom and Photoshop differ"), so there's no hard-and-fast rule about the order in which you make adjustments—you can perform them in any order you want, though generally speaking, you'll make global adjustments before making local ones.

Although you could start with a top-down panel approach—beginning with the Basic panel and working your way down through the other panels—you won't need to use every panel on every photo. The use of any sliders in the Develop module is largely dependent on the type of problem you are trying to tackle in your picture.

What are camera profiles?

When shooting in JPEG mode, the camera applies color, contrast, and sharpening to the files it produces. When you switch to shooting in raw, your camera captures all of the raw data in the file, but builds a small JPEG preview as well. This JPEG preview—with all of the color, contrast, and sharpening—is what you see in the LCD on the back of the camera.

When you import a raw file, Lightroom initially shows you that JPEG preview as a thumbnail. Behind the scenes, it starts to render the raw data into pixels you can view and work with onscreen (a process known as *demosaicing*). To do this, Lightroom looks at the image's metadata—white balance and everything buried in your camera's color menu—and interprets it as best it can.

Because Lightroom can't interpret some proprietary camera settings, the preview almost never looks like the JPEG that you saw on the back of your camera. This is why your thumbnails shift in color shortly after (or during) the import process.

This shift frustrated many photographers before Lightroom's developers added camera profiles (presets that attempt to mimic the settings included in a camera's JPEGs). While not 100 percent accurate, they let you get closer to what you saw on the back of your camera. They used to be located in the Camera Calibration panel.

As more photographers started using them, some created profiles for artistic effects. Adobe realized that users wanted to add profiles first—for both color fidelity and artistic expression—and moved them to the top of the Basic panel.

The new profiles in Lightroom

The April 2018 release of Lightroom Classic CC greatly expanded how photographers use camera profiles in their workflow by creating three categories to explore:

- Adobe Raw Profiles: These profiles are not camera-dependent and aim to give users of any camera a more unified look and feel for their images.

- Camera Matching Profiles: These profiles mimic the profiles built in to your camera, and vary by camera manufacturer.

- Creative Profiles: These profiles are built for artistic expression and leverage Lightroom's ability to include 3D LUTs for even more coloring effects.

Now that we know what these tools can do, let's spend some time exploring how to use them to make our work really stand out: Select the first image in the Develop Module Practice collection, and press the D key to make sure you are in the Develop module. To make it easier for you to see the changes we are making, close the left-side panels and the Filmstrip by clicking the gray triangles in the middle of each side.

Note: Color lookup tables (LUTs) are tables that remap or transform color in an image. Originally used in the video space to attempt to make footage from different video sources look similar, LUTs gained popularity as Photoshop users began using them to colorize their images as an effect. These effects sometimes are known as *cinematic color grading*.

At the top of the Basic panel (directly under Treatment) is the Profile area. On the left is the Profile pop-up menu, where you choose a profile that mimics your camera settings from the list of Adobe Raw profiles (these appear only when working on a raw file). On the right is the Profile Browser icon (it looks like four squares), where you can access a variety of profiles, including the Adobe Raw Profiles.

Josh Haftel, principal product manager for Adobe, wrote a blog post explaining the new color profiles:

> "*Adobe Monochrome* has been carefully tuned to be a great starting point for any black and white photograph, resulting in better tonal separation and contrast than photos that started off in Adobe Standard and were converted into black and white.

Adobe Portrait is optimized for all skin tones, providing more control and better reproduction of skin tones. With less contrast and saturation applied to skin tones throughout the photo, you get more control and precision for critical portraiture.

Adobe Landscape, as the name implies, was designed for landscape photos, with more vibrant skies and foliage tones.

Adobe Neutral provides a starting point with a very low amount of contrast, useful for photos where you want the most control or that have very difficult tonal ranges.

Adobe Vivid provides a punchy, saturated starting point."

While I believe that Adobe has done a great job with the Adobe Raw profiles, many photographers will want to go directly to the Camera Matching profiles. To do this, click the Profile Browser icon.

The new Profile Browser gives you access to all the profiles Adobe created. We already discussed the Adobe Raw profiles at the top of the Profile Browser. The Camera Matching profiles include any profiles that are specific to your camera make, so the number of profiles available will vary by camera type.

At the bottom of the Profile Browser are the creative profiles, separated by category: Artistic, B&W, Modern, and Vintage. If you expand any of them, you'll see a series of thumbnails showing what each profile will look like on your photo (as seen below).

I encourage you to experiment with all of the profiles. While the Camera Matching profiles might offer you a one-click solution to get closer to what you saw on the back of your camera, the creative profiles might spark a new interpretation of your image. My other favorite part? The creative profiles have an Amount slider, allowing you to dial in the effect to your liking. Once you choose a profile, click the Close button at the upper right of the browser to return to the Basic panel.

Setting your picture's white balance

White balance refers to the color of light in a photo. Different kinds of light—fluorescent or tungsten lighting, overcast skies, and so on—create a different color cast in your photo. White balance adjustment is done by adjusting the temperature and tint to bring the color back to what you intended. You can do this with the WB menu. If you shoot in a raw format, you have more choices in the menu—the ones that you typically find in your camera (these are not available with a JPEG). Simply choose the one that most closely matches the lighting you shot in. You can also make your own adjustments to the Temp and Tint sliders.

Note: On raw images, you can use the WB menu to access white balance presets, although it's usually quicker to set it manually using the White Balance Selector. Your camera's white balance is baked into JPEGs, so this menu has far fewer options for them.

If you don't like the results, in the Basic panel, click the White Balance Selector (it looks like a turkey baster) or press W on your keyboard. Move your cursor over your image, and click an area that *should* be neutral in color, such as a light or medium gray.

In the example on the next page, I clicked the back wall, to the right of my daughter's head (shown circled). Lightroom automatically adjusts the temperature and tint to give you a better result. If it doesn't look right, click in another area that should be neutral. If it's still not right, you can fine-tune the color of the light using the Temp and Tint sliders, if necessary.

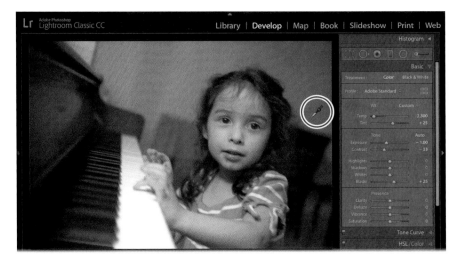

Setting exposure and contrast

Exposure is determined by how much light your camera's sensor captures and is measured in f-stops (which indicate how much light your camera's lens lets in). In fact, the slider values simulate stops on a camera: a setting of +1.00 is like exposing one stop over the metered exposure in-camera. In Lightroom, the Exposure slider affects midtone brightness (in portraits, that's skin tones). Drag it to the right to increase brightness, or drag it to the left to decrease brightness (you can see this in the slider itself—white is to the right and black is to the left).

If you move your cursor over the middle of the histogram at the top of the right-side panels, the area affected by the Exposure slider is highlighted in light gray and the word "Exposure" appears below the lower-left corner of the histogram.

> **Tip:** To have Lightroom perform an auto adjustment for a single slider, no matter where it appears in the adjustment panels, Shift-double-click it. This is especially helpful in setting contrast—if, say, you opt to set exposure and contrast manually rather than using the Auto button—because contrast can be tough to get right (because you can easily mess up your highlights and shadows).

Contrast adjusts the difference in brightness between the darkest and lightest tones in your picture. When you drag this slider to the right (increasing contrast), you "stretch out" the histogram's data, creating darker blacks and brighter whites. If you drag this slider to the left (decreasing contrast), you scrunch the histogram's data inward, shortening the distance between the darkest (pure black) and lightest (pure white) endpoints, making the photo's tones look flat or muddy.

Lightroom's Auto button often does a good job adjusting your image, and you may need to fine-tune only the exposure. However, if the auto adjustment is too far off, undo it by pressing Ctrl+Z/Command+Z, and then manually adjust the exposure and contrast.

Alternatively, Alt/Option-click the word Tone to reset the tone sliders to 0.

Adjusting shadows and highlights

The Highlights and Shadows sliders let you recover details in areas that may be clipped. Clipping occurs when there are areas in the picture that are too dark or too light. If an area is too dark (sometimes you'll hear it referred to as *blocked*), there is not enough variation in the shadows to provide detail. The area is too black, muddy, and no good. If there is an area that is clipped in the highlights (sometimes referred to as *blown out*), it is so bright, there is no detail in it. Printing this part of a picture would show nothing—no ink would hit the page.

The general goal is to make sure that both your shadows and highlights have the most amount of detail possible without affecting the rest of the image. This picture of a cave in Monument Valley, Utah, was exposed for the blue sky. Because of the camera's limited dynamic range (and the lack of light in the cave), the interior of the cave is really dark, clipping the shadows. You can see this by moving your cursor over the shadow clipping warning at the upper left of the histogram, which turns the clipped shadows in your image blue (as seen in the inset).

Tip: You can click either clipping warning to leave the warning on while you work. When you are finished using the shadow and highlight clipping warnings, make sure you go back and turn them off.

Saving Develop settings as defaults and presets

If you repeatedly set the same panels to the same settings, consider saving them as default values or including them in a preset. Both maneuvers can save you a lot of time.

For example, any settings you make in the panels on the right side of the Develop module can be saved as defaults so that they're automatically applied when you open an image in the Develop module. Although you (probably) wouldn't want to save tone and color changes as defaults, camera calibration profiles and the Lens Corrections panel's Enable Profile Corrections and Remove Chromatic Aberration options are great candidates for saving as defaults. This is especially true if you tend to take the same kind of pictures with the same camera (say, you always shoot portraits with your Canon 5D Mark III).

To save settings as defaults:

1   Ensure all other panels on the right are at their default settings.

2   Adjust the settings you want to capture as defaults.

3   Press and hold Alt/Option to change the Reset button at the lower right to Set Default.

4   Click Set Default, and in the resulting dialog, click Update To Current Settings.

From this point on, those settings will be applied to any photo you take with that camera the second you open it in the Develop module.

Another option is to save certain settings as a preset that you apply whenever you want or on import. For example, if you find a camera calibration profile that you like for landscapes but prefer a different one for portraits, you could set up two presets: one for landscape shots and another for portraits. And you could apply either of those presets on import.

To save a preset:

1   Adjust the settings in the panels on the right however you like.

2   Click the plus sign (+) in the Presets panel header and choose Create Preset.

3   In the resulting dialog box, enter a meaningful name for the preset.

4   Click Check None at lower left.

5   Turn on the settings you want included in the preset—here, that's Lens Profile Corrections, Chromatic Aberration, and Calibration.

6   Click Create.

To install presets you've downloaded from elsewhere:

1   Uncompress them, and then choose Edit > Preferences (Windows) or Lightroom > Preferences (macOS).

2   In the dialog box that appears, click the Presets tab.

3   Click the Show Lightroom Develop Presets button.

4 In the Explorer or Finder window that appears, drag your presets into it.

5 Restart Lightroom.

To apply the preset:

1 Select an image (or several).

2 Open the Presets panel.

3 Click the triangle to the left of User Presets to expand it.

4 Click the preset you want to apply, and Lightroom makes it so.

To apply a preset on import, choose it from the Import Preset menu at the bottom of the Import window.

Adjusting the picture's exposure overexposes the sky and eliminates the blue I am looking for. Dragging the Shadows slider, though, brings back all the detail in the cave without sacrificing the blue in the sky.

This picture (of the Narrows at Zion National Park) is a little overexposed at the top. Move your cursor over the highlight clipping warning (at the upper right of the histogram), and red appears where there is no information.

▶ **Tip:** You can turn clipping warnings on and off by pressing J on your keyboard.

Highlights slider to the rescue! Dragging the Highlights slider to the left darkens only that portion of the image, yet leaves all of the shadow detail intact. The result is more yellow at the top of the mountain and less blown-out highlights, without having to make any additional changes.

These four sliders encompass the largest number of adjustments you'll make to your pictures. I think it will come as a big shock just how much information you can get out of raw files, so make sure you're shooting in raw!

Adjusting whites and blacks

Now that you've adjusted exposure, contrast, highlights, and shadows, we'll move on to the Whites and Blacks sliders.

Adjusting whites and blacks can be controversial because many photographers set their whites and blacks *first*. Those first four sliders work so well for me, I find I use the Whites and Blacks sliders less and less. More often than not, I only use them to do some slight tweaking to the file.

In the picture here, there's a pretty good range of light, but I could use a little bit more information in both the blacks

and whites, if you're looking at the histogram. By dragging those sliders, we can solve that problem pretty quickly.

The whites and blacks are the brightest and the darkest parts of the picture, but it can be difficult to see exactly where they are. Here are two tips to help you with this: First, hold down the Alt/Option key and click the Whites slider. As soon as you click, the image turns completely black. As you drag the Whites slider to the right, you'll see some color changes.

What you're looking for is the first area that turns white. White tells you that portion of the picture is clipping, so that is the brightest you can make the whites without losing information. If other colors appear before you see white, Lightroom is letting you know that they are predominately bright in the image. Looking at the original image, it feels like it has a film of color over it. This is known as a *color cast*. The yellows that appear when we do this clipping trick suggest there is a bit of bright yellow in the picture, but I am okay with that. You may see other colors as you drag, but what you're looking for is white.

Once you're done with the whites, Alt-click/Option-click the Blacks slider and drag it to the left. This time, the image turns white, and what you're looking for is the first spot of black. This tells you how far you can drag the Blacks slider.

Now you have your limits and you can use the Shadows and Highlights sliders to bring back as much information in the file as you can.

The second method for setting your white and black points is to let Lightroom automatically make these adjustments for you. Hold down the Shift key and double-click the Whites or Blacks slider, and Lightroom makes the change. Sometimes, it's good; most of the time, I'd rather make these changes myself. It's easy enough to do.

Clarity, vibrance, and saturation

Once you've dialed in your picture's tonality, you can move on to making some of the final Basic panel adjustments to the shot. Clarity, vibrance, and saturation round out the basic editing of a picture.

Setting the picture's general exposure adds contrast in the shadows and highlights, and affects the whites and blacks. The one part that doesn't get a lot of attention is the midtones and, sometimes, adding a little punch in the midtones is very helpful.

The Clarity slider controls midtone contrast. It's great for adding a bit of a gritty element to your pictures—things like metals, textures, brick walls, and hair all can do with a little bit of a clarity boost.

Keep in mind, though, when you're using the Clarity slider, that out-of-focus areas in a picture generally don't look good with clarity applied to them. It also doesn't do well with softer elements, such as clouds, water, and fluffy kitties.

The Saturation and Vibrance sliders both deal with the application of color to a picture, but they work a little differently. Dragging the Saturation slider to the right intensifies all of the colors in your image evenly, including skin tones. The problem is it really doesn't take into account whether a color is overused already. It's an easy way for you to overcook a picture in Lightroom. You'll need a more subtle hand at this, and that's where the Vibrance slider comes in.

As you drag the Vibrance slider to the right, any under-represented colors are intensified more. Any colors that are over-represented are not adjusted as much. If there are any skin tones in the picture, Vibrance tries not to affect them as much.

Add a more generous Vibrance boost to your picture to see how it looks before adding any Saturation adjustments. If there is an individual color you want to boost, adjust it individually in the Saturation section of the HSL/Color panel or paint in a color change with the Adjustment Brush, which we'll cover later.

Adding detail to your images

When you shoot in JPEG mode, the camera adds color, contrast, and sharpening to the final image. Photographers are quick to make the tonal adjustments we just discussed, but a shocking number of them forget the most vital component: detail.

Lightroom adds a small amount of detail to raw files, but it is never really enough for input sharpening.

In the Detail panel, there is a Sharpening area with four sliders: Amount, Radius, Detail, and Masking. Above the Sharpening sliders, there is a 100% preview of the picture (click the little triangle to its right to show/hide it). This small preview isn't a really good way for you to see how much sharpness is being applied. Instead, click the larger image in the center preview area once to zoom in to 100%. Drag around the picture to find an area where you can see the sharpening you're applying better and evaluate its effect.

Let's look at the sliders. The Amount slider is pretty straightforward: it dictates how much sharpening you want to apply to the picture.

The Radius slider lets you change how far from the center of the pixel you want to apply that sharpening. It's really hard to see this by just dragging the Radius slider, so try this: hold down the Alt/Option key and drag the slider. Drag it to the left, and your image turns gray; drag it to the right, and you start seeing more edge information. The visible edge information is the area that is sharpened. Anything that's gray won't be sharpened. This gives you a better way to create the sharpness that you need.

Once you have the Radius set, move on to the Detail slider. The Detail slider brings out more texture or detail in a picture as you drag it to the right. However, if you move it too far, or all the way to the right, it will start introducing a little bit of noise. You'll want to be careful with that.

Use the Radius and the Detail sliders to define the areas that you want to see sharpened, first. Then, go back and adjust your sharpening amount.

If you want to limit how that sharpening is applied, use the Masking slider. It creates a black-and-white mask, where the black areas won't be sharpened and the white areas will be sharpened, confining your sharpening to just the edges.

Again, hold down the Alt/Option key and drag the Masking slider to the right, and you can dictate where you want that sharpening to occur. Once you release the Alt/Option key, you'll see a much sharper picture without the noise you might get from sharpening everything evenly.

To see a before/after of your sharpening, click the power switch at the far left of the Detail panel's header. Click it again to turn the sharpening back on, and now you can see whether you've added enough sharpening.

Input, creative & output sharpening

When you import a raw photo, Lightroom automatically applies a little sharpening to your photo so you can see the details it contains. This sharpening is attempting to mimic the sharpening that your camera would normally apply to an image if it were shot as a JPEG, and is commonly referred to as *input sharpening*. In my opinion, this level of sharpening is never enough as input sharpening, which means that you have to take it into your own hands at the start of the import process.

As you start working with your image, you may decide that you would like to sharpen more in some areas and not as much in others. For example, I would sharpen the bark on a tree more than I would sharpen the sky that is behind the tree. This is commonly known as *creative sharpening*—sharpening you perform to highlight a specific thing in a picture.

When you're completely finished adjusting the photo, you can add more sharpening according to how you'll output it, which is cleverly referred to as *output sharpening*. For example, a photo that's destined to become a canvas gallery wrap needs more sharpening than one you'll print on glossy or metallic stock.

How much to sharpen these images, when to sharpen them, and what process to use in doing so in Photoshop could be the subject of an entirely new book.

I believe Jeff Shewe is one of the masters in this space and *The Digital Print* (by Peachpit Press) is a book that will take you through this entire process, from start to finish.

Once you're done with sharpening, go ahead and tackle noise. Noise in a picture appears for one of two reasons: you used a camera with a really high ISO setting (you shot in low light) or you added a lot of sharpening to your photo. In this example, we're using a picture taken at 12,800 ISO, so it's pretty high.

The Noise Reduction section has a two different types of noise you can affect, the first of which is luminance. Drag the Luminance slider to the right, and the noise starts disappearing. You'll use this slider for 90% of the noise you want to remove.

If you feel you have lost too much detail after dragging the Luminance slider, grab the Detail slider below it and drag it to the right. If you want add contrast back after these adjustments, drag the that slider to the right a bit. Increasing the Detail and the Contrast reduces some of the effect of the luminance noise reduction (they tend to counterbalance each other). Click the Detail panel's switch to turn your adjustments off and back on to see your results.

The Color, Detail, and Smoothness sliders deal with the fact that some camera sensors display noise not just in black, white, or gray dots, but in red, green, or blue dots, as well. To mitigate that, drag the Color slider to the right until those dots are desaturated, then add a bit of detail and smoothness back in.

Noise reduction brings back some smoothness to a file with a high ISO, but it's also something you have to do if you excessively sharpen a picture. The more you sharpen a picture, the more noise gets introduced, especially if you use the Detail slider. So every time you go into the Detail panel's sharpening section and create a lot of sharpening, add a little bit of noise reduction too. You'll be surprised at the quality of the results you'll get.

Cropping your image

The best thing you can do to your pictures is to make sure that you only leave in what needs to be left in. To do that, it is absolutely essential you crop them.

Press the R key on the keyboard and the Crop & Straighten tools appear. A crop overlay appears on your image, letting you change the crop. Here are a couple things to keep in mind when cropping a picture:

- Hide the entire interface to better see your picture. Press Shift+Tab to hide all the panels, then press the L key twice to go into Lights Out mode. To finish your crop, press Enter/Return, and then press L again to turn the lights back on and Shift+Tab again to bring the panels back.

- By default, dragging inward from a corner lets you crop the picture proportionally, but there are times when you don't want a proportional crop. There are a set of predefined crop ratios in the Aspect menu. Even better, if you choose Custom from the menu, a dialog box appears that lets you enter your own values. Once you choose an aspect, the lock icon appears closed, letting you know you cannot change the proportions as you drag. To crop without a set aspect, click the lock icon to unlock it.

- Seeing a crop overlay (Rule of Thirds, Golden Spiral, and so on) over the picture can be really helpful. Press the O key to cycle through them.

One last bit of advice on cropping: if an element in the picture doesn't add to the picture, it takes away from it. Crop those away. Cropping is essential.

Lens corrections and transformations

Every lens you use creates problems that need some form of adjustment. One lens may distort pictures a little, while another may darken pictures' edges (which is where the vignette effect comes from). Some older or more cost-concious lenses cause colored pixels to appear along the edges of objects (called *chromatic abberation*). Lightroom provides an easy way for you to correct these problems.

● **Note:** While Lightroom contains a large collection of lens profiles, sometimes your specific lens isn't listed. Newer lenses usually take an update or two before they appear in the Lens Corrections panel.

In the Lens Corrections panel's Profile tab, select Enable Profile Corrections, and Lightroom reads the image's embedded EXIF information to determine what make and model of the lens you used. It then chooses one of the built-in profiles and automatically adjusts the picture, often yielding a better-looking file. If it can't find your lens, choose the closest one from the Make and Model menus.

There are times, however, when the problem with your image has little to do with your lens and more to do with your position when you made the picture. In the picture above, the camera was angled upward on the side of the Grand Mosque in Abu Dhabi, creating exaggerated vertical lines and a tilt to the picture that require additional transformation. This is where the Transform panel can help.

The buttons in the Upright area of the Transform panel tilt and skew your image in an attempt to fix it. There are four options to choose from:

- Auto: Balances level, vertical, and horizontal perspective corrections, and keeps the aspect ratio as much as possible.

- Level: Perspective corrections are weighted toward horizontal details.
- Vertical: Perspective corrections are weighted toward vertical details and level corrections.
- Full: Combination of full Level, Vertical, and Auto perspective corrections.

It's often best to try each option to find the best one for your situation.

If none of the options fully solves your problem, try the Guided option to really move things along. Guided transformation allows you to draw up to four lines on the picture, tracing areas that should be straight. As you draw the lines, the image adjusts itself to what it believes is a straight picture.

Once the transformation is complete, use the Transform sliders to make any final tweaks. This image ended up with a lot of white background in the bottom corners that needs to be cropped, or click the Constrain Crop option to have Lightroom automatically remove the white areas. The final image will be smaller than the original one, but it will certainly be straighter.

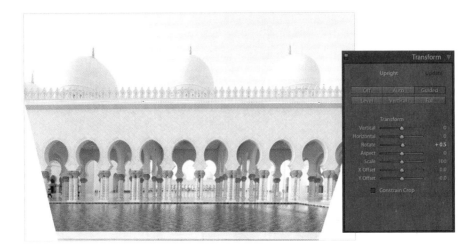

Using virtual copies for variations

Lightroom does a great job of keeping your library organized by keeping the number of duplicate images down to zero. One image can be referenced in multiple collections, and making a change in the file in one collection automatically cascades that change to the file in all other collections.

What if you want a copy of the file to try out a different look without changing the original? This is where another powerful feature comes in handy: the virtual copy.

Create a new collection called **Virtual Copy Test** and place the Monument Valley picture we edited earlier in it, so we can keep the changes we make to this picture separate.

Right-click the image thumbnail, either in the Library module's Grid view or in the Filmstrip in the Develop module, and choose Create Virtual Copy from the menu. A duplicate thumbnail will appear to the right of the original. It will look exactly the same as the original, but with the lower-left corner of the thumbnail curling up.

This new file is a virtual copy. You can make changes to it in the Develop module and it will be treated as a separate image. The plus side to this? While it looks like a separate image—a full copy not tied to the original image—it actually refers to the same physical copy of the image. That's the virtual part.

You can create multiple virtual copies of a photo to try out different edits without taking up much additional space on your hard drive. You can make better judgements about which edits you prefer by having these virtual copies side by side.

Using snapshots for variations

To save different edits to a photo without making separate copies of the image for comparison, snapshots are a great option.

Edit the image to a point you want to save, and then click the plus sign (+) on the right side of the Snapshots panel header. A dialog box will appear with the date and time that you created the snapshot in the Name text box. You can either keep that date and time or rename the snapshot and click Create.

Continue editing your picture and when you are ready to save another change, click the plus sign (+) again to save a new snapshot. This is a great way to save variations and keep tabs on your progress, although I prefer the side-by-side nature of working with virtual copies.

Syncing changes to multiple photos

Lightroom has a number of features that make quick work of sharing adjustments across multiple photos, including Sync, Copy/Paste, Previous, and Auto Sync. If you're adjusting photos that were taken under the same lighting conditions, these features can save you loads of editing time.

To apply the same changes to two or more photos, use the following steps to sync changes manually. Let's practice on the pictures of Sabine at the piano.

1   Go back to your Develop Module Practice collection and select all of the images of Sabine at the piano. Click the plus sign (+) at the right side of the Collections panel's header, and create a collection called **Sync Test**.

> **Tip:** To save some time, leave the Include Selected Photos option selected.

2   Select the first picture of Sabine that we edited for white balance, and add contrast, clarity, and vibrance adjustments in the Basic panel.

3   Shift-click the last thumbnail in the Filmstrip to automatically select all of the images in between those two images.

> **Tip:** You can also Ctrl-click/Command-click to select nonconsecutive thumbnails in the Filmstrip.

4   Make sure the photo you corrected in step 2 is the most-selected thumbnail— the one with the lightest thumbnail frame in the Filmstrip (circled here).

5   Click the Sync button at the bottom of the right-side panels. If the button reads Auto Sync, click the panel switch to the left of the button to change it to Sync.

6   In the resulting dialog box, click Check None, and then pick the changes you want to sync. For this lesson, select the White Balance, Clarity, Vibrance, and Process Version options.

7   Click Synchronize to automatically apply those changes to the selected photos.

If the result, including the crop, needs fine-tuning on any affected photos, select the photo in the Filmstrip (remember to click in the gray area outside the thumbnail to deselect all others and select only this one) and then adjust the settings.

Your other options for applying changes to multiple photos include:

• Copy/Paste: Select the photo you adjusted, and then click Copy at the bottom of the left-side panels. In the resulting dialog box, select the changes you want to copy, and then click Copy. Select other photos in the Filmstrip, and then click the Paste button, also at lower left.

• Previous: This option lets you apply the most recent changes you've made to *one* other photo. Immediately after adjusting an image, click to select another photo in the Filmstrip, and then click the Previous button (where the Sync button is if

▶ **Tip:** You can sync local adjustments, too. As you'll learn in the next lesson, each local adjustment you make sports a pin that you can drag to move the adjustment to another area (say, if your subject moved a little bit between the photos you're syncing).

you select multiple photos). Lightroom applies *all* the changes you made to the previous photo to the one that's currently selected—you don't get a dialog box that lets you pick which edits to apply.

- Auto Sync: If you select multiple photos in the Filmstrip and then click the gray switch on the Sync button, it changes to Auto Sync. Click it, and Lightroom applies all the changes you make to the most selected photo, from this point forward—until you remember to turn off Auto Sync—to all the other selected photos. This is a perilous option because it's incredibly easy to forget you have other photos selected or that you have Auto Sync turned on. For that reason, it's best to avoid this feature.

You can sync changes in the Library module too. To do that, select the photos in the Filmstrip or Grid view, and then click the Sync Settings button at the bottom of the right-side panels.

Now that you have a good grasp of how to make global adjustments, you're ready to dive into the realm of adjusting specific areas of a photo, which is a lot of fun.

The significance of process version

Process version (PV) refers to Lightroom's underlying image processing technology. The instructions in this book, particularly those that concern the Basic panel, are for the current Lightroom process version, Process Version 5, which was introduced in 2018. You can find the process version of the image by going to the Camera Calibration panel in the Develop module.

If you used Lightroom to adjust photos prior to 2018, a different process version was used. In fact, if you used a version of Lightroom that dated back to 2012 and looked at the Develop module, some of the Basic panel sliders would look and behave differently than Lightroom CC. Some sliders have different names, their starting points are different, and the Clarity slider, in particular, uses a completely different algorithm in earlier process versions.

If you like the way a photo looks with its older processing, you can leave it alone. If you want to take advantage of the improvements in Process Version 5, you can change the photo's process version, although doing so may significantly change the way it looks.

Review questions

1. When importing raw files, why do the thumbnails shift in color shortly after (or during) the import process?
2. What is the difference between Lightroom's Camera Matching profiles and creative profiles?
3. Is there a way to save multiple versions of a photo?
4. How do you find the white point in your photo?
5. Is there one right way to white balance a photo?
6. How do you reset a panel's sliders?
7. How can you avoid sharpening your entire photo evenly?
8. What are the four ways to apply changes to multiple images?

Review answers

1. Because Lightroom initially shows you the JPEG preview of the raw files made by the camera. If Lightroom can't interpret all of the proprietary camera settings, the rendered raw files may look slightly different than the JPEG preview.
2. The Camera Matching profiles mimic the profiles built in to your camera by the manufacturer. Creative profiles were created for artistic expression.
3. Yes. You can use snapshots or virtual copies. Snapshots let you save different versions of the photo that are accessible in the original file via the Snapshots panel. Virtual copies, on the other hand, create a separate shortcut (alias) of the file, which you can adjust any way you want.
4. Alt-click/Option-click the Whites slider and drag to the right. As soon as you begin to see white appear, you have found your white point. Also, you can double-click the Whites slider to have Lightroom set it automatically.
5. No. White balancing is subjective. Lightroom's White Balance controls can neutralize a color cast in a photo, but there are times when a color cast is desirable as a way to communicate the mood and message that you, as the photographer, choose to convey.
6. By double-clicking the slider itself.
7. By using the Masking slider in the Detail panel's Sharpening section.
8. Sync, Copy/Paste, Previous, and Auto Sync.

4 USING LIGHTROOM'S DEVELOP MODULE FOR LOCAL AND CREATIVE ADJUSTMENTS

Lesson overview

The adjustments you learned about in the previous lesson are *global*—they affect the entire photo. To accentuate a certain area, you can perform *local* adjustments. Lightroom includes an impressive array of tools for this purpose. By mastering and maximizing these techniques in Lightroom, you'll spend less time in Photoshop.

In this lesson you'll learn how to:

- Adjust skies and foregrounds using the Graduated Filter.

- Create custom vignettes using the Radial Filter.

- Use the Adjustment Brush and Range Mask tools to apply targeted adjustments.

- Remove distractions with the Spot Removal tool.

- Convert a color photo to black and white, and apply effects like split-toning, vignettes, and grain.

 This lesson will take about 2 hours to complete. Please log in to your account on peachpit.com to download the files for this lesson, or go to the "Getting Started" section at the beginning of this book and follow the instructions under "Accessing the lesson files and Web Edition." Store the files on your computer in a convenient location. Your Account page is also where you'll find any updates to the lessons or to the lesson files. Look on the Lesson & Update Files tab to access the most current content.

Lightroom's local adjustment tools let you edit
specific areas of your photo, and its powerful color
controls let you create interesting effects.

Preparing for this lesson

1 Follow the instructions in the "Getting Started" section at the beginning of this book for setting up an LPCIB folder on your computer, downloading the lesson files to that LPCIB folder, and creating an LPCIB catalog in Lightroom.

2 Download the Lesson 04 folder from your Account page at peachpit.com to *username*/Documents/LPCIB/Lessons.

3 Launch Lightroom, and open the LPCIB catalog you created in "Getting Started" by choosing File > Open Catalog and navigating to the LPCIB Catalog. Alternatively, you can choose File > Open Recent > LPCIB Catalog.

4 Add the Lesson 4 files to the LPCIB catalog using the steps in the Lesson 1 section "Importing photos from a hard drive."

5 In the Library module's Folders panel, select Lesson 04.

6 Create a collection called **Lesson 04 Images** and place the images from the Lesson 04 folder in the collection.

7 Set the Sort menu beneath the image preview to File Name.

Now that you have plenty of files to play with, you're ready to learn how to use Lightroom's tools to perform local adjustments. You'll start with the Graduated Filter and Radial Filter tools.

Using the Graduated Filter tool

The Graduated Filter tool lets you apply adjustments to part of a picture in a linear direction. The effect uses sliders that are similar to the ones in the Basic panel, but that let you fade out the effect in the direction you drag. In this exercise, you'll apply two Graduated Filter tool adjustments to a single photo.

1   Select the picture labeled slc.dng, an image of Salt Lake City, Utah. The sky is a little bright in this image. We want to darken that sky a bit, slowly fading the darkening as it reaches the horizon. This will draw the viewer's attention toward the horizon.

2   Activate the Graduated Filter tool in the tool strip beneath the Histogram panel (it's the fourth tool from the left), or press M on your keyboard. The Graduated Filter panel appears beneath the tool strip.

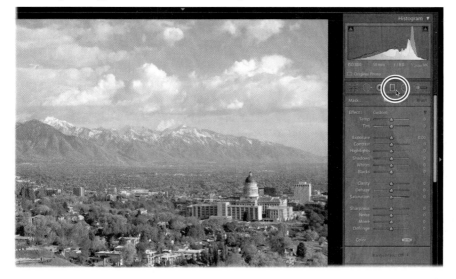

▶ **Tip:** This exercise file is a great candidate for using the Dehaze slider at the bottom of the Basic panel. Try setting it at +25 to give the photo a much-needed contrast and color boost.

● **Note:** If you prefer to work through this adjustment, activate the Graduated Filter tool, and click Reset at the bottom of the Graduated Filter panel to delete the ones that were applied for you. If you already clicked the Reset button and want to return to the edited version, click Snapshot 1 in the Snapshots panel.

3   In the Graduated Filter panel, double-click the Effect label at the upper left to set all the sliders to 0 (you can also Alt-click/Option-click the Effect label, which changes to Reset, to do the same thing).

The sliders for all the local adjustment tools are sticky, so it's important to remember to reset them. To reset an individual slider to its default value, double-click the slider label or the slider itself.

4   Drag the Exposure slider to the left to about −1.00. Setting one (or several) sliders before you use the tool loads it with those settings so they're applied as soon as you drag on your photo.

5   To apply the filter, Shift-drag from the top middle of the photo down to slightly past the top of the trees, so the adjustment covers the sky and mountains (holding down the Shift key keeps the filter straight).

▶ **Tip:** Press O on your keyboard to turn on the gradient mask overlay in light red. Press the same key to turn it back off (alternatively, turn on Show Selected Mask Overlay at the left side of the toolbar, beneath the photo). To change the mask color, press Shift+O on your keyboard (this is helpful when the mask color also appears in your photo).

Lightroom adds a mask in a linear gradient over the area where you dragged. This gradient mask controls where the adjustment is visible. Drag the pin in the middle of the gradient to reposition the filter. When the pin is selected, it's black, and you can adjust the filter's sliders. When it's unselected, it's light gray. To delete a filter, click its pin and press the Backspace/Delete key.

▶ **Tip:** Lightroom automatically hides the pins when you move your mouse away from the preview area. To change this, use the Show Edit Pins menu in the toolbar at the lower left of the photo. (If you don't see the toolbar beneath your photo, press T on your keyboard to turn it on.)

The filter's three white lines represent the strength of the adjustment: 100%, fading to 50%, and then down to 0%. You can contract or extend the filter's gradient by dragging the top or bottom lines toward or away from the center line. To rotate the filter, move your cursor near the center line, and when it turns into a curved arrow, drag it clockwise or counterclockwise.

6   To add another graduated filter, click New at the upper right of the panel, and then drag another filter from the bottom of the picture to the center of it. This deselects the first pin, which changes to light gray.

▶ **Tip:** You can create overlapping graduated filters, too!

7   Double-click Effect to reset all the sliders, and then drag the Exposure slider to the left, to about −1.00, to darken the foreground.

8 Click the panel switch at the bottom left of the Graduated Filter panel to turn both filters off, and then click it again to turn both filters back on.

To finish this off, click the top gradient's pin and drag the Dehaze slider to 33. This is a much better way to add Dehaze, as it only applies it where you need it—on the sky. Drag the Whites slider to 43 to bring back some brightness.

9 To close the Graduated Filter panel, click Close at the lower right of the panel or click the Graduated Filter tool itself in the tool strip to put it away.

The Graduated Filter tool can help accentuate portions of your picture and make them stand out. Here are a few more things that are helpful to know about using this tool (these tips work with the Radial Filter and Adjustment Brush, too):

• You can use a brush to erase portions of a filter. If the filter bleeds onto an area where you don't want it, click the filter's pin to select it. Click Brush at the upper right of the filter's panel (shown on the next page). Click Erase in the Brush section at the bottom of the panel to switch to Erase mode. Paint over any areas where you want to remove the filter (notice the minus sign [–] inside your brush cursor).

• You can lower the strength of all the settings of a single filter at once by select-ing its pin and clicking the black triangle at the upper right of the tool panel (just above the sliders; shown circled on the next page) to reveal an Amount slider. Drag it to the left to reduce the opacity of *all* the settings you applied with that filter.

• You can save tool settings as a preset. To do that, click the Effect menu near the top of the tool's panel (shown on the next page) and choose Save Current Set-tings as New Preset. In the resulting dialog box, enter a meaningful name and click Create. From this point on, your preset will be available in the Effect menu. This also is useful if you're making several adjustments with a single filter.

Click to save adjustment for this tool

Panel switch

The next section teaches you how to use the Radial Filter tool, which works in a similar manner.

Using the Radial Filter tool

You can use the Radial Filter tool to apply the same adjustments as the Graduated Filter tool, but in a circular pattern instead of a linear gradient. The Radial Filter tool is handy for spotlighting a specific area of your photo by brightening, darkening, blurring, and shifting the color of a background, and for creating an edge vignette that you can move around (say, to draw attention to a subject that is off-center).

In this exercise, you'll learn how to add a radial filter that draws your attention to a non-circular area. This area will be off-center (common in photography).

1   Select the flamingo image in the Filmstrip. While a post-crop vignette may seem appropriate here, the fact that the flamingo is off-center would make the effect look contrived. Ideally, we want the darkening to happen off-center, and only in the area around the middle flamingo.

2   Activate the Radial Filter tool in the tool strip beneath the Histogram panel (it's the fifth tool from the left) or press Shift+M on your keyboard. The Radial Filter panel appears beneath the tool strip.

3   In the filter's panel, double-click the Effect label at the upper left to set all sliders to 0.

4   Near the bottom of the tool options, set the Feather to around 75. This ensures a gradual, soft transition at the outside edge of your radial filter.

5   Click the field to the right of the Exposure slider to highlight it, and enter **–1.00**. Press Tab on your keyboard, and enter **15** for Contrast; press Tab again, and enter **–59** for Highlights; press Tab twice, and enter **35** for Whites.

▶ **Tip:** Using the Tab key will let you move down the specific fields and manually enter a number. If you'd like to move up in those fields, press Shift+Tab.

6   Position your cursor near the center of the flamingo and then drag diagonally downward and to its right side (the filter is created from the center out).

The adjustments you made immediately darken the area around the flamingo. The Highlights adjustment will also pull back some of the blown-out areas in the flamingo on the right. While this looks good, we will want to turn this circle into an oval to better cover the flamingo.

7   Reposition and resize the filter to your liking using the following techniques:

    • Reposition the filter by dragging its pin to a different area.

- Resize the filter by moving your cursor over one of the square anchor points on the filter's outline. When your cursor changes to a double-headed arrow, drag toward or away from the center of the filter to resize it. Do this to adjacent anchor points to reshape the filter.

- Rotate the filter by moving your cursor outside the filter's outline. When your cursor changes to a curved arrow, drag to rotate the filter.

8   Click the panel switch at the lower left of the Radial Filter panel to turn it off; click the switch again to turn it back on.

Note: You can erase portions of a Radial Filter adjustment by clicking Brush at the upper right of the tool's panel and then clicking Erase near the lower right of the panel, as described at the end of the previous section.

Let's try it on a different photo to see what else we can do with it. As with the Graduated Filter tool, you can add multiple Radial Filter adjustments to a single photo. To do that, after you finish adjusting your first Radial Filter, click New at the upper right of the filter's panel, and then double-click the Effect label to reset all the sliders to 0. Adjust the sliders for the next filter (you can tweak them later), and then drag over your photo to apply it.

I took a picture of my buddies Cameron and Owen. Both of their faces are dark, but one is seated higher than the other, so we need to brighten them separately.

1   Select the Portrait-2Boys image in the Filmstrip.

2 With the Radial Filter tool active, double-click Effect at the upper left of the panel to reset all the sliders to 0. At the bottom of the panel, make sure Feather is set to 75, and select Invert. This will apply the radial effect on the inside of the oval versus the outside of the oval.

3 Set the Exposure slider to approximately 1.25.

4 Drag to apply the filter to your photo around Cameron's head and torso (he's the child on the left).

5 Move the pin to the center of the subject and adjust the circle until it creates an oval that covers him (as shown here).

6 Once you have completed the adjustments for the first child, create a second inverted Radial Filter for the second child. Apply the same exposure of 1.25 for the second child. One of the benefits here is that you can combine both regular and inverted Radial Filters to apply different effects to the image.

7 Because the children were in shadow, both of them could benefit from a white balance adjustment. Create a third Radial Filter, leaving the Invert option selected.

8 Reset the Exposure slider and add a little warmth to the filter by adjusting the Temp slider to 14.

9 Drag an oval across both subjects and you'll notice that both children get a warmer tone.

If you have a series of portraits that need the same custom

vignette, you could sync a Radial Filter to multiple images (see the Lesson 3 section "Syncing changes to multiple photos").

In the next section, you'll learn how to retouch portraits using the Adjustment Brush tool.

Using the Adjustment Brush tool

While the Graduated Filter and Radial Filter allow you to make specific adjustments to an image, they do not have the fine control that is sometimes needed. Ideally, you would pinpoint all of the adjustments in the Basic and Detail panels to specific areas. This is where the Adjustment Brush really comes in handy.

The Adjustment Brush is perfect for making precise changes to specific areas, such as lightening and darkening (dodging and burning), blurring, sharpening, reducing noise, boosting color, and so on. In this section, you'll learn how to use it to do some photo finishing. Photoshop is a fantastic tool for pixel-perfect adjustments, but if you can complete a large portion of your work inside Lightroom, all the better.

Select the Indoors1.NEF file and go into the Develop module. Directly below the Histogram panel, you'll see a brush icon in the tool strip. Click it to get the Adjustment Brush, and the same sliders you saw with the Graduated and Radial Filters appear. You can paint all of these effects with the Adjustment Brush. Start by dragging the Exposure slider to −2.68 and painting over everything in the image, except for the monkey. All of the areas you paint on now will be underexposed.

A pin is dropped on the picture, letting you know that an adjustment has been painted. If you move your cursor over the pin, an overlay appears, showing you where you applied the effect. Press Shift-O wihle your cursor is over the pin to cycle through the different overlay colors.

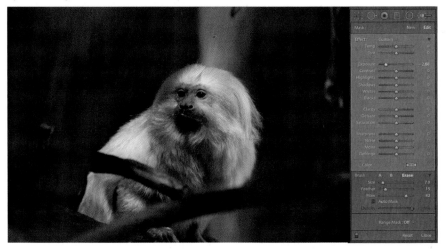

Let's reduce the highlights on the monkey, to the right of its face. We'll need a new Adjustment Brush selection and settings, so click New at the upper right of the panel. To reset the Exposure slider, double-click it. To reset all of the sliders in one shot, double-click the Effects label in the upper left. Take the Highlights slider down to –62 and the Temp to 36, and paint over the monkey's fur on the right, pulling some of the highlights back and warming it up (as shown here).

There is a color cast on the branch in the front, so let's tone it down and increase the temperature. Create a new brush and underexpose it a little further by dragging the Exposure slider to –1.65, dropping the Highlights slider to –44, and increasing the Temp slider to 55. Painting over the branch now darkens it and adds a little bit of a yellow tone to it, matching the scene.

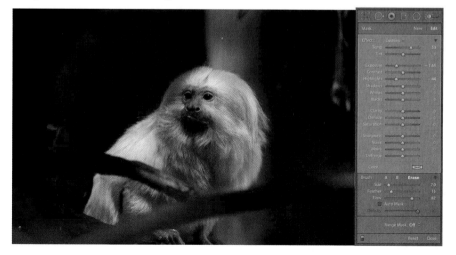

Finally, let's add a little clarity to the fur. Clarity boosts the midtone contrast. It's great for textured items, fur, metals, or anything that needs an extra bit of sharpness to it. Oftentimes, I choose not to use clarity as a global adjustment, as it makes the picture look too fake. Painting it in locally with the Adjustment Brush keeps it more realistic. Also add a little Contrast and Sharpness.

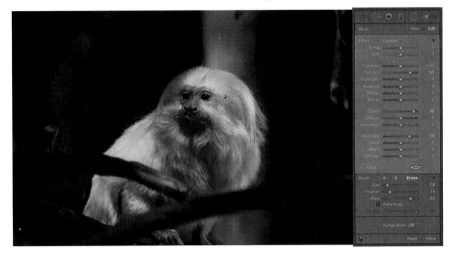

Moving your cursor over each pin shows you an overlay of the area affected by that pin. To add another effect to an area, simply select the pin that covers that area. To delete the effects in a single area, select the pin for that area and press Backspace/Delete on the keyboard.

To see how your changes look, create a virtual copy of the picture by right-clicking and selecting Create Virtual Copy. With the virtual copy selected in the Develop module, click Reset at the bottom of the Adjustment Brush panel to remove your changes. Then, Ctrl-click/Command-click the adjusted photo in the Filmstrip to select both, and press the letter C to go into Compare view. The Adjustment Brush can be a powerful tool to bring out selective details inside an image!

Adjustment pin tips and tricks

The following tips work on any adjustment that creates a pin, so you can use them on adjustments made with the Graduated Filter, Radial Filter, and Adjustment Brush tools.

To move a pin, drag it to the desired location in the photo.

To duplicate a pin, right-click it, choose Duplicate from the menu that appears, and then drag the new pin elsewhere in the photo.

To reduce the intensity of all settings, Alt/Option-click the pin, and when your cursor turns into a double-sided arrow, drag left. Any sliders you've changed move toward their default value of 0 as you drag.

To increase the intensity of all settings, Alt/Option-drag the pin to the right. Any sliders you've changed move toward their maximum settings as you drag.

Removing distractions with the Spot Removal tool

Although Lightroom lacks Photoshop's advanced Content-Aware technology for removing and moving objects in your photos (see the section "Where Photoshop excels" in "Getting Started"), its Spot Removal tool does a nice job of removing smaller distractions such as sensor dust spots, objects with lots of open space around them (say, power lines), blemishes, and so on. It also can be used to perform some quick photo retouching of subjects.

The Spot Removal tool works in both Heal and Clone modes, which lets you determine whether you want an automatic blending of surrounding pixels or a straight copy and paste, respectively.

Removing sensor spots and syncing changes

In this exercise, you'll use the Spot Removal tool to get rid of sensor spots, and then sync those changes to another photo with the same spots in the same locations.

1   Select the desert photo (sands-1.dng) in the Filmstrip. Adjust the image to your liking, following the workflow in Lesson 3 to adjust tone and color.

2   Activate the Spot Removal tool in the tool strip beneath the Histogram panel (it's the second tool from the left) or press Q on your keyboard. The Spot Removal panel appears beneath the tool strip.

3   In the Spot Removal panel, click Heal so Lightroom blends the change with surrounding pixels. Set the Feather slider to around 10, and the Opacity to 100.

Since Lightroom automatically blends your changes with surrounding pixels when the tool is in Heal mode, you can get away with a lower Feather amount, especially when you're removing tiny dust spots.

▶ **Tip:** If you don't see a toolbar beneath your image in the preview area, press T on your keyboard to summon it.

4 In the toolbar beneath the image preview, select Visualize Spots. Lightroom inverts the image in black and white so the outlines of its content are visible. Any sensor spots in the photo appear as white circles or grayish dots. Drag the Visualize Spots slider to the right to increase sensitivity and see more spots; drag to the left if you are seeing too many spots.

The Visualize Spots feature is critical for revealing spots caused by dust on your lens, sensor, or scanner. Although these tiny imperfections may not be noticeable onscreen, they often show up when you print the photo.

▶ **Tip:** When a local adjustment tool is active, you can also zoom in by pressing the Spacebar on your keyboard as you click the photo, and then continue to hold it down to move around. When a local adjustment tool isn't active, simply clicking the photo zooms in and out.

5 Zoom in to the photo by clicking 1:1 in the Navigator panel at the upper left. Hold down the Spacebar on your keyboard, and drag to reposition the photo so you can see one of the spots.

6 Move your cursor over one of the spots, resize it so it's slightly bigger than the spot itself, and then click the spot to remove it.

> ▶ **Tip:** You can resize your cursor by pressing the Left Bracket key ([) on your keyboard to decrease size or the Right Bracket key (]) to increase it.

Lightroom copies content from a nearby area in the photo and uses it to remove the spot. You see two circles: One marks the area you clicked (the destination), and another marks the area Lightroom used to remove the spot (the source), with an arrow that points to where the spot used to be (shown below left).

● **Note:** Because the Tool Overlay menu in the toolbar beneath the photo is set to Auto here, the circles disappear when you mouse away from the preview area, just like the pins of the Graduated Filter, Radial Filter, and Adjustment Brush tools. To change this behavior, click the Tool Overlay menu and choose Always, Never, or Selected (to see only the selected fix).

Destination

Source

7 If you don't like the results, try changing the area Lightroom used for the fix, or try changing the tool size. To do that, click the destination circle to select the spot and then:

- Press the Forward Slash (/) key on your keyboard to have Lightroom pick a different source area. Keep tapping the key until the removal looks good to you.

- Manually change the source area by moving your cursor over the source circle and, when your cursor turns into a tiny hand, dragging the circle to another location in the photo (shown above right).

- To resize the destination or the source, move your cursor over either circle, and when your cursor changes to a double-sided arrow, drag outward to increase or inward to decrease the size of the circles. Alternatively, you can drag the Size slider in the Spot Removal panel.

Of course, you can always start over by removing the fix. To do that, select the destination circle and then press the Delete/Backspace key on your keyboard.

▶ **Tip:** To thoroughly inspect a photo for spots (if, say, you'll print it or submit it to a stock photography service), press the Home key on your keyboard to start at the upper-left corner of the photo. Press the Page Down button on the keyboard to page through the photo from top to bottom in a column-like pattern.

8 Spacebar-drag to reposition the photo, and repeat these instructions to remove all the spots.

9 Turn off Visualize Spots in the toolbar to return to regular view, and see if all the spots are gone.

You can remove spots in either view, or you can switch back and forth between views as you work by turning Visualize Spots on and off.

10 To sync these changes with the other desert photos, Shift-click the last desert photo in the Filmstrip and then click the Sync button at the lower right. In the resulting dialog, click Check None, select Spot Removal, and then click Synchronize.

Be sure to inspect the other photos to ensure the spots were successfully removed. If, by chance, the spots weren't in exactly the same place in the other photos, you can reposition the removals by dragging the destination circles.

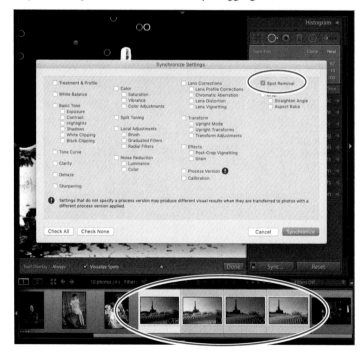

11 Don't put away the Spot Removal tool yet, because you'll use it in the next exercise.

Removing objects from photos

Now let's take a look at how you can use the Spot Removal tool to remove slightly larger objects by dragging.

1   Select the clone-1.raf photo in the Filmstrip, and follow the adjustment workflow in Lesson 3 to adjust the tone and color to your liking.

2   In the Spot Removal panel, increase Feather to 28 or so. This softens the transition edges a little more so the removal looks realistic.

3   Use the instructions in the previous section to set your brush size, and then drag to remove the top portion of the couple in the center of the photo. As you drag, Lightroom marks the area with white. When you release your mouse button, the white disappears and you see an outline of where you dragged, the destination area. The source area is also visible as an outline, with an arrow pointing to the destination. You can reposition either area by dragging the pin inside each outline. In this example, try dragging the source area to the base of another statue.

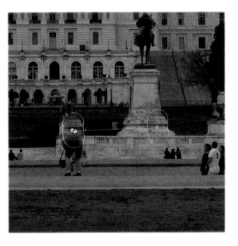

4   Once the top portion of the couple is removed, brush the bottom half of them to remove it and use a new source area. This figure shows all the pins it took to remove all the tourists.

5   Assess your work by turning the panel's switch off and on. If necessary, click one of the pins to select the removal, and reposition the source area to make it better match the tone and color.

● **Note:** You don't have to perform the adjustment workflow on this photo, but it's good practice.

▶ **Tip:** You can adjust the Feather slider after you drag to remove an object, which is helpful to add more or less smoothing in the transition area.

▶ **Tip:** Remember that you can also press the Forward Slash (/) key on your keyboard to have Lightroom pick a different source area if you don't like the initial results.

Creative color and black & white effects

As you work through your photographic exploration, it's a good idea to work in black and white. According to famed environmental portrait photographer Gregory Heisler, black-and-white imagery "allows you to see the structure of the image in a way that color cannot." While we often see photographs in black and white as nostalgic, the lack of color in the image allows the viewer to focus on stronger components of the picture—composition, structure, gesture, and so on.

Your digital camera may have a setting that allows you to make black-and-white pictures. These settings, however, are only for images shot in JPEG format. More importantly, allowing your digital camera to produce a black-and-white image robs you of the ability to target specific colors in a picture and decide how you want them to appear. Think of this as an opportunity to use your own creativity.

Taking this technique further, Lightroom lets you add individual colors to an image, creating a hand-tinted picture that can expand your exploration. These coloring techniques can start with a single color, and move on to several more to produce retro effects in a snap. You'll start this section by creating a black-and-white photo, and then move on to other creative color effects from there.

Converting a color photo to black and white

● **Note:** In previous versions of Lightroom, creating a black-and-white image required you to go to the HSL panel to start. With the 2019 release, this option is now located in the Basic panel. Clicking Black & White at the upper right of the panel will change the HSL/ Color panel into the B&W panel for you to adjust the black-and-white mix.

As a general rule, you should adjust the image that you want to make black and white prior to the conversion. Often, I'll oversaturate the image to better see the color representation of the photo. I also adjust Highlights, Shadows, Blacks, Whites, and Dehaze to make sure every bit of detail in the image is available. All of the color will disappear shortly, but it's good to see this beforehand.

1 Select the clone-1.raf file we used previously in the Filmstrip. Adjust the image as you see here.

Softening with negative Clarity and Dehaze

The Clarity and Dehaze sliders increase contrast and saturation. A negative Clarity adjustment can do wonders to soften skin and other elements in a portrait. You also can use Dehaze to fix a foggy or hazy photo.

What you may not realize is that you also can use a negative Clarity setting to produce a watercolor look and a negative Dehaze setting to create a foggy-dreamy look. To get your creative juices flowing, consider these examples, which you can try on the photo of the lone tree (you can use the Snapshots panel to see different versions of the photo that were prepared for you).

In the Basic panel, Clarity was set to −71 to make the photo resemble a watercolor painting. And in the Effects panel, Dehaze was set to −26.

While you obviously wouldn't want to soften every photo, it's good to know that these kinds of special effects can be performed in Lightroom.

Original corrected photo   Negative Clarity

Negative Clarity + Dehaze

2 Once the image is adjusted, click Black & White in the Treatment section at the top of the Basic panel. The image undergoes a basic black-and-white adjustment and the HSL/Color panel changes to B&W.

3 Expand the B&W panel, and there are a series of sliders representing different colors that you can mix. Dragging any of the sliders to the right will make any color in that range more white. Dragging a color slider to the left will make that individual color more black.

4 The biggest problem that we run into here is that we are attempting to adjust color sliders in an image that is now in black and white. This is where the Targeted Adjustment tool (TAT) can come in quite handy (it looks like a dartboard and is circled in the panel shown at right).

5 Click the Targeted Adjustment tool (TAT) at the upper left of the panel to activate it. This tool lets you make adjustments to specific colors by dragging up or down over the photo itself.

6 Click the darker blue area of the sky, and while holding down your mouse button, drag downward to darken all the colors beneath the tool, in the sky and wherever else they appear in the photo.

7 Click the Capitol Building and drag the mouse upward slightly to lighten the individual colors that make up the building, wherever they are in your image.

8 Finally, click the grassy area at the bottom of the picture and drag those colors toward black.

9   Assess your custom black-and-white work by clicking the panel switch at the upper left of the B&W panel to turn your adjustments off and back on again. This will toggle you between the regular black-and-white conversion Lightroom performed and your custom black-and-white conversion.

After you complete a black-and-white conversion on your image, go back to the Basic panel and perform some additional adjustments to your image. Often I find that black-and-white images can do with a little more contrast, clarity, exposure adjustments, detail, and grain (which we'll talk about later) to really finish them off.

Note: If you decide that you no longer want to have this image as a black and white, simply click Color in the Treatment section of the Basic panel. The image will return to color, and the B&W panel will reset itself to HSL/Color once again.

Applying split-toning and retro effects

Lightroom's Split Toning panel lets you add a color tint to the highlights and another one to the shadows in your photo. The best results often come from using colors that are opposite each other on a color wheel, such as orange and blue, yellow and purple, green and red, and so on.

To create a split-tone, follow these steps:

1   Perform a custom black-and-white conversion on your image. In this instance, we'll continue with the image of the Capitol Building (if you'd like to save this work before tinting, simply create a virtual copy).

2   The Split Toning panel allows you to specify the hue and saturation you want to add to the shadows or highlights in a series of sliders. The Hue slider for each shows you a sample of the colors that you can choose in the slider itself. I prefer to click the color swatch to the right of Shadows to open the Shadows color picker, or to the right of Highlights to open the Highlights color picker, giving me a more direct way to select a color.

3   With the color picker available, you can use the Eyedropper tool that appears to sample the different colors you can use for your image. The image preview will show you how your tinted image is going to look.

4   Click a sample color for your shadows and highlights. In this case, I selected a Shadows Hue of 173 with a Saturation of 10 and a Highlights Hue of 296 with a Saturation of 15.

5   To redistribute the balance of colors, drag the Balance slider to the right to emphasize the Highlights color or to the left to emphasize the Shadows color. A value of −33 was used here.

Range selection for specific control

Lightroom's ability to adjust localized color with brushes and gradients has really minimized the amount of work you need to do in Photoshop. That said, neither program had a quick way to localize adjustments based on color and luminosity. With the 2018 release of Lightroom, though, users now have the ability to use color and luminosity controls in all of the local adjustment tools, taking your editing that much further.

1   Select the Jade-1 image and use the Adjustment Brush to paint over an area where you want to make a localized adjustment (in this case, the sky). To see this adjustment better, select Show Selected Mask Overlay in the toolbar below the image preview. Make sure you also have Auto Mask selected near the bottom of the Adjustment Brush panel as you paint over the sky—you'll find it easier and faster to get all of it selected without selecting the mountains or water.

2 Turn off the overlay, and decrease the exposure of the sky area by −2. While this adjustment may be a little too harsh, it does offer a good way for you to see how the effect works. Using this localized adjustment, I wanted to darken the blue in the sky, but the underexposure makes the clouds look really dark.

Although this is something that we are doing with an Adjustment Brush, you'll run into the same problem with Linear and Radial Gradients, as well. Lightroom now offers three ways for you to limit these adjustments with range masking:

- Luminance (another word for brightness) allows you to select specific areas based on the luminance range you select.

- Color allows you to create a selection mask based on the colors that you sample within the mask area.

Note: According to the Adobe website: Depth Range Mask is available for only those photos that have embedded depth map data. As of this writing, this is limited to HEIC files captured on Apple iPhone 7+, 8+, X, XS, XS MAX, and XR using Portrait mode in the built-in iOS camera app. If there is no available depth info for an image, the Depth option is disabled in the Range Mask menu.

- The Depth Range option was released in October 2018. It allows you to select an area based on depth range information.

3 Select Luminance from the Range Mask menu near the bottom of the panel, and select Show Luminance Mask to see it in action. The areas that are affected have the red overlay. We'll need to limit the effect to just the darker areas of the blue sky.

4 The Luminance Range Selector (it looks like a big eye-dropper) is a great way to get the precise luminance values you are looking for. Click the tool to activate it, then click the dark blue portion of the sky in the upper right.

5 The Range slider has two knobs that dictate the luminance range affected. Dragging the left one to the right eliminates the darker portion of the range; dragging the right one to the left eliminates the whiter portion of the range.

The Smoothness slider adjusts how smooth the falloff is at either end of the selected luminance range. Drag the Range and Smoothness sliders until only the dark cloud areas are covered in the red overlay.

6 With the new range selection created, adjust Exposure to –1.48, Shadows to 60, and Saturation to 39. Although this increases the amount of color in the sky, the whites in the clouds are not affected.

You also can use Color in the Range Mask menu to isolate and apply adjustments to a specific color or sets of colors.

7 Click New at the upper right of the panel, and zero out all the sliders, then paint a mask over the bottom half of the picture. With the Auto Mask option selected, it shoud be pretty easy to get all of the mountains in a selection. You may have to release the mouse and click again to paint in the water.

8 Switch the Range Mask menu to Color, and use the Color Range Selector (the eyedropper) to select the green at the front of the image. This will apply the effect to anything in that color. If you hold down the Shift key, you can add more colors into the range to be affected.

9 If you'd like a visual representation of the colors that are affected, hold down the Alt/Option key and drag the Amount slider. The image will turn into a black-and-white mask—white areas will have the effect applied; black areas will not. Keep the Alt/Option key held down and adjust the Amount slider until you get the exact amount of white in the mask that you want to affect.

10 Adjust the mountains in the image to taste, or you can use the settings I've applied in the picture:

Contrast: 39
Shadows: 39
Dehaze: 28
Saturation: 28

Once that's complete, remove the flare at the center front of the mountain range by using the Spot Removal tool.

It will take a couple of tries with range masking to get the hang of how to work with luminance and color, and when to use each, but I guarantee you it is an incredibly powerful tool that gets the very best out of specific areas in an image.

Could you do this in Photoshop? Absolutely. But the trick is to work efficiently on your images. Any time you can use a local adjustment to complete the work you need to do in one spot and save yourself a trip to Photoshop, it's a good thing.

The Effects Panel

The Effects panel in Lightroom allows you to add grain and post-crop vignetting to your images. Post-crop vignetting is a great feature when you want to add a specific focus to the center of the picture, but it requires a lot of care or you risk your image looking kitschy.

Let's walk through how to use post-crop vignetting on a black-and-white image I was working on for a magazine cover, and then see how it can be overused and quickly go to the *Dogs Playing Poker* kitsch level (not that there's anything wrong with that, if that is your intent) on a landscape image.

Open the lili-1.dng image in your Lesson 04 collection, and turn it into a black-and-white image. I added a Contrast amount of 39 to finish the image off.

This picture orginally was to be used for a magazine cover, so it needed a lot of headroom for the masthead and additional text. We won't need that here, so use the Crop Overlay tool to get rid of some of that excess space and bring the focus back to the center of the portrait.

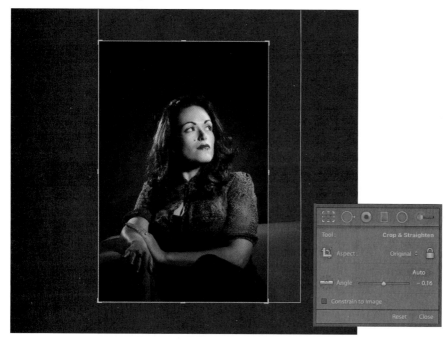

Post-crop vignetting is an effect that evolved from the undesirable darkening in the corners of images taken using specific lenses. As a style, people started to like this effect of "burning the edges" in, as it drew attention to the center of the picture.

Lightroom introduced a Vignetting slider in the original release of the program that was supposed to be used to correct the effect, not add it. When photographers used it to apply a vignetting effect and then cropped their pictures, the vignette effect disappeared.

Lightroom has since moved the Vignetting sliders (to remove vignetting) into the Lens Corrections panel and added Post-Crop Vignetting (which retains the size and centeredness of the vignetting even if you crop the image) in the Effects panel.

There are three Style menu choices available under Post-Crop Vignetting:

- Highlight Priority can bring back some blown-out highlights, but can lead to color shifts in darkened areas of a photo. It's good for images with bright areas, such as clipped specular highlights.

- Color Priority minimizes color shifts in darkened areas of a photo, but cannot perform highlight recovery.

- Paint Overlay mixes the cropped image values with black or white pixels and can result in a flat appearance.

There are five sliders available to you under Post-Crop Vignetting:

- Amount darkens the picture as you drag to the left, and lightens as you drag to the right.

- Midpoint adjusts how tight to the corners the effect is created. A low number moves it away from the corners; a higher number moves it closer to the corners.

- Roundness adjusts whether the effect looks like an oval or a circle. Drag to the left and it becomes more of an oval; drag to the right and you get a circle.

- Feather adjusts how soft the effect transition appears. Drag to the right and the effect appears softer.

- Highlights is available only when Highlight Priority or Color Priority are chosen in the menu. This slider controls the degree of highlight contrast that is preserved.

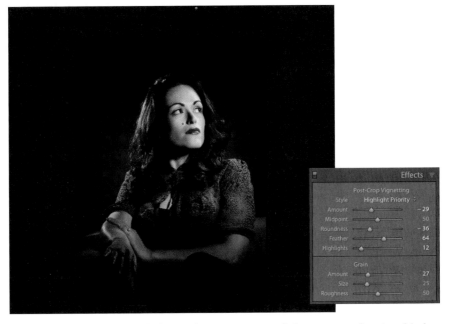

Grain is a little more straightforward. You can control the amount of grain added to your image, how big the individual grains are, and how jagged they are. The grain looks pretty realistic and can add an extra punch to images, especially if you're working in black and white.

This is a (slightly exaggerated) example of what you should avoid when working in the Effects panel.

- Post-Crop Vignetting is always focused on the center of the picture. If you have items that are off-center, the look will not work well.

- If you exaggerate the amount of vignetting, you should adjust the feather as well. If you don't, the image tends to look like it's lit with a flashlight, and it won't have a lot of believability.

- For as good as the grain is in Lightroom, overusing it can take away from the believability of the image.

- If you are looking to offset the darkening of the image, as well as control things like shadows and colors, use the Radial Gradient tool.

You now have a solid plan for working on images in your collections. You know how to make global and localized adjustments to your images, as well as save yourself a ton of time by synchronizing those changes across multiple images. In the next lesson, we'll cover some common photographic problems and how you can fix them in Lightroom.

Review questions

1 What's the best tool to use to improve a boring sky?

2 Can you create overlapping adjustments? If so, with what tools?

3 Once you've used a local adjustment tool, can you reposition the adjustment in your photo?

4 When you want to blur something in a photo, do you need to pass the photo off to Photoshop?

5 Can you realistically remove elements from a photo in Lightroom?

6 Is it possible to adjust a specific area in your photo based on color?

7 How do you make certain color areas in your photo lighter or darker after converting to black and white?

Review answers

1   The Graduated Filter tool.

2   Yes. You can create overlapping adjustments with all of Lightroom's local adjustment tools: the Graduated Filter, Radial Filter, and Adjustment Brush.

3   Yes. To do that, select the appropriate adjustment pin and then drag it to another position in your photo.

4   No. You can use the Graduated Filter, Radial Filter, and Adjustment Brush tools to blur certain areas of the photo. To do so, set the Sharpness slider to −100.

5   Yes, by using the Spot Removal tool in either Heal or Clone mode.

6   Yes, using a local adjustment tool with the Range Mask menu set to Color.

7   After converting your image to black and white, use the Targeted Adjustment tool (TAT) to drag upward on an area you want to be lighter or downward on an area you want to be darker.

5 FIXING COMMON PHOTOGRAPHY PROBLEMS

Lesson overview

With a better command of global and local adjustments, you're ready to get the very best out of your images. As you go through them, you'll run into common problems with simple solutions that can be achieved inside Lightroom. This lesson is not meant to be an exhaustive list of all the things you'll encounter, but once you see how easy it is to apply these techniques, you can develop a system for tackling your unique situation. The goal is to solve these problems fast and get back to doing what you really want to do: make more images.

In this lesson, you'll learn how to:

- Brighten discolored teeth.

- Smooth out wrinkles in skin.

- Remove flyaway hairs and distractions with the Spot Removal tool.

- Add brightness and contrast to eyes.

- Implement all of these skills in a start-to-finish workflow.

 This lesson will take about 90 minutes to complete. Please log in to your account on peachpit.com to download the files for this lesson, or go to the "Getting Started" section at the beginning of this book and follow the instructions under "Accessing the lesson files and Web Edition." Store the files on your computer in a convenient location. Your Account page is also where you'll find any updates to the lessons or to the lesson files. Look on the Lesson & Update Files tab to access the most current content.

Whether it is a landscape, product shot, or environmental portrait, every image should go through a workflow to make sure that you get the most detail out of every portion of the image. Adjusting every component allows you to tell an even better story.

Preparing for this lesson

To get the most out of this lesson, be sure you do the following:

1 Follow the instructions in the "Getting Started" section at the beginning of this book for setting up an LPCIB folder on your computer, downloading the lesson files to that LPCIB folder, and creating an LPCIB catalog in Lightroom.

2 Download the Lesson 05 folder from your Account page at peachpit.com to *username*/Documents/LPCIB/Lessons.

3 Launch Lightroom, and open the LPCIB catalog you created in "Getting Started" by choosing File > Open Catalog and navigating to the LPCIB Catalog. Alternatively, you can choose File > Open Recent > LPCIB Catalog.

4 Add the Lesson 5 files to the LPCIB catalog using the steps in the Lesson 1 section "Importing photos from a hard drive."

5 In the Library module's Folders panel, select Lesson 05.

6 Create a collection called **Lesson 05 Images** and place the images from the Lesson 05 folder in the collection.

7 Set the Sort menu beneath the image preview to File Name.

Now that you have a good command of how to work on images from a global to a local level, it's time to address some common photographic problems. Try as you might to avoid them, you will run into these problems, and it's good to have a set of skills in your back pocket to deal with them.

Lightening teeth

The ability to lighten a photo in a specific area is tremendously helpful. Not only can you lighten underexposed areas, but you can also lighten shadows on your subject's neck to reduce the appearance of a double chin, lighten eyes to enhance them, and so on. Here, you'll learn how to lighten your subject's teeth.

1 Select the exercise file Teeth.jpg from the Lesson 05 Images collection (the image was cropped to protect the innocent). Click 1:1 in the Navigator panel to zoom in a little farther, so you're viewing it at 100 percent. Spacebar-drag within the photo to reposition it so you're viewing his teeth.

2 Activate the Adjustment Brush tool in the tool strip beneath the Histogram panel (it's the last tool on the right) or press the letter K on your keyboard. The Adjustment Brush panel appears beneath the tool strip.

3 Double-click the Effect label at the upper left of the panel to reset all the sliders to 0. To lighten his teeth, set the Exposure slider to roughly 0.40 and the Saturation slider to around −50. Decreasing the saturation removes any color cast the teeth may have.

▶ **Tip:** Remember, you can reset any slider to its default value by double-clicking the text label to the left of the slider or by double-clicking the slider itself.

▶ **Tip:** The A and B buttons in the Brush section of the Adjustment Brush panel let you customize two brushes—for example, a big one and a smaller one for detail work. Once you get the settings correct for your first brush (A), click B and then adjust its settings as necessary. To switch between the two brushes, click the A or B buttons.

● **Note:** Although the Density slider does indeed affect the intensity of the adjustments as you're applying them, you can't use it to change the overall opacity of an adjustment you've already made without brushing over it again.

4 Set the brush functions in the Brush section at the bottom of the panel:

- Change your brush size using the Size slider or keyboard shortcuts: press the Left Bracket key ([) to decrease the size or the Right Bracket key (]) to increase it. Set it to 9 for this exercise.

- Use the Feather slider to set the softness of the brush edge. To change the feather amount using keyboard shortcuts, press Shift+Left Bracket ([) to decrease the feathering or Shift+Right Bracket (]) to increase it. Set it to 19 for this technique.

- The Flow slider controls the rate at which adjustments are applied. If you decrease the flow, the brush acts like an airbrush, building up the opacity of the adjustments over multiple strokes. Set it to 100% here.

- The Density slider controls the intensity of the brush itself while you're using it. For example, with both Flow and Density set at 100%, your brushstrokes are *not* cumulative—they don't build up like an airbrush—so the adjustment is applied at full strength.

  If you lower the Density to 50% and brush across an area you've already brushed across, the intensity of that adjustment is changed to 50%, no matter how many times you brush across it. If you then change the Density to 75% and brush across that area again, the adjustment is changed to 75%.

  This keeps you from having to change the sliders in the Effect section of the Adjustment Brush panel to alter the adjustment's intensity (if, say, one eye needs more or less of the same adjustment than the other). For this exercise, set the Density to 100%.

- The Auto Mask option instructs Lightroom to use a hard-edged brush to confine your adjustment to areas that match the tone and color beneath your cursor (Lightroom continuously samples pixels as you paint with the brush). Turn it on when you want to adjust a defined area (say, an object against a solid background). Leave it turned off for this technique.

5 Brush across the top row of teeth in the photo, using a brush size of 9. Reduce the size to about 3, and then brush across the bottom row of teeth.

A pin appears to mark the area you adjusted.

If you make a mistake and brush across an area you didn't mean to, press Alt/ Option to put the brush into Erase mode (you'll see a minus sign [–] inside the cursor), and then brush across that area again.

Alternatively, you can put the brush into Erase mode by clicking Erase in the Brush section of the tool's panel.

● **Note:** The brush size in Erase mode won't match what you use in standard (add) mode, so you'll need to alter its size as necessary to erase the adjustment.

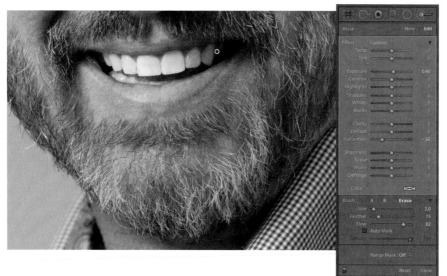

6   To change the overall opacity of the adjustment (so both
    the exposure and saturation change), click the black triangle at the upper right
    of the panel, and in the Amount slider that appears, lower it to around 40%.

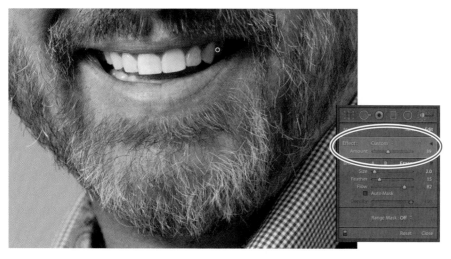

7   Click the panel switch at the lower left of the Adjustment Brush panel to turn
    off the adjustment, and then click it again to turn it on.

Lightening the whites of eyes

Now let's use the same technique to brighten the whites of a subject's eyes. This is a
great way to give your subject a little more sleep than they actually got, and handy
when your white balance has caused a color cast in the whites of the eyes.

1 In the Filmstrip, select the Eye Contrast.dng file to start the retouch. Use the Spacebar-drag technique to reposition the photo so you can see the eyes.

2 Click Reset at the lower right corner of the Adjustment Brush panel to undo the Adjustment Brush changes made to this file for you. Click the triangle at the right of the Amount slider to expand the tool's panel, if necessary.

3 Follow the steps in the previous technique to lighten the whites of both eyes. Set the Exposure to 0.36 and Saturation to −50 to remove the slight blue cast in the whites of her eyes.

It's helpful to turn on the mask overlay, which you learned about in "Using the Graduated Filter tool" in Lesson 4, to ensure you don't accidentally lighten the iris rims. To do that, press O on your keyboard. The mask appears in red, which helps you see the brush strokes you're making.

▶ **Tip:** You can press Shift+O repeatedly to cycle through various mask overlay colors.

If you do accidentally brush over the irises, hold down the Alt/Option key to switch the brush to Erase mode, and brush over the spillover.

4 Use the panel switch to see a before and after of the eye whitening.

Enhancing irises

Let's continue with this portrait, and add a second adjustment to enhance the irises of each eye.

1   To create another adjustment, click New at the upper right of the tool's panel, and then double-click the Effect label to reset the sliders.

2   To enhance the irises, set the Blacks slider to −15, the Clarity slider to 50, and the Saturation slider to −48.

3   Turn on the mask overlay so you can see your brush strokes, and brush over the strongest light reflection in each iris. If one iris needs less lightening than the other, reduce the Density slider in the Brush section of the tool's panel.

4   Use the panel switch to see a before (left) and after (right) of the adjustment.

Skin softening with the Adjustment Brush

You can also use the Adjustment Brush to quickly soften skin, but it's important to note that this technique can be overdone very quickly.

People often attempt to soften skin in an image because it's supposed to give a fresher look. Unfortunately, excessive softening of skin yields a very porcelain look that is not realistic.

The goal with softening skin should be to produce an even tone in your image while retaining pore detail. In this example, we should only slightly soften the skin, as it's really not needed. I'm doing it here to show you how.

1   Select Flyaway.dng in the Filmstrip, and then double-click the Effect label to reset the tool's sliders.

2   Set Clarity to −100 to reduce edge contrast, which is a great way to soften skin.

3   In the Navigator panel, click the Fill button so you can see more of the photo.

4 Quickly brush over all the skin, adjusting the brush size as you go. Brush over the eyes and mouth, too. Hold down Alt/Option to put the brush in Erase mode, make sure the Size is small and the Feather is a lower number, and then brush over any areas you don't want softened, such as the model's eyes, eyebrows, lips, and the edges of her nostrils.

5 Once the negative Clarity setting has been applied to the skin, click the black triangle to the right of Effect and adjust the Amount slider, ensuring that you see as much pore detail as possible.

Removing flyaway hairs with the Spot Removal tool

If you are shooting in an outdoor scenario, you will often encounter flyaway hairs in your portraits. Removing these distractions used to be extremely time-consuming in Photoshop, but now you can remove them with the Spot Removal tool.

There are two things to keep in mind when you are trying to remove flyaway hairs in this manner:

• You have to constantly move the sample area to best find an area that matches the flyaway hairs.

• You have to adjust your feathering and opacity to create the best match with the sample area.

1 Let's stick with the previous image and remove the flyaway hairs on the right side of the picture.

2 Switch to the Spot Removal tool (press Q on your keyboard) and select a brush small enough to cover the flyaway hair on the right side. Be sure not to include much of the background of the picture as you brush, as Lightroom will need it to sample from to create its fix.

3 The tool's sample area will almost always be off with larger brushstrokes, but you can drag it to an area that makes more sense.

4 Once the sample area is appropriately placed, you can adjust the feathering and opacity of the fix so that it blends with the background.

The success of the Spot Removal tool will largely depend on the type of background that you have to work with. In a case where you have a background with as shallow a depth of field as the one here, you can rely on the Heal option and the Feather and Opacity sliders. For sharper backgrounds, you may need to set the Spot Removal tool to Clone and use a lower Feather amount.

Once the hair has been taken care of, decrease some of the vibrance of the picture to remove the yellow sun glow and add an oval radial gradient to darken the image at an angle.

The key here is to make sure that anything we do in terms of skin adjustments is as subtle as possible, and to make sure that any distracting elements are removed.

Reducing wrinkles beneath eyes

The Spot Removal tool can also be used to reduce the appearance of wrinkles and dark areas beneath your subject's eyes. It's important to note that (almost) everyone has some difference in skin tone in the area under the eye. The exception is usually when it is covered by makeup.

When removing wrinkles and dark areas under the eyes, the goal is to make sure that extreme color changes are minimized but not removed entirely. Removing all traces of them looks like bad plastic surgery.

Give yourself a general rule when working on under-eye areas: make sure your subjects look like they had a good night's rest, not like they had too much surgery. Keep that in mind, and your retouching will always look realistic.

1   Select the Tito.nef image in the Lesson 05 Images collection.

2   With the Spot Removal tool in Heal mode, set the Feather to 44 and the Opacity to 100, and then brush over the area beneath Tito's eye on the left. Reposition the source point so it's beneath the area you're fixing.

3   To make the change more realistic, reduce the Opacity in the tool's options panel to approximately 30.

4   Assess your work by turning the tool's panel switch off and back on. If necessary, click one of the pins to select that removal, and then reposition the source area or adjust the Feather and Opacity sliders to your liking.

5   Repeat this process for the right eye, adjusting the Feather and Opacity sliders, and the source area, to best match the texture that you need for the darker area in the picture.

Putting it all together—start to finish

▶ **Tip:** If you want to follow along with this process, make sure you access the videos that accompany this lesson online. See the "Getting Started" section at the beginning of the book for how to access them.

Now that you have a good command of how to fix common photographic problems, let's spend some time going through a full portrait retouch, employing all of the techniques that we have learned:

1 Select the Start-Finish.dng image in the Lesson 05 Images collection.

2 In the Basic panel, set the following global settings for your picture:

- Set the Exposure to +0.35 to provide an overall brightness to the scene.

- Increase the Contrast setting to +12 to provide some edge detail.

- Open up the Shadows by dragging the slider to +21.

- Set the Whites to +24 to brighten the image slightly.

- Drag the Vibrance slider to +7 to enhance some of the color.

Let's perform some local adjustments, including slight skin retouching and some finishing to the color details in the image.

3 Double-click Effect to reset the sliders. Select the Adjustment Brush, set Exposure to 0.22, and drag the Shadows slider to +51

to open up the face. Turn on the mask overlay to ensure that you are applying the effect where you need it. Brush over her face and neck to apply the changes.

4 Use the Spot Removal tool to soften the skin area under her eyes. Press Z to zoom in to the image to ensure that you accurately select the source and destination areas.

5 Make sure you feather the selection and adjust the opacity in the tool options to properly blend it into the portrait.

6 Create a new adjustment brush and reset its sliders by double-clicking the Effect label at the upper left of the Adjustment Brush panel. Use this new adjustment brush to add a little more color, contrast, and detail to the yellow areas and the jeans in the portrait:

   • Open up the shadows in the image by dragging that slider to +21.

   • Increase the Whites slider to +24 to brighten the image slightly.

   • Drag the Saturation slider to +7 to enhance some of the color.

7 Turn off the mask overlay and brush your adjustments into the area around your previous adjustment.

Once you finish, take a look at how far you have come with the adjustment: right-click the image and select Create Virtual Copy from the menu to create a second version of it. The virtual copy appears after the image you selected.

We'll use these two copies to see a before and after. With the original image active, click the Reset button below the right-side panels and all the changes you made to this image will disappear, bringing you back to square one. Don't worry, the virtual copy contains all the changes. We'll select both images by Ctrl-clicking/Command-clicking them.

Note: If you want to learn more about Survey and Compare modes, and take a deep dive into the world of Lightroom, make sure you check out *Adobe Photoshop Lightroom Classic CC Classroom in a Book (2018 release)* by John Evans and Katrin Straub.

Press the N key to go into Survey mode in the Library module, which we talked about in the "Customizing your view" section of Lesson 1. Survey mode allows you to see multiple images in the preview area. It is often used for selecting the best of a series of pictures. In this instance, since both images are vertical, you'll get a good side-by-side comparison of where you started and how many changes you made to the image.

As you can see, Lightroom's Adjustment Brush tool is extremely powerful and lets you get the very best out of your images.

Review questions

1 What Adjustment Brush slider do you use to remove a color cast from teeth?

2 When using the Adjustment Brush, how do you tell if you have brushed over an area you didn't want to include in your adjustment?

3 What Adjustment Brush setting do you use to soften skin?

4 When using the Spot Removal tool to remove things along the edge of a person, like flyaway hairs, how do you know whether to set it to Heal or to Clone?

5 What else can you do to ensure your Spot Removal fix blends with your background?

6 What is the best way to ensure your retouching with the Adjustment Brush tool and the Spot Removal tool looks natural?

7 How can you see a before/after of a single local adjustment?

Review answers

1 To remove a color cast from teeth, use the Saturation slider.

2 To see where you have brushed, select the Show Selected Mask Overlay option.

3 To soften skin with the Adjustment Brush, set the Clarity slider to –100.

4 If your background is very soft (you have a shallow depth of field), set the Spot Removal tool to Heal. If your background is sharper, set it to Clone.

5 To ensure the Spot Removal tool blends its adjustment with the background, adjust the tool's Feather and Opacity settings.

6 To keep your Adjustment Brush tool work looking natural, click the little black triangle to the right of Effect to close the adjustment sliders, and then use the Amount slider to reduce the opacity of your changes. To do the same with the Spot Removal tool, use the Opacity slider to reduce the effect of the fix.

7 Turn the panel's switch off and on to see a before/after of your changes.

6 LIGHTROOM–PHOTOSHOP ROUNDTRIP WORKFLOW

Lesson overview

This may be the most important lesson in this book because it covers the mechanics of a typical roundtrip workflow between Lightroom and Photoshop. It teaches you how to adjust settings in both programs to ensure you pass the highest-quality files between the two. You'll learn how to send files from Lightroom to Photoshop in a variety of formats and then reopen the edited files in Lightroom.

In this lesson, you'll learn how to:

- Configure Lightroom's External Editing preferences and Photoshop's Maximize Compatibility preference.

- Match Photoshop's color settings to Lightroom's.

- Keep Lightroom in sync with Photoshop's Camera Raw plug-in.

- Send a raw file or JPEG from Lightroom to Photoshop, and then pass the file back to and reopen it in Lightroom.

- Send a raw file from Lightroom to Photoshop as a Smart Object.

 This lesson will take 1 to 2 hours to complete. Please log in to your account on peachpit.com to download the files for this lesson, or go to the "Getting Started" section at the beginning of this book and follow the instructions under "Accessing the lesson files and Web Edition." Store the files on your computer in a convenient location. Your Account page is also where you'll find any updates to the lessons or to the lesson files. Look on the Lesson & Update Files tab to access the most current content.

Setting up Lightroom and Photoshop to work together ensures you're passing the highest-quality photos back and forth between the two programs.

Preparing for this lesson

To get the most out of this lesson, be sure you do the following:

1 Follow the instructions in the "Getting Started" section at the beginning of this book for setting up an LPCIB folder on your computer, downloading the lesson files to that LPCIB folder, and creating an LPCIB catalog in Lightroom.

2 Download the Lesson 06 folder from your Account page at peachpit.com to *username*/Documents/LPCIB/Lessons.

3 Launch Lightroom, and open the LPCIB catalog you created in "Getting Started" by choosing File > Open Catalog and navigating to the LPCIB Catalog. Alternatively, you can choose File > Open Recent > LPCIB Catalog.

4 Add the Lesson 6 files to the LPCIB catalog using the steps in the Lesson 1 section "Importing photos from a hard drive."

5 In the Library module's Folders panel, select Lesson 06.

6 Create a collection called **Lesson 06 Images** and place the images from the Lesson 06 folder in the collection.

7 Set the Sort menu beneath the image preview to File Name.

In the next section, you'll learn how to set up various preferences and settings in both Lightroom and Photoshop so they work together as a team.

Setting up Lightroom and Photoshop for smooth integration

Before you start sending photos back and forth between Lightroom and Photoshop, there are some settings to adjust in both programs to ensure you're moving between them at the highest possible quality.

In the next few sections, you'll learn how to adjust Lightroom's preferences to control the kind of file it sends to Photoshop. You'll also adjust Photoshop's settings so the color space you're using in Lightroom matches that of Photoshop. Next, you'll learn how to keep Lightroom's and Photoshop's Camera Raw plug-ins in sync, and then you'll dig into how to send files back and forth between the two programs.

While these sections don't cover the most exciting topics in this book, they are important for your success in using the programs together. Once all this is set up, you won't have to worry about it again.

Configuring Lightroom's External Editing preferences

Lightroom's External Editing preferences determine exactly how files are passed from Lightroom to Photoshop. You can control file format, bit depth, color space—all of which are explained in this section—as well as file naming conventions and how the Photoshop files are displayed back in Lightroom.

You can set up an additional external editor if you are more comfortable with it. Truth be told, the intergration between Photoshop and Lightroom is so tight, you'll rarely need to use a different editor.

Setting your primary External Editing preferences

Lightroom automatically scours your hard drive for the latest version of Photoshop (or Photoshop Elements) and picks it as the primary external editor. To control exactly how Lightroom sends files to Photoshop, use these steps:

1   In Lightroom, choose Edit > Preferences (Windows) or Lightroom > Preferences (macOS), and click the External Editing tab.

    The settings in the top section of the resulting dialog determine the properties with which a file opens in Photoshop when you use Lightroom's Photo > Edit In command and choose to edit in Photoshop. (If you don't change these settings, their default values are used.)

2   Choose PSD from the File Format menu to preserve the quality you get in Lightroom, as well as any layers you add in Photoshop.

Tip: TIFF supports layers too, but it creates a larger file size than PSD does.

3   From the Color Space menu, choose the range of colors you want to work with. If you're shooting in raw, choose ProPhoto RGB. If you're shooting in JPEG, choose Adobe RGB (1998) instead.

    As you can see in the sidebar "Choosing a color space," ProPhoto RGB encompasses the widest possible range of colors and protects colors captured by your camera from being clipped or compressed. Since a raw file doesn't have a conventional color profile until it's rendered by a pixel editor (such as Photoshop) or it's exported from Lightroom, choosing ProPhoto RGB here preserves that broad color range when you edit it in Photoshop.

    JPEGs, on the other hand, can't use the broad color range that raw files do. If you're shooting in JPEG format, your largest color-range option is Adobe RGB.

Note: Anytime you convert an image in a large color space to a smaller one, its colors may shift. That's why it's important to view the image in the smaller color space (a process known as soft proofing) before you export it.

Choosing a color space

Color space refers to the range of colors you want to work with. Here's what you need to know about choosing the one that's right for you:

- Adobe RGB (1998) is the most popular workspace. It includes a wide range of colors, so it's perfect for designers and photographers. It's also great for printing on inkjet printers and commercial presses.

  You can also change your digital camera's color profile to match what you use in Photoshop. For example, most cameras are initially set to sRGB mode, but you can switch to Adobe RGB instead. Alas, you'll have to dig out your owner's manual (or find it online) to learn how, but the increased range of colors and monitor consistency can be worth it.

- ProPhoto RGB is currently the largest workspace in use and is the one used by programs that process raw images. It's the native workspace of Lightroom and of Photoshop's Camera Raw plug-in. In the infographic shown here, the ProPhoto RGB workspace is shown in white with the other workspaces superimposed atop it.

- sRGB is slightly smaller than Adobe RGB (1998). It is the Internet standard, so it's perfect for prepping images for use on the web, in presentation programs, and in videos, and for submitting to online printing companies (labs such as mpix.com and nationsphotolab.com). This is the RGB workspace that Photoshop uses unless you pick another one.

The CMYK workspace, on the other hand, represents the smaller number of colors that are reproducible with ink on a commercial printing press. The lower-right image shows the ProPhoto RGB workspace compared to the color gamut of the truly incredible human eye.

ProPhoto RGB vs. AdobeRGB (1998)   ProPhoto RGB vs. sRGB

ProPhoto RGB vs. CMYK   ProPhoto RGB vs. human eye

4   From the Bit Depth menu, choose 16 bits/component if you're shooting in raw format or 8 bits/component if you're shooting in JPEG format.

Bit depth refers to how many colors the image itself contains. The goal is to keep as much color detail as you can for as *long* as you can.

JPEGs are 8-bit images that can contain more than 16 million colors. Raw images, on the other hand, can be 16-bit and contain over 280 trillion colors. If you have 16-bit files, send them to Photoshop and reduce them to 8-bit *only* if you need to do something in Photoshop that doesn't work on 16-bit files (say, running a filter) or when you're ready to export the image from Lightroom for use elsewhere.

5   Leave Resolution set to its default value of 240.

Resolution determines pixel density and thus pixel size when the image is *printed*. Leave it at 240 ppi, which is a reasonable starting point for a typical inkjet printer, and then adjust the resolution as necessary when you export the edited file from Lightroom.

6   Don't close the dialog yet; you'll use it in the next section.

From this point forward, whenever you select a thumbnail (or several) in Lightroom's Library module and choose Photo > Edit In > Edit In Adobe Photoshop, or when you press the keyboard shortcut Ctrl+E/Command+E, Lightroom uses these settings.

Setting additional external editor preferences

You can designate one or more additional external editors that also appear in Lightroom's Photo > Edit In menu. Doing so gives you a choice of editors or a choice of settings for the same editor.

Additional editors can be third-party programs or plug-ins such as Adobe Photoshop Elements, Nik Color Efex Pro, ON1 software, and so on. You can even create additional configurations for Photoshop, each with settings geared toward particular kinds of photos or uses.

For example, you may set up Photoshop as an additional external editor with options suitable for photos destined for the web.

> **Note:** PPI stands for pixels per inch. DPI stands for dots per inch. The latter term is used when referencing printers, because many printers use a dot pattern to reproduce an image with ink on paper.

> **Note:** Only Photoshop or Photoshop Elements can be your primary external editor. If you don't have one of them installed, the commands for editing in a primary external editor aren't available in the first section of the Photo > Edit In menu. You can still designate other applications in the Additional External Editor section and then choose them from the second section of the Photo > Edit In menu.

> **Tip:** You can use the Additional External Editor section to configure as many external editing preferences as you like. Simply use the Preset menu to save each one as a preset. You won't see them all separately in the Preferences dialog, but they stack up in the second section of Lightroom's Edit In menu.

Configuring Adobe Photoshop Elements as an external editor

You can configure Lightroom to use Adobe Photoshop Elements as your primary or additional external editor. The process is roughly the same, but there are a few things to keep in mind.

First, if you have Elements but not Photoshop on your computer, Lightroom automatically picks Elements as the primary external editor.

Second, if you have both Elements and Photoshop on your computer, you can designate Elements as an additional external editor. To do that, be sure to navigate to the Elements Editor application file, not the alias (shortcut) in the root level of the Elements Editor folder. To find the *real* application file, use these paths:

- C:\Program Files\Adobe\Photoshop Elements\Photoshop Elements Editor.exe (Windows)
- Applications/Adobe Photoshop Elements/Support Files/Adobe Photoshop Elements Editor (macOS)

If you pick the alias or shortcut instead, and then try to send a file from Lightroom to Elements, the application will open but the photo won't.

Third, Elements works only in the Adobe RGB (1998) and sRGB color spaces. So if you're sending files from Lightroom to Elements, choose Adobe RGB (1998), not ProPhoto RGB. You'll also notice these commands missing from Lightroom's Photo > Edit In menu: Open as a Smart Object, Merge to Panorama, and Merge to HDR Pro.

Setting the stacking preference

Note: You can expand and collapse a stack by selecting it in the Library module's Grid view and then pressing S on your keyboard.

When you send a file from Lightroom to Photoshop, the PSD that comes back to Lightroom appears next to the original file in the Library module. In some cases, you may also generate copies of the PSD—if, say, you want to create different versions of it.

To reduce the clutter in your library, you may want to select Stack With Original to have Lightroom stack your PSDs into a pile with the original photo.

Doing so creates a collapsible group, known as a *stack*, of thumbnails. When you expand a stack, your PSDs are displayed side by side in the Library module in Grid view and in the Filmstrip. This makes related files easy to spot.

However, when a stack is collapsed, only one thumbnail is visible in the grid and the Filmstrip, so you can't see all of its associated files. Therefore, you may want to leave Stack With Original unselected, and instead rely on the Library module's Sort menu to keep original photos and their associated PSDs together.

To do that, click the Sort menu in the toolbar at the bottom of the Library module, and choose File Name or Capture Time.

● **Note:** If you don't see the toolbar in the Library module, press T on your keyboard.

Setting the file naming preference

The Template menu at the bottom of the External Editing Preferences dialog box lets you specify how Lightroom names the files you've edited in Photoshop. It adds "-Edit" by default, but you can change the naming scheme to whatever you want (the sample filename is given the PSD extension automatically).

For the purposes of this lesson, stick with the default file naming scheme. However, if you want to change it later on, in the Template menu, choose Edit to open the Filename Template Editor, where you can choose what you want your filenames to look like and save that as a template.

```
Edit Externally File Naming: IMG_0002-Edit.psd
    Template:  Custom Settings                                                    ◇
    Custom Text:                                      Start Number:
```

The next section teaches you about the changes you need to make to Photoshop to work well with Lightroom.

Configuring Photoshop's color settings

Now that Lightroom's settings are configured, you can turn your attention to Photoshop. In this section, you'll learn how to make Photoshop's color space match the one you told Lightroom to use when it sends a file to Photoshop.

1　In Photoshop, choose Edit > Color Settings.

2　In the Working Spaces section, choose ProPhoto RGB or Adobe RGB (1998) from the RGB menu. The choice you make here should match the choice you made earlier in Lightroom's External Editing preferences.

3　In the Color Management Policies section, choose Preserve Embedded Profiles from the RGB menu.

● **Note:** If you're using Photoshop Elements as an external editor, you need to adjust its color settings too. To do that, launch the Elements Editor and choose Edit > Color Settings. In the dialog box that appears, choose Always Optimize for Printing, and click OK. This makes Elements use the Adobe RGB (1998) color space. (Choosing Always Optimize for Computer Screen uses the smaller sRGB color space instead.)

4　For Missing Profiles, select Ask When Opening and leave the other options unselected.

With these settings, the files you send from Lightroom to Photoshop should open in the correct color space. And if Photoshop encounters a file that doesn't have an embedded profile, you get a dialog asking how you'd like to proceed. In that case, choose Assign Working RGB, and click OK.

5　Click OK in the Color Settings dialog box to close it.

Now let's take a look at how to create Photoshop files that Lightroom can preview.

Configuring Photoshop's Maximize Compatibility preference

If you followed the advice of this book and told Lightroom to send files to Photoshop in PSD format, there's one more Photoshop setting to adjust.

Lightroom doesn't understand the concept of layers, so in order for layered PSDs to be visible in Lightroom, Photoshop needs to embed a flattened layer into each document. This flattened layer is what you see in Lightroom.

● **Note:** If you assigned Photoshop Elements as your external editor, you need to do this in Elements too. In the Elements Editor, choose Edit > Preferences > Saving Files (Windows) or Adobe Photoshop Elements Editor > Preferences > Saving Files (macOS).

1　In Photoshop, choose Edit > Preferences > File Handling (Windows) or Photoshop > Preferences > File Handling (macOS).

2　In the File Handling Preferences dialog box, change the Maximize PSD and PSB File Compatibility menu from Ask to Always.

3　Click OK to close the dialog box.

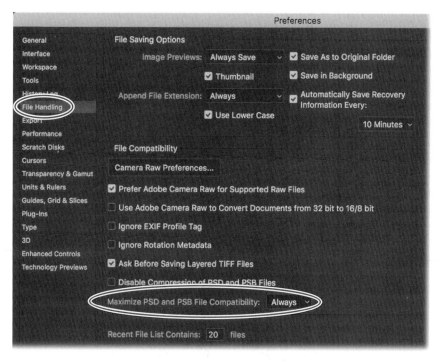

Once you do this, you'll be able to see your PSDs in Lightroom.

The next section teaches you how to keep your version of Lightroom synced with Photoshop's Camera Raw plug-in.

Keeping Lightroom and Camera Raw in sync

Lightroom, at its heart, is a raw converter whose job is to convert the data in a raw file into an image that can be viewed and edited onscreen. Photoshop has a raw converter too: a plug-in named Camera Raw. Camera Raw and Lightroom use the same raw conversion engine, and when Adobe updates one, it usually updates the other with a matching version.

This is important because when you send a raw photo from Lightroom to Photoshop, Photoshop uses Camera Raw to render the raw data into pixels you can see and work with onscreen. If you don't have matching versions of Lightroom and Camera Raw, you may encounter a mismatch warning in Lightroom and you may have content issues as you pass the file back and forth. For more on this topic, see the sidebar "Encountering a Lightroom–Camera Raw mismatch."

To check which versions of Lightroom and Camera Raw are installed on your computer, follow these steps:

1   In Lightroom, choose Help > About Adobe Photoshop Lightroom (Windows) or Lightroom > About Adobe Photoshop Lightroom (macOS). A window opens that shows your version of Lightroom. It also reports the version of Camera Raw

that's fully compatible with your version of Lightroom. Click the X in the upper right (Windows) or the window itself (macOS) to close it.

2 In Photoshop, choose Help > About Photoshop (Windows) or Photoshop > About Photoshop (macOS). Your version of Photoshop appears in the window that opens. Close the window by clicking the X in the upper right (Windows) or clicking the window itself (macOS).

3 Also in Photoshop, choose Help > About Plug-Ins > Camera Raw (Windows) or Photoshop > About Plug-Ins > Camera Raw (macOS). Your version of the Camera Raw plug-in is reported in the window that opens. Click the window to close it.

Encountering a Lightroom–Camera Raw mismatch

If you have mismatched versions of Lightroom and Camera Raw installed on your computer, you may get a mismatch warning in Lightroom when you try to send a raw file to Photoshop.

Although that's not the end of the world, it's important to understand the options Lightroom gives you, which are:

- Cancel closes the warning dialog without sending the file to Photoshop. You can then upgrade your software before trying again.

- Render Using Lightroom sends the raw file to Photoshop, but instead of Camera Raw rendering it, Lightroom does it itself. The advantage of letting Lightroom render the file is that doing so ensures that all your Lightroom adjustments are included in the rendered image, even if you used a feature in the most recent version of Lightroom that isn't in the version of Camera Raw on your computer. A potential downside is that as soon as you click the Render Using Lightroom button in the warning dialog, an RGB copy of the image is added in your Lightroom catalog, and it stays there even if you change your mind and close the image in Photoshop without saving. In that case, you now have the extra step of deleting the RGB copy from your Lightroom catalog.

- Open Anyway sends the raw file to Photoshop, and Camera Raw, not Lightroom, renders the file. This option doesn't guarantee that all your Lightroom adjustments are included in the rendered image. For example, if you have a newer version of Lightroom than Camera Raw, any new features you used in Lightroom that aren't in your version of Camera Raw won't appear in the image when it opens in Photoshop.

The moral of this story is that it's easier to keep your versions of Lightroom and Camera Raw in sync if at all possible.

If you subscribe to Adobe Creative Cloud, you can use the Adobe Creative Cloud app to update your software. If you're not a subscriber, choose Help > Updates in

Lightroom or Photoshop (CS6 or earlier) instead. When you update Photoshop, you get the latest version of Camera Raw, as well.

Sending a raw file from Lightroom to Photoshop

Once you adjust a raw photo in Lightroom, you may determine that you need to send it to Photoshop for additional pixel-level editing.

The process of sending raw files from Lightroom to Photoshop is easy, and it's the same process for a camera manufacturer's proprietary raw file (say, a .CR2 from Canon or an .NEF from Nikon) or a DNG file. This section teaches you how to do that.

When you're working with your own photos, begin by adjusting the photo's tone and color in Lightroom, which you learned about in the previous lessons.

The basic adjustments have been completed for you on this photo of a box of mini doughnuts; however, one of the mini doughnuts (circled in red here) is missing some sprinkes. This would be best added at a pixel level using the Clone Stamp tool in Photoshop.

Note: You can easily send other file formats, such as JPEGs, from Lightroom to Photoshop too. That topic is covered later in this lesson.

Note: Once you send a photo from Lightroom to Photoshop, any Lightroom adjustments you've made to it become permanent in the PSD file Photoshop sends back to Lightroom. For that reason, you may want to wait to make some adjustments—say, adding an edge vignette—until the file is returned to Lightroom.

1   Choose Photo > Edit In > Edit in Adobe Photoshop CC (or whatever version you're using). Alternatively, you can press Ctrl+E/Command+E.

Photoshop opens (it also launches if it isn't already running), and Lightroom passes the raw file to Photoshop.

Behind the scenes, the Camera Raw plug-in renders the raw file so you can see and edit it in Photoshop. Any adjustments you made in Lightroom are made permanent in the image that opens in Photoshop. (Of course, your adjustments are flexible in the original file back in Lightroom.)

2   In Photoshop, create a new blank layer by choosing Layer > New > Layer or pressing Shift+Ctrl+N/Shift+Command+N.

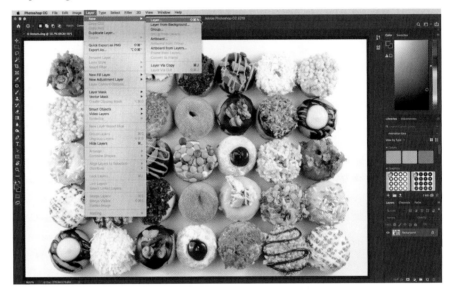

3   Select the Clone Stamp tool by pressing the S key. Then, hold down Ctrl+Spacebar/Command+Spacebar and click the image to zoom in to the doughnut in question.

4   In the brush options for the Clone Stamp tool, select a soft brush a little wider than a sprinkle. Also, make sure that the Sample menu is set to All Layers in the options bar at the top.

5   Hold down the Alt/Option key and click one of the sprinkles on the doughnut. This will sample that specific

area and load it into your brush. Because you created a new layer and set it to sample all layers, the results will be painted onto a blank layer.

▶ **Tip:** If you want to follow along with this tutorial, make sure you access the videos that accompany this lesson online. Refer to the "Getting Started" section at the beginning of this book for how to access the videos.

6 Switch to the Eraser tool by pressing the E key, and erase out some of the areas alongside the new sprinkles to make sure that they blend in with the old ones.

Now that the doughnut is fixed, you're ready to send the photo back to Lightroom.

● **Note:** You can also send a raw file from Lightroom to Photoshop as a Smart Object, which has some unique benefits. You'll learn how to do that later in this lesson.

Send the photo back to Lightroom

When you're finished editing in Photoshop, all you have to do is save and close the photo. As long as Lightroom is open and running when you do this, the PSD appears in your Lightroom catalog next to the original photo.

1 In Photoshop, choose File > Save (or press Ctrl+S/Command+S) to save the file. Close the Photoshop document by choosing File > Close or by pressing Ctrl+W/Command+W.

   Technically, you can use the File > Save As command to rename the file, but it's important that you don't change the file's *location*. If you do, Lightroom won't be able to find it.

2 In Lightroom, press G to return to the Library module's Grid view, and the PSD appears next to the original raw file.

   Notice the file formats at the upper right of each thumbnail: one is a PSD, and the other is a DNG.

▶ **Tip:** If you are following my suggestion
for creating collection
sets for each shoot
and collections for
different parts of the
shoot, this would be a
good time to create a
specific collection called
Photoshop Files within
the parent collection
set. That way, you have
a quick way of accessing
all of the Photoshop
files from the shoot in
one place.

The raw file displays the adjustments you made to it in Lightroom before you sent it to Photoshop. The Photoshop file reflects your Lightroom adjustments as well as the cloning you did in Photoshop. As mentioned, your Lightroom edits are permanent in the PSD file. That said, you can reopen the PSD file and continue editing it if you need to, which you'll do next.

3   Leave the photo open because you'll use it in the next exercise.

Reopen the PSD for more editing in Photoshop

If you determine that you have more pixel editing to do in the PSD that came back to Lightroom, you can easily reopen it in Photoshop. For example, you may decide to do a bit more cloning on the doughnut. Follow these steps to do that:

1   Select the PSD in Lightroom's Library module, and press Ctrl+E/Command+E.

2   In the dialog box that opens, choose Edit Original, and click Edit to open the layered PSD in Photoshop. Choosing *any* other option here opens a flattened copy of the PSD, not the layered PSD. (You'll use the other options later.)

3   When the layered PSD opens in Photoshop, use the Clone Stamp tool to add a couple more sprinkles on the layer we added.

4   Save the PSD by pressing Ctrl+S/Command+S. Close the document by pressing Ctrl+W/Command+W.

The updated PSD returns to Lightroom with your changes intact. Now you're ready to add final adjustments to the PSD in Lightroom.

Add final adjustments to the PSD in Lightroom

Once you've taken a raw file from Lightroom to Photoshop and back again, you may be finished editing; however, you may have a thing or two left to do in Lightroom. Some examples of the editing you may do to a PSD are finishing touches, such as an edge vignette, a quick crop, or color adjustments you need to print the file.

Generally speaking, try to avoid redoing any of the *original* adjustments you made in Lightroom's Basic panel because that can complicate your workflow. If you need to reopen the PSD in Photoshop, it won't include any additional Lightroom adjustments (this is due to the special flattened layer Photoshop includes in the file, which you learned about in the section "Configuring Photoshop's Maximize Compatibility preference"). And, if you open a copy of the PSD that *includes* the Lightroom adjustments, you lose the layers you originally made in Photoshop.

Let's get the doughnut photo ready for printing:

1   In Lightroom, select the PSD of the doughnut file and press D to open the photo in the Develop module, if you aren't already there.

2   Let's finish off the toning of the document in the Basic panel: move Exposure to +0.25, Contrast to +10, Whites to +5, Blacks to −17, and Clarity to +10.

Note: If you add the edge vignette to the PSD and then realize you have more cloning to do, you'll have to add the edge vignette again to the updated PSD that comes back to Lightroom.

3 My client would like to print this picture large, so I want to be able to see the detail in each of the doughnuts. Go into the Detail panel and adjust the Sharpening Amount to 57.

4 Holding down the Alt/Option key, drag the Radius slider until you see the edges of the doughnuts (I used a setting of 1.3).

5 Holding down the Alt/Option key, drag the Detail slider until you see enough detail to taste (I returned mine to 25 after dragging to the right).

If you find that noise has been introduced into the image, mitigate it using the Noise Reduction slider. Also, it's important to keep in mind that, depending on what paper you'll print on, you may need to do additional sharpening. The point? Sharpen, but don't go overboard here.

Sending a JPEG or TIFF from Lightroom to Photoshop

When you send any file format *other* than a raw photo from Lightroom to Photoshop, Lightroom questions you as to *what* it should send to Photoshop. The choice you make determines whether or not the edits you've made in Lightroom tag along for the ride over to Photoshop.

In this section, you'll send a JPEG to Photoshop for the purpose of using Photoshop to get rid of an element in a picture, as well as apply a toning preset.

1 In Lightroom's Library module or the Filmstrip in the Develop module, select the Church1.jpg photo.

2 Open the photo in Photoshop by pressing Ctrl+E/Command+E.

3 In the Edit Photo with Adobe Photoshop dialog box that appears, choose Edit A Copy With Lightroom Adjustments, and click Edit.

Note: This dialog is exactly the same one you encountered when you reopened a PSD from inside Lightroom earlier in this lesson.

The image opens in Photoshop with your Lightroom adjustments applied. Choosing any other option in the Edit Photo dialog box would prevent your adjustments from being visible once the file opens in Photoshop.

4 In Photoshop, choose Layer > New > Layer Via Copy or press Ctrl+J/Command+J.

5 Let's flip this copy of the picture so that we have a clean left border. Press Ctrl+T/Command+T to enter Free Transform. Then, right-click anywhere on the picture and select Flip Horizontal. Press Enter/Return to exit Free Transform.

6 I want to show only the left side of the picture, but hide the right side with a mask. So, hold down the Alt/Option key and click the Add Layer Mask icon at the bottom of the Layers panel to add a black mask to the duplicate layer.

7 Press D on your keyboard to make sure the Foreground and Background colors are set to black and white. Then, press G to get the Gradient tool (click the three dots icon near the bottom of the toolbar to add it, if needed). Click the arrow next to the gradient thumbnail in the options bar to open the Gradient Picker, and choose the Foreground To Background gradient in the upper left.

8 Click to the left of the church's steeple and, while holding down the Shift key, drag toward the center of the steeple. If your Foreground color is set to black and your Background color is set to white, this should reveal the contents of that layer on the left and slowly hide it as you move to the right.

9 Let's finish this image off with a photographic effect. Click the Create New Adjustment Layer icon (the black-and-white circle) at the bottom of the Layers panel and select Gradient Map near the bottom of the menu.

10 In the Properties panel, click the arrow next to the gradient thumbnail to open the Gradient Picker, then click the little gear icon and choose Photographic Toning from the menu. Make sure that you click Append (not Replace).

11 The gradients here are really interesting takes on tinted effects. I tend to like the Selenium gradients instead of the Sepia ones, but experiment with them to find one that speaks to you. At the upper right of the Layers panel, lower the layer's Opacity setting to around 75% to let some of the original colors show through.

> **Tip:** If your colors are reversed in the Gradient settings in the options bar, you may need to swap your Foreground and Background colors. Press the X key to swap them.

12 You now have several layers in this JPEG file: the original Background layer, the masked copy layer, and a Gradient Map layer at the top. Press Ctrl+S/Command+S to save the file. Close the file by pressing Ctrl+W/Command+W. Because of the layers, Photoshop saves it as a PSD. In Lightroom, the PSD appears next to the original JPEG in the Filmstrip or Grid view.

13 If you decide you want to change the opacity of the Gradient Map adjustment layer you applied in Photoshop, select the PSD in Lightroom, and reopen it in Photoshop by pressing Ctrl+E/Command+E.

14 This time, in the Edit Photo dialog box, choose Edit Original and click Edit.

15 In Photoshop, select the Gradient Map adjustment layer in the Layers panel, and then lower the Opacity setting at the upper right of the panel to around 52%.

16 Press Ctrl+S/Command+S again, and then close the file by pressing Ctrl+W/Command+W.

Your changes are updated in the PSD that appears in Lightroom.

Sending a photo from Lightroom to Photoshop as a Smart Object

Another way to send files of any format to Photoshop is as Smart Objects, which you can think of as a protective wrapper. Anything you do to a Smart Object happens to the wrapper and not to the photo inside it. Smart Objects also let you do stuff like resize and run filters on the photo without harming the original.

When you send a *raw* file to Photoshop as a Smart Object, the Smart Object stays in raw format, too. This enables you to fine-tune it using Photoshop's Camera Raw plug-in if the photo needs a last-minute tweak while you're in Photoshop.

This feature also lets you access any snapshots (saved image states or versions) you've made in Lightroom via the Camera Raw plug-in's Snapshots panel. This can be another good way to experiment with different treatments of the image while you're still in Photoshop.

● **Note:** Adobe Photoshop Elements doesn't support Smart Objects, so you won't see this option if you're using Elements as your external editor.

Working with snapshots in Lightroom and Photoshop

Before we start working with snapshots, I want to use one of the images that we worked on in Lesson 4—the flamingo.

1 Navigate to the Lesson 04 Images collection and drag the Flamingo.NEF file into the Lesson 06 Images collection. This not only adds it to a new collection, but any changes that we make will appear in both collections.

▶ **Tip:** If you want to keep the changes you made to the flamingo image in the Lesson 04 Images collection, create a virtual copy of it after you drag it into the Lesson 06 Images collection.

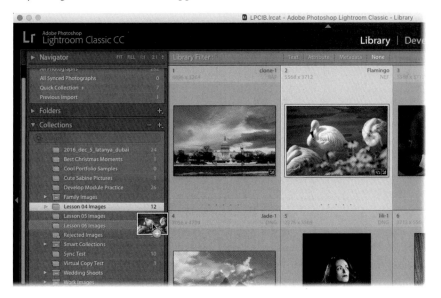

2 Edit the image in the Develop module to taste. I increased the Exposure setting to +0.35, decreased the Highlights setting to −71, and increased the Whites

setting to +14 to begin. I'd like to save this version of the file in the event I want to get back to these edit settings, so I will make a snapshot of them. In the Snapshots panel on the left side of Lightroom's Develop module, click the plus sign (+) and create a new snapshot called **Full Color**.

3 Expand the Presets panel to find a creative preset to apply. Click the triangle next to Creative, and let's apply the Creative-Warm Contrast preset.

4 Repeat step 2 to create a new snapshot named **Warm Contrast**.

In the Snapshots panel, you now have two different color treatments that you can go back to quickly and easily. The only drawback? You can't compare two snapshots with one another in Survey mode, as you can with virtual copies. However, it's a great speed tool, so let's make a Smart Object from this file.

5 Right-click the photo and choose Edit In > Open as Smart Object in Photoshop.

6   In Photoshop, apply a filter to the image by choosing Filter > Pixelate > Crystallize. This makes the image appear as if it is constructed of a series of small crystals. Changing the size of the crystals gives you different looks.

7   Change the Cell Size value in the Crystallize dialog box to **25** and press the Enter/Return key.

8   Because the image is a Smart Object, Photoshop applies what is called a Smart Filter to it. Filters are normally applied to pixel-based images. A Smart Filter gives you all of the options of pixel-based filters, but on raw images. The Smart Filter even includes a mask that lets you paint the filter in, in specific areas.

9 Double-click the word *Crystallize* in the Layers panel and it will bring back the Crystallize filter dialog box, letting you change the values for your filter. This time, change the size of the cells to **75** and click OK.

10 The image will automatically change, and the new settings will be applied to the Smart Object. You can paint on the white mask that appears above the filter with a black brush to hide the effect from part of the picture. If you want to reapply that effect to the area, switch your brush color to white and paint over the black on the mask. We'll cover layer masking in a later lesson.

While being able to re-edit Smart Objects and alter Smart Filters is useful, the ability to read snapshot information inside Camera Raw is just as powerful.

Earlier, we saved a couple of snapshots inside the raw file in Lightroom before we opened it as a Smart Object in Photoshop. Let's open the Smart Object and change the snapshot to apply a new look to the image.

11 Double-click the Smart Object layer's thumbnail and you will be taken into Camera Raw. You'll notice that the sliders there are very similar to the ones in the Develop module in Lightroom. Click the far right icon at the top of the panel area, and you will see the snapshots we saved in Lightroom.

12 Select the Full Color snapshot that you made inside Lightroom and click the OK button at the lower right of the Camera Raw window.

13 Save and close the file in Photoshop and the Lightroom thumbnail will reflect the changes that you made in Photoshop.

● **Note:** You can send any file format to Photoshop as a Smart Object; it doesn't have to be a raw file.

While it's easy to access snapshots you make in Lightroom via the Camera Raw plug-in while you're in Photoshop, it bears repeating that this maneuver works *only* on raw files.

Using third-party plug-ins

If you use a third-party plug-in in Photoshop—say, Alien Skin's Exposure X or the Google Nik collection—simply use the plug-in as you normally would and the results are saved in the PSD that Photoshop sends back to Lightroom. If you use a third-party plug-in in Lightroom, you can access it in the Photo > Edit In menu. Lightroom asks you to set the options you want to use when you open the image: file format, color space, and so on. Some plug-ins, such as Exposure X, can't read PSD files, so you'll have to use TIFF files instead. The end result is an additional file in your catalog.

Review questions

1 Can you set up more than one configuration of Photoshop settings for opening photographs from Lightroom in Photoshop?

2 What is the keyboard shortcut for Photo > Edit In > Edit in Adobe Photoshop CC (or the latest version of Photoshop installed on your computer)?

3 When you hand off a raw file from Lightroom to Photoshop by pressing Ctrl+E/Command+E, which program is rendering the photograph so you can see and work with it in Photoshop?

4 After you pass a raw file from Lightroom to Photoshop and save it in Photoshop, what format file appears in your Lightroom catalog alongside the raw file?

5 If you reopen a PSD in Photoshop that you made additional Lightroom adjustments to, can you see those final adjustments in Photoshop using the Edit Original command?

6 Is it possible to access snapshots you made in Lightroom while you're in Photoshop?

Review answers

1 Yes. In addition to configuring the primary external editor, you can set up additional configurations for the same editor, or a different one, in the Additional External Editor section. When you save additional configurations as a preset, they appear as a menu item in Lightroom's Photo > Edit In menu.

2 The shortcut is Ctrl+E/Command+E.

3 Photoshop's Camera Raw plug-in renders the photo.

4 Passing a raw file from Lightroom to Photoshop and saving it in Photoshop generates a PSD file, unless you changed Lightroom's External Editing preferences to TIFF.

5 No. When you reopen a PSD using the Edit Original option in the Edit Photo dialog box, any adjustments made in Lightroom after editing in Photoshop aren't visible in Photoshop due to the special flattened layer that it includes in the document. Therefore, you'll have to redo those adjustments once the edited PSD returns to Lightroom.

6 Yes, but only for raw files. If you create snapshots for a raw file and then send it to Photoshop as a Smart Object, you can double-click the Smart Object in Photoshop to open the Camera Raw plug-in. When it opens, click the Snapshots icon, and you'll see all the snapshots it contains.

7 LIGHTROOM TO PHOTOSHOP FOR SELECTING AND MASKING

Lesson overview

Photoshop lets you isolate a complex object or tonal range with far more precision than Lightroom's local adjustment tools. Indeed, you can tell Photoshop exactly which part of an image you want to tinker with by making a selection. With a selection, you can use masking to hide the selected area and replace it with another image or restrict an adjustment to it. This lets you swap backgrounds, change an object's color, fill an area with a color or pattern, create scenes that don't exist in real life, and a whole lot more. In this lesson you'll learn how to:

- Select by shape using the Rectangular Marquee and Pen tools, and select by color using the Magic Wand and Quick Selection tools.

- Select what's in focus using the Select Subject command and select hair using the Select And Mask workspace.

- Replace a selected area with another photo and change the color of a selected area.

- Make targeted adjustments using selections with adjustment layers.

This lesson will take 2 to 2 1/2 hours to complete. Please log in to your account on peachpit.com to download the files for this lesson, or go to the "Getting Started" section at the beginning of this book and follow the instructions under "Accessing the lesson files and Web Edition." Store the files on your computer in a convenient location. Your Account page is also where you'll find any updates to the lessons or to the lesson files. Look on the Lesson & Update Files tab to access the most current content.

©2014 RAFAEL CONCEPCION, ABOUTRC.COM

A great reason to send a photo from Lightroom to Photoshop is to take advantage of Photoshop's sophisticated selection and masking capabilities, which let you swap backgrounds realistically.

Preparing for this lesson

To get the most out of this lesson, be sure you do the following:

1 Follow the instructions in the "Getting Started" section at the beginning of this book for setting up an LPCIB folder on your computer, downloading the lesson files to that LPCIB folder, and creating an LPCIB catalog in Lightroom.

2 Download the Lesson 07 folder from your Account page at peachpit.com to *username*/Documents/LPCIB/Lessons.

3 Launch Lightroom, and open the LPCIB catalog you created in "Getting Started" by choosing File > Open Catalog and navigating to the LPCIB Catalog. Alternatively, you can choose File > Open Recent > LPCIB Catalog.

4 Add the Lesson 07 files to the LPCIB catalog using the steps in the Lesson 1 section "Importing photos from a hard drive."

5 In the Library module's Folders panel, select Lesson 07.

6 Create a collection called **Lesson 07 Images** and place the images from the Lesson 07 folder in the collection.

7 Set the Sort menu beneath the image preview to File Name.

Let's get the selecting and masking party started by covering some selection basics that will serve you well throughout your Photoshop career.

Selection basics

Photoshop includes a wide array of tools and commands that you can use to create selections. When you create a selection, a series of animated "marching ants," appear on the image. This marching ants selection circles the edge of the selected area, isolating it. When you have an active selection, whatever you do next affects only the area inside the selection. If you right-click inside the selection, a menu of frequently used selection-related commands appears. The commands at the top change according to which selection tool is active (here, that's the Magic Wand).

Note: Selections don't hang around forever—when you click somewhere outside the selection with a selection tool, the original selection disappears.

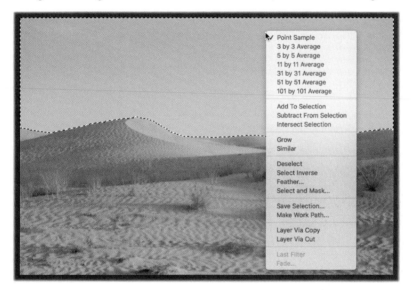

Here are some commands you'll use often when making selections:

- Select All. This command selects the entirety of the currently active layer and places marching ants around the perimeter of your document. To run this command, choose Select > All or press Ctrl+A/Command+A.

- Deselect. To get rid of the marching ants after you've finished working with a selection, choose Select > Deselect or press Ctrl+D/Command+D. Alternatively, you can click once outside the selection to get rid of it.

- Reselect. To resurrect your last selection, choose Select > Reselect or press Shift+Ctrl+D/Shift+Command+D. This command reactivates the last selection you made, even if it was five filters and 20 brushstrokes ago (unless you've used the Crop or Type tools since then, which render this command powerless). Reselecting is helpful if you accidentally deselect a selection that took you a long time to create.

- Inverse. This command, which you run by choosing Select > Inverse or pressing Shift+Ctrl+I/Shift+Command+I, flip-flops a selection to select everything that

Tip: You can also use the Undo command (Ctrl+Z/Command+Z) to resurrect a selection that you accidentally dismissed.

wasn't selected before. You'll often find it easier to select what you don't want and then inverse the selection to get what you do want.

- Load a layer as a selection. This command puts marching ants around everything on a particular layer; that way, whatever you do next affects only that content. To do it, Ctrl-click/Command-click the layer's thumbnail. Alternatively, you can right-click the layer's thumbnail and then choose Select Pixels from the resulting menu.

- Save Selection. If you spent a long time creating a selection, you may want to save it so you can reload it again later (that said, you can always copy a mask from one layer to another by Alt-dragging/Option-dragging it). To do that, choose Select > Save Selection. In the resulting dialog box, give the selection a meaningful name, and click OK. To reload the selection, choose Select > Load Selection, choose your selection from the Channel menu, and click OK.

● **Note:** Before selecting and masking your own images, be sure to adjust the tone and color of each photo as discussed in Lesson 3.

Once you make a selection, you can modify it—expand it, contract it, and so on—using the commands in the Select menu or the controls in the Select And Mask workspace, which you'll learn about toward the end of this lesson.

In the sections that follow, you'll learn how to use Photoshop's most practical and useful selection methods; there's simply not room in this book to cover them all. The next section teaches you how to select areas based on shape.

Selecting by shape

The success of your selection work in Photoshop will largely depend on which selection tool or command you start with, so take a moment to assess the area you want to select. If it's a certain shape—say, rectangular or oval, or it has a lot of straight edges—then use a selection tool that's based on shape.

These tools include the Rectangular and Elliptical Marquee tools, the Polygonal Lasso tool, and the Pen tool. You can also use Photoshop's shape tools to create a selection based on shape.

Since the Rectangular Marquee tool is the easiest one to use, that's where you'll start.

Using the Rectangular Marquee tool

Photoshop's most basic selection tools are the Rectangular Marquee and the Elliptical Marquee. Any time you need to make a selection that's squarish or roundish, you should use these tools.

In the following exercise, you'll use the Rectangular Marquee tool to select a photo on a wall in one image and replace it with another photo as a sample proof. You can use these same steps to create a circular selection using the Elliptical Marquee tool.

1 Click the sleeps.jpg image in Lightroom's Library module, and then Ctrl-click/
   Command-click to select the friends.dng photo.

2 Press Ctrl+E/Command+E and click Edit in the resulting dialog box to open
   both photos as separate documents in Photoshop.

3 In the friends photo document, choose Select > All or press Ctrl+A/
   Command+A, and Photoshop places marching ants around the photo. Copy
   the selection to your computer's memory by choosing Edit > Copy or by pressing Ctrl+C/Command+C. Get rid of the marching ants by choosing Select >
   Deselect or by pressing Ctrl+D/Command+D.

4 Using the document tabs at the top of the Photoshop workspace, click the tab of
   the other open document so that you're viewing the sleeps.jpg photo. Zoom in
   to the photo by pressing Ctrl++/Command++. Spacebar-drag to reposition the
   photo so you can see the edges of the canvas above the bed.

5 Activate the Rectangular Marquee tool by pressing M or by clicking it in the
   Tools panel. Click in the upper-left corner of the picture hanging on the wall,
   and then drag to the lower-right corner of it. Release your mouse button.

> **Tip:** You can cycle between Photoshop's marquee tools by pressing Shift and then tapping M on your keyboard.

   Photoshop starts the selection where you clicked and continues it in the direction you drag as long as you hold down the mouse button. To reposition the
   selection while you're drawing it, keep holding down your mouse button and
   then hold down the Spacebar while you drag the selection to where you want it.

Release your mouse button, and you're finished. To reposition the selection after you release your mouse button, drag inside the selection or use the arrow keys.

6 Paste the photo inside the active selection by choosing Edit > Paste Special > Paste Into.

The freinds photo appears on its own layer, masked with your selection (the mask is circled here).

7 Resize the photo so it fits within the canvas. Summon Free Transform by pressing Ctrl+T/Command+T. Press Ctrl+0/Command+0 to have Photoshop resize your document so you can see all four corner handles of the bounding box. Drag the corner handles inward until the photo fits the canvas. As necessary, zoom in or out of the document so you can see the corners of the image. To reposition the photo on the canvas, drag within the Free Transform bounding box. Press Enter/Return to accept the transformation.

● **Note:** One of the changes in the October 2018 (version 20.0) release of Photoshop revolves around how you transform images. In previous versions, you had to hold down the Shift key as you dragged to keep your transformations proportional. In this new release, you no longer have to.

8 The new picture is a little bright against the wall, making it stand out. Let's add a gray color overlay to it to mute the colors and make them blend in with the image better. With the friends photo layer active, click the *fx* (Add a Layer Style) icon at the bottom of the Layers panel and choose Color Overlay in the menu. In the resulting dialog box, click the color swatch and enter **383838** in the Hex (#) field at lower right, and then set Blend Mode to Darken and Opacity to 27%. Click OK to close the dialog box, and Photoshop adds the color overlay to the image and your Layers panel, making the photo swap more realistic.

9 Choose File > Save (or press Ctrl+S/Command+S) to save the swapped photo document, and then choose File > Close (or press Ctrl+W/Command+W) to close the document in Photoshop. Close the friends photo as well.

The edited photo is saved back to the same folder as the original, and the PSD appears in Lightroom. You can see them both in Survey view here, with the original on the right, and the edited photo on the left.

In the next exercise, you'll place a new photo on a computer monitor using a different selection tool, and you'll adjust its perspective.

Using the Pen tool

Note: You can also use the Pen tool to draw complicated shapes in order to create art from scratch.

The Pen tool is the most precise of all the tools you can use to create a selection, but it can be a frustrating tool to learn to use because of how it works. Instead of dragging to create a selection, you create anchor points and control handles, which are collectively referred to as vector paths or Bezier curves (named for their inventor). The handles aren't actually part of the line; they're levers you use to control each line segment's curvature. Once you create the path shape you want, you can convert it into a perfectly smooth selection.

Creating a straight-edged selection

Note: You can also use the Polygonal Lasso tool to create a straight-edged selection, but it's really difficult to be precise with it. That's why this book advises using the Pen tool for straight-edged selections.

To get started with the Pen tool, try using it to create a straight-edged selection, as described in the following exercise.

1 Click the monitor.tiff image in Lightroom's Library module, and then choose Photo > Edit In > Edit in Adobe Photoshop CC or press Ctrl+E/Command+E. Choose to Edit A Copy With Lightroom Adjustments and click Edit. Once in Photoshop, zoom in to the photo, and Spacebar-drag to reposition it so you can see the corners of the computer monitor.

2 Activate the Pen tool by pressing P or by clicking it in the Tools panel. In the options bar, choose Path from the unlabeled mode menu on the left.

3 Click one corner of the monitor screen to start your path, then move to the next corner and click it. Photoshop puts a thin line between the two points. Move in the same direction around the screen, click the other two corners, then close the selection by clicking atop the starting point. (You'll see a tiny circle appear beneath your cursor, as shown here.)

4 Activate the Direct Selection tool (circled here), and then click outside the path to *deselect* it (the corner points disappear, but the outline remains). Zoom in to your document more so you can see the corners, click any point not snug in its corner—it becomes solid, but the rest of the corner points are see-through—and then drag the point to adjust its position. When you do, only the selected point moves. Adjust the other three points, as necessary.

▶ **Tip:** If you need to move the whole path, Ctrl-click/Command-click it so all four corner points become solid, and then drag the path into the desired position.

5 When the path is just right, load it as a selection by pressing Ctrl+Enter/ Command+Return.

Alternatively, you can switch back to the Pen tool, and next to Make, click Selection in the options bar. If you go that route, a dialog box appears asking if you want to feather (soften) the selection edges. Enter **0** in the Feather Radius field, and then click OK. Either way, marching ants surround the monitor screen.

6 In Lightroom, select the treeline.dng image and press Ctrl+E/Command+E to open it in Photoshop.

7 Press Ctrl+A/Command+A to select the entire image, and press Ctrl+C/ Command+C to copy it into the clipboard.

8 Move to the monitor image and choose Edit > Paste Special > Paste Into, and the treeline photo lands on a new layer, masked with the selection you made.

9 Summon Free Transform by pressing Ctrl+T/Command+T, and then press Ctrl+0/Command+0 so you can see all four corner handles. Drag the corner handles inward to resize the treeline photo so it's a little bigger than the monitor—it needs to be a little bigger because you'll distort the photo to fix the perspective in the next step. Don't accept the transformation yet!

10 Right-click inside the Free Transform bounding box, and choose Distort from the resulting menu. Click each corner handle in turn, and drag them inward toward the corners of the monitor screen, making sure they are snug into the corners of the screen. Press Enter/Return when you're finished.

11 Save and close the document in Photoshop. Close the document containing the trees photo as well. When Photoshop asks if you want to save the trees photo, click Don't Save.

Here's the result. As you may imagine, this technique is useful for real estate photographers, although you can use this technique to swap out any portion of an image for something else.

Creating a curved selection

Note: Some photographers pay companies to create precise paths with the Pen tool—they typically use the "zoom in really far and click, click, click" method too. The company saves the path and returns a JPEG to the photographer, who then uses Photoshop's Paths panel to load the path and convert it into a selection. If you're a busy commercial photographer who does product shots for the catalog industry, this may be a time-saving solution!

When it comes to creating a *curved* selection with the Pen tool—or one that's a combination of straight and curved paths—there are a couple of ways to get it done. You can drag to create the control handles mentioned earlier, which takes practice and skill. Alternatively, you can zoom *really* far in to a photo and then click, click, click with the tool to make small straight path segments that fit snugly against the object. This method takes a lot of time, but it doesn't require any skill.

The following exercise walks you through using control handles to create a path around an iPhone lens destined for a white background for use in a catalog.

1 Select the photo of the iPhone lens in Lightroom's Library module, and then choose Photo > Edit In > Edit in Adobe Photoshop CC. Choose to Edit A Copy With Lightroom adjustments and click Edit. In Photoshop, zoom in to the photo and Spacebar-drag to reposition it so you can see the edge of the lens.

2 Activate the Pen tool, and in the options bar, make sure the mode menu at left is set to Path.

3 Click an edge of the iPhone lens to set a starting anchor point. To create a straight-line segment, move to a spot along the object edge and click.

Tip: If you set some anchor points incorrectly, press Ctrl+Z/Command+Z to undo the last anchor point; press it again to undo preceding points. You can also press Escape on your keyboard twice to delete the entire path.

4 To create a curved segment, move to the next spot where the object edge changes direction. This time, instead of clicking, drag in the direction you want the curved segment to go. This creates an anchor point with two handles, and you are automatically controlling one of the handles. The direction and length of the handles determine the shape of the curved segment, so keep dragging and rotating until the curve matches the curve of your object. Continue around the object, creating curved and straight segments.

If you get to a place on the lens edge where you need to change direction, set the ending anchor point for the preceding segment, as you've been doing, then Alt-click/Option-click that anchor point to convert it into a corner point. Continue in the new direction, creating segments as before.

5   When you arrive back where you started the path, point your cursor at the starting anchor point, and when a small circle appears near the cursor, click the anchor point to close the path.

6   Use the Direct Selection tool as described in the previous section to reposition points on the path. Zoom further in to your document so you can see the points and paths more clearly in order to adjust them so they're snug against the lens.

To change the direction and length of a control handle, click to activate the point, and then drag either end of the handle to adjust it.

7 Switch back to the Pen tool, and click the Mask button in the options bar. Photoshop adds a vector mask to the lens layer, and the background drops out and becomes transparent.

8 Save the document in Photoshop, but leave it open. If you peek at the resulting PSD in Lightroom, you see the len's original background, since Lightroom doesn't support transparency (empty pixels). Don't panic; if you reopen the PSD into Photoshop, it'll open with the vector mask and a transparent background.

9 Switch back to Photoshop, and give the lens a solid white background. To do that, click the half-black/half-white circle at the bottom of the Layers panel, and choose Solid Color from the resulting menu. In the Color Picker that appears, enter **ffffff** in the Hex (#) field at lower right (for pure white), and click OK.

10 Drag the Solid Color fill layer's thumbnail beneath the lens layer.

If, later on, you want to change the background color, double-click the Solid Color fill layer's thumbnail to reopen the Color Picker.

11 Save the document, but leave it open. Take a peek in Lightroom, and you see that the PSD now has a white background.

12 Switch back to Photoshop, and save a copy of the photo with a transparent background. To do that, click the visibility eye to the left of the Solid Color fill layer to turn it off. Choose File > Export > Export As. In the resulting dialog box, choose PNG from the Format menu in the upper right, and make sure Transparency is selected. Click Export All. In the resulting dialog box, tell Photoshop where you want to save the PNG, and click Export.

Photoshop saves a copy of the document as a PNG with a transparent background, which is something Lightroom can't do.

13 Close the Photoshop document, and in the resulting dialog box, click Don't Save.

This by no means is meant to be a comprehensive guide for using the Pen tool, though this information gives you enough to get started. For more on the Pen tool, see *Adobe Photoshop CC Classroom in a Book*.

There is also a great online game that you can play that lets you practice making shapes with Bezier curves. Go to https://bezier.method.ac/ and get as much practice as you can.

In the next section, you'll learn how to create a selection based on color.

Selecting by color

Photoshop also has several tools that you can use to create a selection based on pixel color. They're helpful when you want to select a chunk of an image that's fairly uniform in color, such as the sky or the paint job on a car. These tools and commands include the Magic Wand tool, Quick Selection tool, Background Eraser tool, Magic Eraser tool, and Color Range command.

This section teaches you how to use the most practical ones, beginning with an oldie but goodie: the Magic Wand tool.

Using the Magic Wand tool

The Magic Wand is Photoshop's oldest selection tool. Some people avoid using it because it can produce rough edges. However, if the area you want to select is a large area of solid color, it works well. In this exercise, you'll use it to select a boring sky in order to replace it with a different one.

1   Select the balloon2.dng photo in Lightroom's Library module, and then Ctrl-click/Command-click to also select treeline.dng. Choose Photo > Edit In > Edit in Adobe Photoshop CC or press Ctrl+E/Command+E to open the photos in Photoshop.

2   In the treeline image, choose Select > All or press Ctrl+A/Command+A. Copy the selection to your computer's memory by choosing Edit > Copy or by pressing Ctrl+C/Command+C. Get rid of the marching ants by choosing Select > Deselect or by pressing Ctrl+D/Command+D.

3   Using the tabs near the top of the Photoshop workspace, switch to the document with the balloon photo. Resize it so you can see all of the sky.

4   Activate the Magic Wand in the Tools panel. This tool lives inside the Quick Selection toolset, so if you haven't used the Magic Wand before, you'll see the Quick Selection tool instead. Click it, and from the menu that appears, choose the Magic Wand.

5   In the options bar, set the Sample Size menu to Point Sample, and turn on Contiguous if it is not already on. Set your Tolerance to **20**.

The Sample Size menu lets you change the way the Magic Wand calculates which pixels to select. From the factory, it's set to Point Sample, which makes the tool determine its selection based only on the color of the specific pixel you clicked. When you change it to 5 by 5 Average, it looks at the original pixel and averages it with the colors of surrounding pixels. When working with your own imagery, you may need to experiment with this setting. In this instance, Point Sample will work well. The Tolerance setting specifies the range of color the Magic Wand will select. Contiguous lets the Magic Wand know that it should only select colors that are next to one another—in this case, the areas around the balloon, but not in the balloon.

▶ **Tip:** To set any Photoshop tool to its default values, select the tool in the Tools panel, right-click the tool icon on the far left of the options bar, and choose Reset Tool.

▶ **Tip:** If you create a selection with the Magic Wand, you can always pop into the Select And Mask workspace described near the end of this lesson and use the Smooth slider to smooth it out a bit.

▶ **Tip:** You can press Shift+W to cycle between the Quick Selection and Magic Wand tools.

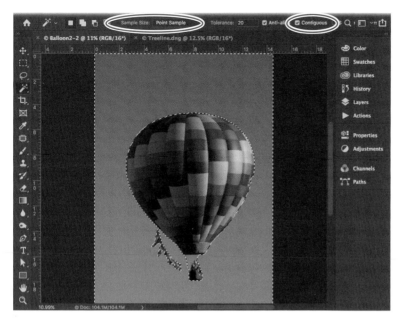

6   Click anywhere within the blue sky. Because the sky is so uniform in color, a single click may select all of it. If there is any sky missing from the selection, hold down the Shift key and click the part of the sky that is missing.

7   Paste the treeline photo inside the active selection by choosing Edit > Paste Special > Paste Into.

8   Resize the sky photo to your liking using Free Transform. Press Ctrl+T/ Command+T, and then press Ctrl+0/Command+0 to resize the document so you can see the corner handles. Drag the lower-right corner handle outward to make the photo larger. Press Enter/Return when you're finished.

● **Note:** You can only click, not drag, with the Magic Wand.

9 Save and close the balloon document, and then close the treeline document without saving it.

The balloon photo is far more exciting with clouds in the sky! In the next section, you'll learn how to use the Quick Selection tool to select by color.

Using the Quick Selection tool

● **Note:** If you don't get a good selection with the Quick Selection tool, you can refine it using the Select And Mask workspace, which you'll learn about toward the end of this lesson.

The Quick Selection tool is easy to use and lets you create complex selections by clicking or dragging. As you drag with this tool, your selection expands to encompass pixels similar in color to the ones you're brushing over. It works well if there's a fair amount of contrast between what you want to select and everything else.

The size of the area the Quick Selection tool selects is proportional to the size of the brush you're using: A larger brush creates a larger selection, and a smaller brush creates a smaller selection. For the best results, use a hard-edged brush to produce well-defined edges and a soft-edged brush to produce slightly transparent edges.

▶ **Tip:** You can switch between hard- and soft-edged brushes using the Brush Preset picker at the left side of the options bar.

One of the many practical reasons to send a photo from Lightroom to Photoshop is to use selections and masks to change the color of an object. This is particularly useful if you're a commercial photographer who takes product shots.

The next two sections teach you how to use the Quick Selection tool, along with a an adjustment layer, to change the color of the iPhone lens we used earlier.

Changing color using an adjustment layer

Adjustment layers are incredibly useful for changing the color of objects in a photo. In this exercise, you'll use one of these handy layers to change the color of an iPhone lens.

1 Select the colorchange-1.jpg in Lightroom's Library module. Choose Photo > Edit In > Edit in Adobe Photoshop CC or press Ctrl+E/Command+E to open it in Photoshop. Zoom in to the photo, and Spacebar-drag to reposition the photo so you can see the red color of the iPhone lens.

2 Activate the Quick Selection tool, which lives in the same toolset as the Magic Wand. If you used the Magic Wand in the previous exercise, press Shift+W to cycle between the tools, and activate the Quick Selection tool. In the options bar, select Auto-Enhance.

Because the Quick Selection tool makes selections extremely quickly, the edges can end up blocky and imperfect. Selecting Auto-Enhance tells Photoshop to take its time and think more carefully about the selections it makes.

3 Use the Left Bracket ([) and Right Bracket (]) keys on your keyboard to make your brush smaller or larger, respectively, and then drag across the largest parts of the lens to select them. Decrease your brush size when you get close to smaller areas.

Selection tips

Oftentimes, you'll need to add to or subtract from a selection in order to select the area you want. Here are a few tips that are helpful for that purpose:

- Choose Select > Grow to make Photoshop expand the selection to all similar-colored pixels adjacent to the current selection.

- Choose Select > Similar to make Photoshop select similar-colored pixels throughout the whole image, even if they're not touching the original selection.

- To add to a selection, hold the Shift key as you select another area that is contiguous to or in a different part of the image from the initial selection. Alternatively, with a selection tool active, click the Add To Selection icon (at the left end of the options bar).

- To subtract from a selection, hold down the Alt/Option key as you click or drag in the area you want to remove from the selection. Alternatively, click the Subtract From Selection icon (at the left end of the options bar).

You can also use the selection tools and commands *together* in order to get the selection you want. For example, you may make an initial selection using the Magic Wand and then fine-tune it manually using the Lasso tool—it lets you draw a selection freehand—adding to and subtracting from the initial selection until it's the shape you want.

Keep in mind that most selection tools (with the exception of the Quick Selection tool) default to New Selection mode. So if you make an initial selection with one tool and then switch to another one and click the image, the initial selection disappears. To keep that from happening, use the Shift key or the Add To Selection icon as described above. The additional selection can be contiguous to or in a different part of the image than the initial selection.

As soon as you create an initial selection with the Quick Selection tool, it automatically goes into Add To Selection mode, so there's no need to use the Shift key to add to your selection.

4 If an area of the lens that is not red ends up in the selection, hold down the Alt/Option key and click or drag across it with a very small brush (say, 50 pixels) to subtract it from the selection.

If too much of the image gets subtracted from the selection, release the modifier key, and drag across the area again to add it to the selection. The great part about the Quick Selection tool is that it is a smart tool. The more you add and remove from the selection, the more precise the selection becomes. Continue to do this until all of the red area is selected.

5 Click the half-black/half-white icon at the bottom of the Layers panel, and choose Hue/Saturation from the resulting menu. Alternatively, you can choose Layer > New Adjustment Layer > Hue/Saturation.

This fills the selection with the Hue/Saturation effect and adds a fill layer to your Layers panel. The new fill layer has an automatic layer mask that is white inside the area you selected and black outside that area, which lets the new color show only atop the red portions of the lens.

6 In the Hue/Saturation options in the Properties panel, drag the Hue slider to experiment with different colors. You can also increase and decrease the lightness of the color, as well as the saturation.

● **Note:** Each adjustment and fill layer comes with its own layer mask. If a selection is active when the adjustment or fill layer is created, the selected area is white within the mask, revealing the content of the fill layer in that area. The area outside the selection is black within the mask, concealing the fill layer in that area. Remember that in the realm of the layer mask, black conceals and white reveals!

7 If you would like to experiment further with how the colors interact with the layer below, you can switch the blend mode of the layer. Click the blend mode menu at the upper left of the Layers panel, and hover over each blend mode to see how the colors change. The most succesful ones for this would be Hue, Color, and Hard Light. The next section teaches you how to create a selection based on what's in focus in the photo.

Note: Another new change with the October 2018 release of Photoshop is the abilty to hover over the blend modes to see the live preview instead of clicking each blend mode to see the result. While the change seems small, it's a definite timesaver.

Using the Select Subject command

Adobe has made great advances in the use of artificial intelligence to speed up much of the tedious work that's done by photographers and designers. Adobe Sensei, its artifical intelligence and machine learning technology, is being used more and more in the background of Photoshop, reducing tasks that used to take hours to mere seconds.

You can see the fruits of this in a new feature in Photoshop: Select Subject. This AI-driven technology analyzes the picture, guesses what the subject of the picture is, and creates a selection for you. Is it perfect? It largely depends on the photo. That said, even at times when it is less than perfect, it shaves off a ton of time in tedious selection work.

In this exercise, you'll use the Select Subject command to select the subject of the picture. Then you'll flip the selection to create a mask and swap out a background.

1 Select bird.dng photo in Lightroom's Library module. Ctrl-click/Command-click to also select the sands.dng. Choose Photo > Edit In > Edit in Adobe Photoshop CC or press Ctrl+E/Command+E to open them in Photoshop.

2 With the bird photo active, choose Select > Subject. Photoshop analyzes your image and automatically generates an initial selection of the hawk. Not bad!

▶ **Tip:** If the arm of the falconer is not selected, you can switch to the Quick Selection tool and paint over it to add it. If a portion of the background is included in the selection, hold down the Alt/Option key and paint over it to remove it.

3 Choose Select > Inverse to make a selection of everything but the falcon.

4 Move back to the sands.dng image in Photoshop, and press Ctrl+A/Command+A to select the entire image. Press Ctrl+C/Command+C to copy it to the clipboard.

5 Return to the bird.dng picture and choose Edit > Paste Special > Paste Into.

6 Resize the sands photo to your liking using Free Transform. Press Ctrl+T/ Command+T, and then press Ctrl+0/Command+0 to resize the document so you can see the corner handles. Hold down the Alt/Option key while dragging from a corner to resize from the center of the image. Press Enter/Return when you're finished.

7 The picture is now taking better shape. Next, we'll add a blur to the sands layer to give the picture the appearance of a shallow depth of field.

Click the sands layer's thumbnail in the Layers panel and choose Filter > Blur > Gaussian Blur. In the dialog box, give the layer a 28-pixel Gaussian blur.

While I like the shallow depth of field the Gaussian blur gives this image, you may want to experiment with different pixel settings to get the right amount of blur for your taste. One of the problems with doing it in this manner, however, is that once the Gaussian Blur filter is applied, there's no way to go back and re-adjust it.

In this instance I think that it is better to turn this layer into a Smart Object. By applying the Gaussian Blur filter to a Smart Object, the effect will be applied as a Smart Filter, allowing you to go back later and adjust the blur amount, as needed.

8 Press Ctrl+Z/Command+Z to undo the blur we added. Then, right-click the sands layer and choose Convert To Smart Object from the menu.

9 Apply the Gaussian Blur filter as before. This time, the filter is applied as a Smart Filter, with its own mask. Double-clicking the words *Gaussian Blur* in the Layers panel reopens the Gaussian Blur dialog box, letting you change the values as you wish. Save and close the file to return to Lightroom.

Tightening selections and masks

Once you make a selection and hide it with a layer mask, you may encounter edge halos (also referred to as fringing or matting), a tiny portion of the background that stubbornly remains even after you try to hide it. Edge halos make a new sky look fake and won't help convince anyone that Elvis actually came to your cookout. Here are a couple of ways to fix them:

- Contract your selection. To do so, open the Select And Mask workspace and drag its Shift Edge slider left, or choose Select > Modify > Contract (the latter method doesn't give you a preview). Use this technique while you still have marching ants—in other words, before you hide the background with a layer mask.

- Run the Minimum filter on a layer mask. Once you've hidden something with a layer mask, activate the mask and choose Filter > Other > Minimum. In the resulting dialog box, choose Roundness from the Preserve menu, and then slowly drag the Radius slider rightward to tighten the mask.

Other fixes include the Layer > Matting > Defringe command and the Layer > Matting > Remove Black Matte or Remove White Matte command. However, these commands don't work on layer masks or an active selection. You can use them only after you've physically deleted pixels or copied the selected area to a new layer.

Selecting hair using the Select And Mask workspace

▶ **Tip:** The Select And Mask workspace isn't only for use on hair. Any time you have a selection tool active and some marching ants on your screen, you'll see a Select And Mask button sitting pretty up in the options bar; simply click and use it to fine-tune any selection.

Hair and objects with soft edges are among the most difficult items to select in Photoshop. Happily, the Select And Mask workspace (formerly known as the Refine Edge dialog box) can help with this task. This specialized workspace combines several selection and edge-adjustment tools that are scattered throughout Photoshop's Tools panel and menus, so you don't have to hunt for them. You can even create a selection from scratch in this workspace because it includes the Quick Selection tool and the Lasso tool, which you can use to draw a selection freehand.

The workspace is also unique in that you can see a live, continuously updated preview of what your selection will look like after fine-tuning. Additionally, you get seven different views to choose from, including Onion Skin (which lets you see through to the layer beneath the active one), Marching Ants, Overlay (the same red overlay you get with Quick Mask mode), On Black, On White, and Black & White (which lets you see the mask itself).

However, the Select And Mask workspace isn't magic. You need a strong contrast between your model's hair and the background to get good results. To be honest, it works best on photos taken on solid backgrounds, so you may want to shoot with this in mind.

In this exercise, you'll learn how to use the Select And Mask workspace, combined with Select Subject, to select a friend of mine from one background and place her on another.

1 Select the DanielleP.dng photo in Lightroom's Library module, and then Ctrl-click/Command-click to also select the Graffiti-1.dng background image. Choose Photo > Edit In > Open As Layers In Photoshop.

2 Choose Select > Subject to make a rough selection of the subject.

3 Choose Select > Select And Mask (or click the Select And Mask button if you have a selection tool active) to open the Select And Mask workspace.

The Overlay view puts a red overlay onto the area that isn't included in the selection. Because the overlay is see-through, you see the hair that isn't yet included in the selection, and therefore you know which areas need work. You can click the View menu and select the view that will best help you with your selection. For me, I want to be able to see the graffiti image directly underneath the Danielle layer.

4 There are a few standout tools in the Select And Mask workspace that you should be aware of:

• In the Properties panel on the right, click the arrow next to Edge Detection to expand that area and then drag the Radius slider to the right. Increasing the radius widens the area you're telling Photoshop to take into consideration as it refines the selection edge. To view that area, select Show Edge at the upper right of the panel (then deselect it).

• Selecting Smart Radius tells Photoshop to adjust the radius for both hard and soft edges. In this photo, I would leave it on.

- To include more hair in the selection, brush over those unselected areas with the Refine Edge Brush tool (R). It's the second tool down in the Tools panel on the left side of the workspace.

- You can also constrain the entire selection you have made on your image by shifting it inward or outward with the Shift Edge slider in the Global Refinements area. Let's constrict it by setting it at –23.

5   Adjust the brush size to finish your image as necessary. For this image, you can get away with using a fairly large brush, though for finer detail you may get better results using a small brush. Brush all the way around the hair (you don't have to do it in one brushstroke), and zoom in if you need to. Also, be sure to brush over areas inside the hair where the background is showing through.

To see how it will look against your background photo and make sure you haven't missed any spots, change the View menu to On Layers. Switch back to Overlay to finish tightening your selection.

▶ **Tip:** If Photoshop suddenly includes a giant swath of the photo in the selection, press Ctrl+Z/ Command+Z to undo your last brushstroke, and try again using a smaller brush or shorter brushstrokes (or both).

6   The Refine Edge Brush is very sensitive, so it's likely that your edge refinements will cause other areas of the photo to be excluded from the selection (in Overlay view, those areas appear with the red overlay). If that happens, click the Brush tool (the third tool down in the Tools panel), and then brush over those areas to include them in the selection again.

7 When the selection looks good, click the arrow next to Output Settings to expand that area, choose Layer Mask from the Output To menu at the bottom of the panel (you may have to scroll down to see it), and then click OK to close the workspace. Photoshop masks the active layer with your newly refined selection, allowing you to see through to the graffiti layer below.

8 Click the graffiti layer and resize it using Free Transform. Press Ctrl+T/ Command+T, and then press Ctrl+0/Command+0 to resize the document so you can see the control handles. Hold down the Alt/Option key while dragging to resize from the center of the image. Press Enter/Return when you're finished.

▶ **Tip:** If you see bits of the original background around the edges of the area you're selecting, turn on Decontaminate Colors near the bottom of the Properties panel on the right to get rid of it. However, doing so deactivates the Selection and Layer Mask options in the Output To menu (in that case, choose New Layer with Layer Mask instead).

I'm happy with the result of the masking, but the subject stands out against the blue of the graffiti wall. I'd like to add a little color cast of blue to her image so that it blends in a little better. We'll create a Color Fill layer to do this, but I'll add a special modifier to make this even more targeted.

▶ **Tip:** If you are on Windows, hold down the Alt key and right-click-and-drag with your mouse to the right and left to change your brush size. If you drag up and down, you can change the hardness of the brush. On macOS, press the Control key on the left of your key-board and the Option key together. Once they are held down, drag to the right/left/up/down.

1 With the subject layer selected, hold down the Alt/Option key. Right-click the black-and-white icon at the bottom of the Layers panel and choose Solid Color.

2 Instead of just creating a Solid Color layer, the New Layer dialog box appears. Select the Use Previous Layer To Create Clipping Mask option, and the Color Fill layer—despite the white mask it creates—will be limited to only the layer that you have selected (your subject).

3 Click OK, and the Color Picker appears. You can select any of the colors from the ramp, but I recommend that you move your cursor out of the dialog box and over the picture itself. An eyedropper appears, allowing you to make a selction from the graffiti background. This ensures that you are sampling a color from the background that really matches it and gives the composite image a more realistic look. Click OK.

4 To blend this sampled color with your subject layer, choose Soft Light from the unlabeled blend mode menu in the upper left of the Layers panel. The subject will appear darker and tinted to fit better with the image behind her. Reduce the layer's Opacity until the color looks natural and matches the background better.

5 Once you're satisfied with the image, press Ctrl+S/Command+S to save the file, and then press Ctrl+W/Command+W to close it and return to Lightroom. You will see the finished Photoshop file in your collection.

Inside Lightroom, you can go back to the Develop module with this PSD file and adjust the picture further. I went back and played with the Develop settings, used the Adjustment Brush in a couple of areas, and gave the image a little Clarity boost to make it stand out a little more than the original. This amount of pixel control is only available in Photoshop, but it's nice to see how streamlined the two applications are at working with one another. Below, you can see the original image (on the right) and the finished composite (on the left).

Review questions

1 What is the most precise method for creating a selection in Photoshop?

2 What is the keyboard shortcut for adding to a selection with one of Photoshop's selection tools?

3 What is the keyboard shortcut for subtracting from a selection with one of Photoshop's selection tools?

4 What does the layer mask on a fill layer or an adjustment layer do?

5 What's the best way to create a selection of hair or fur?

6 How do you fix edge halos with a selection and with a layer mask?

Review answers

1 The most precise way to create a selection in Photoshop is to use the Pen tool to create points and paths that you then load as a vector mask.

2 To add to a selection, hold down the Shift key as you use a selection tool.

3 To subtract from a selection, hold down the Alt/Option key as you use the tool.

4 The layer mask that comes with a fill or adjustment layer determines where the adjustment is visible. White on the layer mask reveals the adjustment, black conceals the adjustment, and gray partially conceals the adjustment.

5 The Select And Mask workspace is the best way to create a selection around hair or fur because you can use it to select partially transparent pixels.

6 To keep from having edge halos when making a selection, choose Select > Modify > Contract or use the Shift Edge slider in the Select And Mask workspace. To remove edge halos when using a layer mask, choose Filter > Other > Minimum, and in the dialog box, choose Roundness from the Preserve menu, and drag the slider to the right.

8 LIGHTROOM TO PHOTOSHOP FOR RETOUCHING

Lesson overview

Photoshop is renowned for its retouching capabilities—you can use it for everything from intricate portrait refinements to larger-scale content removal and repositioning. So when your desire to change the reality of a photo exceeds the abilities of Lightroom's Spot Removal tool, you can send the photo over to Photoshop for more serious pixel-pushing voodoo.

In this lesson, you'll learn how to use Photoshop to:

- Remove objects using the Spot Healing Brush, Healing Brush, Clone Stamp, and Patch tools.

- Remove objects using the Content-Aware Fill command.

- Reposition objects using the Content-Aware Move tool.

- Resize your image using the Content-Aware Scale command.

- Smooth skin without losing texture.

- Sculpt a portrait using the Liquify filter.

This lesson will take 1 to 1 1/2 hours to complete. Please log in to your account on peachpit.com to download the files for this lesson, or go to the "Getting Started" section at the beginning of this book and follow the instructions under "Accessing the lesson files and Web Edition." Store the files on your computer in a convenient location. Your Account page is also where you'll find any updates to the lessons or to the lesson files. Look on the Lesson & Update Files tab to access the most current content.

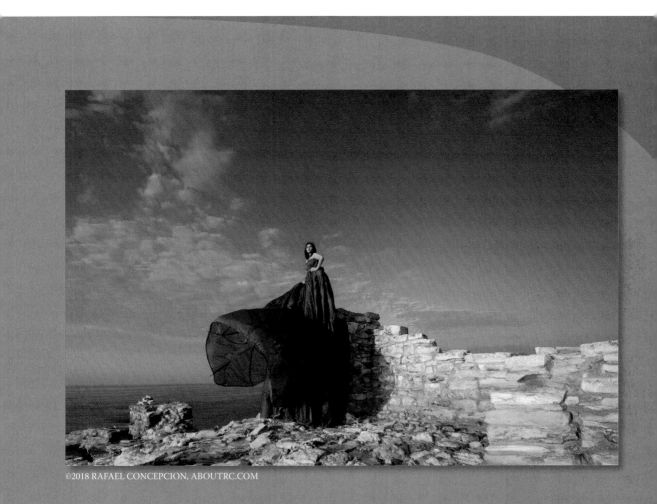

When your goal is to change the content of a photo, you need Photoshop's sophisticated retouching capabilities. In this image, some elements were removed and the picture was extended for dramatic effect.

Preparing for this lesson

In order to follow along with the techniques in this lesson, make sure you do the following:

1 Follow the instructions in the "Getting Started" section at the beginning of this book for setting up an LPCIB folder on your computer, downloading the lesson files to that LPCIB folder, and creating an LPCIB catalog in Lightroom.

2 Download the Lesson 08 folder from your Account page at peachpit.com to *username*/Documents/LPCIB/Lessons.

3 Launch Lightroom, and open the LPCIB catalog you created in "Getting Started" by choosing File > Open Catalog and navigating to the LPCIB Catalog. Alternatively, you can choose File > Open Recent > LPCIB Catalog.

4 Add the Lesson 8 files to the LPCIB catalog using the steps in the Lesson 1 section "Importing photos from a hard drive."

5 In the Library module's Folders panel, select Lesson 08.

6 Create a collection called **Lesson 08 Images** and place the images from the Lesson 08 folder in the collection.

7 Set the Sort menu beneath the image preview to File Name.

● **Note:** Before sending images to Photoshop for retouching, be sure to adjust the tone and color of each photo. Save finishing touches, such as adding an edge vignette, until after you're finished retouching it.

The next section teaches you how to use a variety of Photoshop tools to get rid of unwanted content in your photos, beginning with the healing tools.

Removing unwanted content in Photoshop

As you learned in "Removing distractions with the Spot Removal tool" in Lesson 4, you can use Lightroom to remove small stuff from your photos. That said, it lacks the advanced Content-Aware technology found in Photoshop, so you may get better results by performing the removal in Photoshop, especially with larger objects.

Indeed, Photoshop includes many tools and commands that you can use to remove objects from your photos, including the Spot Healing Brush and Healing Brush tools, the Clone Stamp and Patch tools, and the Content-Aware Fill command. The one you reach for depends on the size of the object, how much open space there is around it, and whether or not you want Photoshop to automatically blend surrounding pixels with the ones you're copying from somewhere else. You'll usually need to use a combination of the tools to produce the results you want.

Note: Once in Photoshop, it's important to maintain editing flexibility and safeguard your original image, so you'll perform each edit on a separate layer.

Let's start by learning how to use two tools that largely rely on healing technology: the Spot Healing Brush tool and the Healing Brush tool.

Using the Spot Healing Brush and Healing Brush tools

Photoshop's Spot Healing Brush and Healing Brush make getting rid of objects very easy. Both tools *blend* copied pixels with surrounding pixels to make your changes look more natural. Whereas the Spot Healing Brush copies pixels directly outside your brush cursor, the Healing Brush lets you copy pixels from anywhere in the photo, which is an important distinction.

Note: The process of telling the Healing Brush where to copy pixels from is referred to as setting a sample point.

In this exercise, you'll use a combination of the two healing brushes to clean up the sand in a desert sunrise image:

1   Select desert-sunrise.dng in Lightroom's Library module, and then send it to Photoshop by choosing Photo > Edit In > Edit In Adobe Photoshop CC or by pressing Ctrl+E/Command+E.

2   In Photoshop, press Shift+Ctrl+N/Shift+Command+N to create a new layer. In the resulting dialog, enter **spot healing** into the Name field, and then click OK.

3   Activate the Spot Healing Brush tool in the Tools panel by pressing J on your keyboard.

4   In the options bar, click Content-Aware for Type and select Sample All Layers. Leave the other settings at their default values.

Tip: You can cycle through all the tools in this toolset by pressing Shift+J repeatedly on your keyboard.

Turning on Sample All Layers tells Photoshop to look through the currently active empty layer to where the pixels live on the layer beneath it.

5   Zoom in to the photo by pressing Ctrl++/Command++. Hold down the Spacebar on your keyboard, and then drag to reposition the photo so you can see the bottom-center portion of the foreground.

6 Move your cursor over one of the green plants. Use the Left Bracket ([) and Right Bracket (]) keys on your keyboard to resize the brush tip so it's slightly larger than the item you're removing.

7 Click or drag atop the plant in the sand to remove it. Be sure to resize your brush cursor as you go. Use the Spacebar-drag trick to reposition the photo onscreen so you can see the left side, and continue to remove plants.

The Spot Healing Brush automatically samples pixels from an area near the outside of the brush cursor, copies them to the area you're brushing over, and blends them with surrounding pixels.

If you don't like the results you get with the Spot Healing Brush, choose Edit > Undo or press Ctrl+Z/Command+Z to undo your brushstroke, and then try again using a larger or smaller brush.

8 While this does a great job with individual small spots of problems, larger trouble spots often look a little off when fixed with the Spot Healing Brush. For larger areas, try the Healing Brush or the Patch tool. Let's tackle the Healing Brush first.

Add another new layer by pressing Shift+Ctrl+N/Shift+Command+N. In the resulting dialog box, enter **healing brush** in the Name field and click OK.

9 Activate the Healing Brush tool in the Tools panel, which is in the same toolset as, and immediately below, the Spot Healing Brush.

You'll use the Healing Brush tool to remove the larger pieces of vegetation, or the smaller ones where you didn't get a good result by using the Spot Healing Brush tool.

The Healing Brush tool is similar to the Spot Healing Brush tool, except it allows you to control the source from which pixels are copied.

10 In the options bar, ensure that the Mode menu is set to Normal, Source is set to Sampled, Aligned is unselected, and the Sample menu is set to All Layers.

With Aligned turned off, the Healing Brush tool will return to the original sample point whenever you release your mouse button and start another stroke.

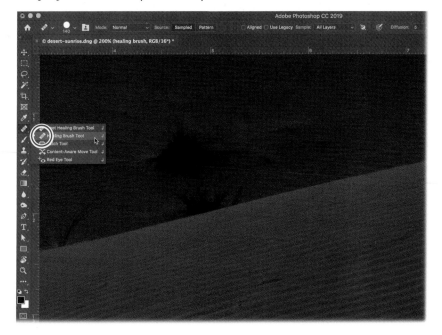

11 To set a sample point, hold down Alt/Option on your keyboard and click a clean area of sand near the larger piece of vegetation (your brush cursor turns into a tiny target). Release the Alt/Option key.

12 Move your cursor over that plant and brush across it to remove it.

As you drag, a small plus sign (+) appears that indicates the source from which pixels are being copied.

▶ **Tip:** Depending on the photo, you may need to keep resetting the sample point to make the removal look realistic and to avoid introducing a repeating pattern.

13 To see a before version, hide all the layers above the Background layer by Alt-clicking/Option-clicking the Background layer's visibility icon (it looks like an eye). To turn the other layers back on, Alt-click/Option-click the same icon again. Choose File > Save (or press Ctrl+S/Command+S) to save the file, and then choose File > Close (or press Ctrl+W/Command+W) to close the document in Photoshop.

The edited photo is saved back to the same folder as the original, and the PSD appears in Lightroom. You can see before (left) and after (right) versions on the following page.

As you can see, the healing brushes and their automatic blending worked well on the textured sand. In the next section, you'll learn how to use the Clone Stamp tool to remove objects without any automatic blending.

Using the Clone Stamp tool

Sometimes the healing brushes' automatic blending creates a blurry area near pixels you want to keep. In order to avoid automatic blending of pixels, you can use the Clone Stamp tool instead.

For example, if you're working with a portrait taken against a (nearly) solid-color background, flyaway hairs around your subject's head can be the bane of your existence. Although you could use Lightroom's Adjustment Brush to blur them, they may still be distracting.

Photoshop's healing brushes can remove the hairs, but you'll end up with a blurry area next to the strands you want to keep. The Clone Stamp tool performs no blending; it simply copies pixels from one area and then pastes them onto another, which makes it better suited for this particular job. Here's how to use it:

1 Select the Flyaway.dng file from the Lesson 05 Images collection. Right-click it and choose Create Virtual Copy. Drag that virtual copy into the Lesson 08 Images collection. Send this image to Photoshop by choosing Photo > Edit In > Edit In Adobe Photoshop CC or by pressing Ctrl+E/Command+E.

2 In Photoshop, press Shift+Ctrl+N/Shift+Command+N to create a new layer. In the resulting dialog, enter **Stray Hairs** into the Name field, and then click OK.

3 Zoom in to the photo by pressing Ctrl++/Command++. Hold down the Spacebar on your keyboard, and then drag to reposition the photo so you can see the left side of the model's head.

4   Activate the Clone Stamp tool in the Tools panel. In the options bar, set the Mode menu to Normal, the Opacity to 100%, and the Flow to 100%, and deselect Aligned. Set the Sample menu to All Layers.

▶ **Tip:** In some cases, you may get a better result by selecting Aligned in the options bar. Doing so causes the source point to move as your brush cursor moves.

5   Resize your brush cursor so it's slightly larger than the strand of hair you want to remove. Next, tell Photoshop where to copy pixels from by setting a sample point. To do that, Alt-click/Option-click a clean area of pixels as close to the hair you're removing as possible to match tone and texture. Brush over the hair you want to remove (short strokes typically work better than long ones).

If the background behind the hair shifts in color or texture, set a new sample point. A plus sign (+) marks the area you're sampling from as you paint (see to the left of her head below).

6   Repeat this process until you remove the most distracting hairs. Be sure to set new sample points as you go. Use the Spacebar-drag trick to reposition the photo so you can see all the stray hairs on the left and top of the model's head.

● **Note:** Be careful not to create an obviously broken strand of hair. If that happens, clone farther into the hair so the strand appears shorter and not broken.

7   When you're finished, choose File > Save (or press Ctrl+S/Command+S), and then choose File > Close (or press Ctrl+W/Command+W) to close the document and return to Lightroom.

This figure shows the before (left) and after (right) versions. Notice how much cleaner the portrait is after using the Clone Stamp tool.

The next section teaches you how to tackle removing larger objects using Photoshop's Patch tool.

Using the Patch tool

The Patch tool is good for removing larger objects from your photos. Like the healing brushes, it performs automatic blending between the copied and surrounding pixels, although you get to control how much blending occurs in both texture and color. You also can tell Photoshop exactly where to copy pixels from with this tool, which is handy if the item you want to remove is close to an item you want to keep.

Removing desert vegetation

In this exercise, you'll use the Patch tool to remove the larger areas of vegetation from the desert sunrise picture we worked on earlier in this lesson:

1   Select the desert sunrise PSD file in Lightroom, and then send it to Photoshop by choosing Photo > Edit In > Edit In Adobe Photoshop CC or by pressing Ctrl+E/Command+E. Choose Edit A Copy With Lightroom Adjustments, and click Edit.

2   In Photoshop, press Shift+Ctrl+N/Shift+Command+N to create a new layer. In the resulting dialog, enter **Patch Tool** into the Name field, and then click OK.

3   Zoom in to the photo by pressing Ctrl++/Command++. Hold down the Spacebar on your keyboard and drag to reposition the photo so you can see the areas of vegetation.

4   Activate the Patch tool in the Tools panel, which is in the same toolset as the healing brushes you used earlier. In the options bar, set the Patch menu to Content-Aware, leave the Structure and Color fields at their default values, and select Sample All Layers.

● **Note:** If you forget to change the Patch menu to Content-Aware, you won't see the Sample All Layers checkbox.

5 Move over your document and drag to create a loose selection around the larger
   vegetation. Be sure to make the selection slightly larger than the item itself;
   otherwise, you may end up with a ghostly outline of it.

▶ **Tip:** You don't have to draw a selection by hand using the Patch tool. You can use whatever
selection tool you want, and then switch to the Patch tool when you're ready.

6 Drag the selection to the area you want to use for the fix, which is to the left of
   the vegetation.

   As you drag, a preview of the potential source area appears inside the selection. If there are any horizontal or vertical lines involved, try to match them
   up. When you release your mouse button, Photoshop performs the patch and
   blends it with the surrounding area. Don't deactivate the selection yet!

7   While the selection is still active, experiment with the Structure and Color fields in the options bar to make the patch look more realistic (values of 4 and 0, respectively, were used here).

To preserve more of the texture from the area you copied pixels from, increase the Structure setting; to preserve less of the texture, decrease it. To perform more color blending between the two areas, increase the Color setting; to perform less, decrease it. As you experiment with these fields, keep an eye inside your selection and you'll see the pixels change.

8   When you're satisfied, deactivate the selection by choosing Select > Deselect (or by pressing Ctrl+D/Command+D).

9   If you see any imperfect areas as a result of the patch, create another new layer, and then use one of the healing brushes or the Clone Stamp tool to fix it. In this example, a combination of the Spot Healing Brush and the Clone Stamp tool was used to clean up a couple of areas.

10 Choose File > Save (or press Ctrl+S/Command+S), and then choose File > Close (or press Ctrl+W/Command+W).

This figure shows the before (right) and after (left) versions. As you can see, the Patch tool did a nice job of removing the larger vegetation.

Removing antennas and lines

In the next exercise, you'll learn how to use the Patch tool to remove a couple of antennas from a photo (you can use the same technique to remove power lines).

1   Select the Venice-1.dng file in Lightroom's Library module, and then send it to Photoshop by choosing Photo > Edit In > Edit In Adobe Photoshop CC or by pressing Ctrl+E/Command+E.

2   In Photoshop, press Shift+Ctrl+N/Shift+Command+N to create a new layer. In the resulting dialog box, enter **Patch Tool** in the Name field, and then click OK.

3   Zoom in to the photo by pressing Ctrl++/Command++. Hold down the Space-bar on your keyboard, and then drag to reposition the photo so you can see the antennas on the roofs on the right. Make sure the Patch tool is activated.

4   To get rid of these antennas successfully, you will have to work in stages. First, draw a selection around the top of an antenna, and drag it to the right to get rid of it and clear the area.

5   Once you have removed the top of the antenna, clear the cables holding the antennas up by making smaller selections around them and removing them.

6   Once the cables are gone, you can make a selection of the antenna pole with the Patch tool and get rid of it by dragging the selection to the right.

7   This makes a clear area of sky. Now you can make a selection of the antenna next to it and remove it entirely by dragging the selection into the clean area.

▶ **Tip:** The October 2018 release of Adobe Photoshop CC eliminated the need to hold down the Alt/Option key to step backward in time. Previously, Ctrl+Z/Command+Z toggled between undo and redo. Now, pressing Ctrl+Z/Command+Z multiple times will step you back through a series of undos.

8   Continue selecting and removing the rest of the antennas on nearby roofs. Keep in mind that this will take a little time and a fair bit of patience. If you mess up

a selection, press Ctrl+Z/Command+Z. When you finish your patch selection, you'll see that the elimination of the antennas gives the sky a cleaner, less distracting look, making for a better scene.

9   To see what the image looked like before, click the visibility icon for the Patch Tool layer to hide it, and see all of the antennas and cables on the rooftop. Save and close the file.

Now let's look at yet another way to remove a fairly large object: using the Content-Aware Fill command.

Using Content-Aware Fill

If you've got plenty of background pixels surrounding the object you want to remove, try using the Fill command's Content-Aware option. Like the Patch tool, this command is quick, and it performs automatic blending between copied and surrounding pixels.

Previously, the drawback of Content-Aware Fill was that you didn't get to choose where Photoshop copied the pixels from. In the October 2018 release of Photoshop, a Content-Aware Fill workspace was added that gives you even greater control.

Let's start by using the Content-Aware Fill command to remove some of the buildings surrounding the Chrysler Building.

1 Select the chrysler.dng photo in Lightroom's Library module, and then send it to Photoshop by choosing Photo > Edit In > Edit In Adobe Photoshop CC or by pressing Ctrl+E/Command+E.

2 Select the Polygonal Lasso tool (it's in the tool group under the Lasso tool) to create a geometric selection. When you click with this tool, it places a dot on the image. Clicking again creates another dot and a connecting line. Think of it as connecting the dots. The goal is to make a selection around the buildings that take the focus away from the Chrysler Building.

To ensure you get the very edge of the image when making the selection, click to create a dot on the outside the image, in the canvas area. This ensures that the selection includes the very edge of the image.

3 Continue making a connect-the-dots selection of the buildings at the lower left of the image, clicking the canvas outside the image to make sure your selection includes the very edges of the image. You can turn this path into a selection by clicking when you reach your starting point and the cursor turns into the Polygonal Lasso tool with a circle next to it.

4 Hold down the Shift key and you'll notice a plus sign (+) next to the tool. This lets you add a new selection to the existing selection on the left side. Click the canvas area outside the upper right of the image and make a selection around the edge of the building there. This creates two distinct selections: one to the left and one to the right of the Chrysler Building.

● **Note:** When the active layer is not a Background layer, the shortcut for opening the Fill dialog is Shift+Backspace/ Shift+Delete.

5 Choose Edit > Fill to open the Fill dialog box (or press the Backspace/Delete key). Choose Content-Aware from the Contents menu, select Color Adaptation, and then click OK.

Photoshop fills the selection with pixels it samples from outside the selection. You get different results each time you use this command, so you may need to undo it by pressing Ctrl+Z/Command+Z and then run it again.

If you still don't like the results, try using a different selection tool, creating a tighter or larger selection, or both. For example, if you first used the Polygonal Lasso tool, you may want to try the Lasso tool in order to make the selection more similar to the shape of the thing you're removing.

6   Deactivate the selection by choosing Select > Deselect or by pressing Ctrl+D/ Command+D.

7   When you're finished, save and close the document in Photoshop to return to Lightroom.

The Content-Aware Fill workspace and the Content-Aware Scale command

While Content-Aware technology can be really helpful fixing problem areas in your images, in the past, it didn't always work well. Behind the scenes, the technology would fill a smaller selection from a larger area, and place random elements in the picture that didn't belong. A tool was needed for finer control—to specify what area of the picture you wanted to sample from to let it perform its magic. The October 2018 release of Photoshop included a new Content-Aware Fill workspace that lets you do just that.

Content-Aware Scale is also incredibly useful to explore, as often, an image may benefit from being extended horizontally or vertically. Transforming a picture by scaling (with Free Transform) can distort it. Making it larger proportionally can reduce its quality. Content-Aware Scale can give you the benefit of a new canvas size, without either of those drawbacks.

Using the Content-Aware Fill workspace

The Content-Aware Fill workspace is an extremely powerful tool, since it lets you restrict the area you want to include as part of the fill, but it requires practice. In the image here, we forgot to remove some backpacks from the shoot area, and there's a black guardrail we need to clean up before we deliver the picture.

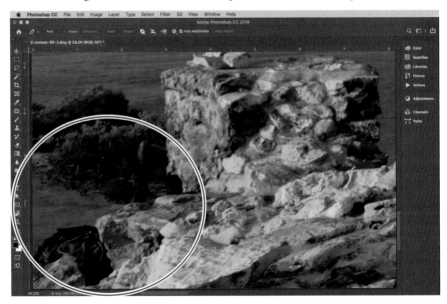

1 Select the content-fill-2.dng image in Lightroom's Library module and send it to Photoshop by choosing Photo > Edit In > Edit In Adobe Photoshop CC or by pressing Ctrl+E/Command+E.

2 Use the Lasso tool (L) to create a selection around the lower-left portion of the picture to remove the backpacks and guardrail areas.

3 Fill this selection using the Edit > Fill command. In the Fill dialog box, set the Contents menu to Content-Aware, select Color Adaptation, and click OK.

4 You'll notice that Photoshop has used different parts of the picture to "fix" the selected area, not always correctly—you may see some of the sky appear, some of the water appear, or perhaps even some of the dress appear. We want to have greater control over what appears inside the fill area.

▶ **Tip:** If you are unhappy with the results of the fill, you can always try a new fill by going to Edit > Fill and using Content-Aware again. It will generate a new fill for you.

5 Instead of pressing Ctrl+Z/Command+Z multiple times to complete multiple undos, choose File > Revert. Revert will take the image back to the point that it was exported from Lightroom and remove anything we have done.

6 Create a new selection around the area that we want to remove in the lower-left portion of the picture.

7 This time, let's use Edit > Content-Aware Fill. This will bring the picture into the Content-Aware Fill workspace, which contains tools and panels that make its use quite easy:

   • The green that you see on the image shows the sampling area by default. The color and opacity of this area can be controlled under Sampling Options in the Content-Aware Fill panel in the workspace.

- The Sampling Brush tool (B) lets you remove parts of the picture that you don't want Photoshop to consider when filling in the selected area, or add areas you do want it to use. You can toggle the brush to add or remove areas from the selection in the options bar at the top, or you can hold down the Alt/Option key as you paint to switch between the add and remove settings.

- If you have not made a selection of an area to fill or need to add to a selection, you can do that with the Lasso tool (L). As with the regular Lasso tool, you can use the Alt/Option key to remove a portion of a selection on the fly.

- The preview in the Preview panel automatically updates depending on the area that you have added to or removed from the sampling area.

- You can change the size of the brush you are using with the tool options at the top of the panel or by holding down Alt-Ctrl/Option-Command while you right-click and drag to the right or left.

- You can reset the panel locations anytime by clicking the second icon from the right in the options bar and choosing Reset Content-Aware Fill. To reset the sampling area and settings in the Content-Aware Fill panel, click the Reset All Settings icon in the lower left of the panel.

Note: The Content-Aware workspace has its own panels and tools for you to use. Take advantage of this new space and adjust the Preview panel, Content-Aware Fill panel, and tools so that they make the most sense to you. I prefer the layout as you see it here.

8 Using the Sample Brush tool, remove all of the water, sky, and dress components from the fill selection. The selection will get a little tighter and only include the rock. If needed, hold down the Alt/Option key while brushing to add more of the rock area at the bottom to get a more realistic look for your image.

9 Choose Currrent Layer from the Output To menu near the bottom of the Content-Aware Fill panel. Click OK to return to the main Photoshop window, and then press Ctrl+D/Command+D to deselect.

10 Save and close the document to return to Lightroom.

We now have a good foundation for the photo, but I'd like to add more sky to add more drama. We can easily achieve this using the Content-Aware Scale command.

Using the Content-Aware Scale command

Scaling a picture inside Photoshop is pretty easy. In the Image > Image Size menu, you have a series of options to make a picture bigger that keep a lot of detail. The problem usually comes when you try to extend the canvas in only one direction.

If you attempt to use Free Transform, the image will stretch unnaturally. The pixels are enlarged and stretched, and both realism and detail are compromised. To extend the image in only one direction, you'd have to get really creative, sampling different portions of the image to extend the canvas as needed.

The Content-Aware Scale technology really stands out in this arena. Rather than stretch the pixels in a given direction, Photoshop analyzes the picture and copies the pixels it believes would look good next to one another to complete the scaling. It reviews elements that it believes are not important to the image and duplicates them to fill the space without compromising the main subjects.

You also can save a selection and protect it from being copied or distorted when the image is scaled, giving you an even more dramatic look without the unrealistic byproducts. In this example, you'll extend the sky vertically to give the picture a more dramatic look.

1   Select content-fill-2-edit.psd (this is the file that you saved in the previous exercise) in Lightroom's Library module, and then send it to Photoshop by choosing Photo > Edit In > Edit In Adobe Photoshop CC or by pressing Ctrl+E/ Command+E. In the dialog that appears, select Edit A Copy With Lightroom Adjustments to keep a separate copy of the work you have done.

2   In Photoshop, select the Crop tool (C) and deselect Delete Cropped Pixels in the options bar. Drag the top-center crop handle upward, and press Enter/Return.

While the Crop tool is commonly used to crop inward, cropping outward will extend the canvas area. It's a great way to extend the picture visually.

3 Once you have the image extended, choose Select > Subject to get a rough outline of the subject in the picture.

4 Choose Select > Save Selection to save the selection for use later. Give it the name **Ixchel** and click OK. Press Ctrl+D/Command+D to deselect.

5 Now choose Edit > Content-Aware Scale and you'll get transformation handles that look similar to the Free Transform ones. As you hold down the Shift key and drag the top-center control handle upward, the Content-Aware technology automatically fills in the sky area with other portions of the sky, instead of stretching the pixels in the image.

6 To ensure that we do not transform the subject, we will select two additional options in the options bar. First, in the Protect menu, choose the Ixchel selection we saved to exclude it from the scaling. Then, click the icon that looks like a person. This option looks for skin-tone elements that look as if they belong to people, and ensures that they are not exaggerated. Press Enter/Return to commit the transformation.

7 Let's repeat using the Crop tool to extend the canvas, this time horizontally to the left of the image, and using Content-Aware Scale, this time to expand the image to the left. Be sure that you set the Protect menu to our selection and click the Protect Skin Tones (person) icon.

8 Once you have transformed the image horizontally and vertically, save and close the file to return to Lightroom.

You need to keep in mind that there is a limit to what Content-Aware technology can do—it's not magic. You may be able to push the boundaries of what you can scale, but after a while, the image will start to break down, so be careful how much you scale.

Skin retouching and body sculpting in Photoshop

While Photoshop is capable of helping you express yourself creatively in incredible ways, it has become strongly identified with its use as a retouching tool that changes how a person looks. In retouching, the two biggest requests are skin softening and body sculpting—we'll cover both here.

Skin softening is a commonly discussed retouching topic, and a great many tutorials tackle the subject, but it's important to highlight that it is not an actual feature inside the program. It is a technique, and you may find different techniques later that may tackle skin softening better for your taste.

When it comes to body sculpting, this has become a feature inside Photoshop through the Liquify tool. In earlier versions of Photoshop, you had to use a brush to push pixels around—think of it like handling a lump of clay. As more users became interested in the tool for body sculpting, the Photoshop team added more features to it to make people-specific transformations easier. These days, a quick trip to the Liquify tool can yield results that used to take hours.

Smoothing skin realistically in Photoshop

One of the biggest complaints about any skin retouching technique is that the resulting skin doesn't retain pore detail. If you are trying to get rid of blemishes, freckles, dark areas, and wrinkles, the results should not be so blurred that you cannot see any texture in the skin. This technique not only allows you to retain pore detail, but gives you the ability to fade it in and out as you see fit.

Let's start with how to minimize dark areas and wrinkles under the eyes in the image.

1 Select the rc.dng portrait (that's me, your author) in Lightroom's Library module, and then send it to Photoshop by choosing Photo > Edit In > Edit In Adobe Photoshop CC or by pressing Ctrl+E/Command+E.

2 In Photoshop, duplicate the image layer by pressing Ctrl+J/Command+J.

3 With the Patch tool selected, draw out a selection of the dark area under the eye on the right, and then drag the selection down slightly, over the cheek, and release it to create a lighter, more even patch of skin. If you find that the area you have selected becomes too dark or light, press Ctrl+Z/Command+Z to undo and try dragging to a new clean area.

4   Because the Patch tool is looking for samples of skin textures, you can actually go across my entire face to find the right patch. For my right eye (the one on the left side of the image), I sampled a patch of skin from my forehead.

5   The picture above shows what the softening of the area under my eyes will look like. Don't worry; while it looks really unrealistic, we'll fix it in a little bit. In the meantime, use the Patch tool to sample any acne spots or freckles that you would like to minimize in the picture. Press Ctrl+D/Command+D to deselect.

6   Hold down the Alt/Option key and click the Add Layer Mask icon at the bottom of the Layers panel and the entire layer will be hidden by a black mask.

7   Select the Brush tool by pressing the letter B. Set the Flow to 8% and the Opacity to 100% in the options bar at the top.

8   Make sure that you have white selected as your Foreground color, then brush under the eyes in the picture and you'll see some of the patch layer start to over-lay the original image.

9   Use the same brush to softly go over all of the spots in the image that you want to correct. Once you're finished, you have an additional level of control with the

With great power comes great responsibility

As artists, we have the opportunity to share our passion with the world, but also a responsiblity to ensure that we do not add to the burden of it. Our society is constantly bombarded by images, and this can bring a host of self-image problems to people who are shown images every day of what the general public considers *beauty* or *beautiful*.

Our youth struggle with issues of self-esteem at levels never seen before as they compare themselves to images that may not seem altogether real. The problem is so pervasive that, in 2017, France instituted a law forcing magazines that use digitally altered images to make it known that they were edited.

Did you know that from 1999 to 2006, hospitalizations for eating disorders among children younger than 12 spiked 119% (Agency for Healthcare Research and Quality, 2009), and it's estimated that almost 1.3 million adolescent girls in the United States have anorexia (Rosen and American Academy of Pediatrics Committee on Adolescence, 2010)? As social tools like Instagram and Facebook dominate our communications, the excessive digital manipulation of images can contribute negatively to people's self-image and lead to depression and eating disorders.

My retouching ethos is largely based on making someone look like they've had a good day's rest. As we age, we all develop dark circles and fine lines under our eyes. A couple of good nights of sleep can certainly minimize such problems, so any retouching work I do is to get to that goal. I'll smooth out and lighten a problem area, then fade the result so the discoloration and lines are never completely gone but are more subdued.

I push and pull pixels in Liquify to correct problems in my photos, such as awkwardly draped or wrinkled clothing, that I didn't address during the posing of my subjects. I try to make the transformations fit the pose, but I never remove excessive weight or alter the body unnaturally.

In fact, whenever I teach these techniques, I usually resort to using pictures of myself. I'm completely okay with you seeing every acne scar, every dark mark, and every blister.

When I sit down to work on an image, I picture my young daughter, Sabine, next to me. I ask myself, are the results of what I am going to do something that I would be comfortable showing her?

You will pick your own ethical line in this controversy, and that's okay. I can only remind you that we share a duty to our future to be as responsible as we can.

Opacity slider in the Layers panel. Turning the layer's opacity down minimizes the effect further.

Frequency separation for skin texture

A popular method for softening skin is commonly known as frequency separation. Think of your skin as two distinct areas: the fine details (high frequency) and the color and tone of it (low frequency). When performing any retouching, you want to make sure that you separate each specific task you need to do to its own frequency.

Just as a high-pass filter in the audio world can be used to remove high frequencies in an audio track (the treble), the High Pass filter in Photoshop can be used to remove high frequencies in an image (fine details; the small, sharp details), which produces a blurring (smoothing) effect.

The technique is broken down into three components. First, the image receives a High Pass filter. Next, you apply a Gaussian Blur to the image. Finally, the image is inverted and set to a specific blend mode. We'll cover each of those steps next, but let's start with inverting and changing the blend mode of the image *first*.

If you work on the image by applying the High Pass and Gaussian Blur filters first, you may not be happy with your slider adjustments once you invert the image and change the blend mode. Then you have to redo the entire technique from scratch. By inverting the image and applying the blend mode first, you can see how it affects the image as you apply your filters.

1 Before we begin, lets take the two layers we had at the end of the previous technique and merge them together into a new layer (in case we need to go back and make any edits). Press Shift+Alt+Ctrl+E/Shift+Option+Command+E, or hold down the Alt/Option key while choosing Layer > Merge Visible. To keep

▶ **Tip:** Retouching, and all of its various undo/redo steps as you test different skin patches, is something you can see a lot better in a video. I've recorded all the steps in this book for all the examples so you can follow along and see how I do them in real time. To access them, make sure that you read the "Getting Started" section at the beginning of the book.

everything in order, double-click the layer name, type **New Portrait Start**, and press Enter/Return.

2   Duplicate this new merged layer by pressing Ctrl+J/Command+J.

3   Using the menu at the upper left of the Layers panel, change the blend mode of the duplicate layer to Overlay, and then invert the information on that layer by pressing Ctrl+I/Command+I. The Overlay blend mode boosts contrast by making dark areas darker and light areas lighter. Inverting the photo's information flip-flops it.

Note: If you find
that the skin gets exces-
sively smooth, you can
adjust this setting to
your liking, but 10 is a
good start.

4   Choose Filter > Other > High Pass, and in the resulting dialog, enter **10** pixels
into the Radius field and click OK.

Note: The Gaussian
Blur filter was named
for the gentleman
who invented this blur
method, Carl Gauss.

5   Choose Filter > Blur > Gaussian Blur, and in the resulting dialog box, drag the
Radius slider all the way to the left, then slowly drag it to the right until you're
happy with the way the skin looks (a setting of 4.5 was used on the next page).
Click OK.

Opacity vs. Flow

When retouching images, a common question is: Which brush setting is better to
use, Opacity or Flow? Let me give you an example I use to explain the two.

Imagine that we are outside and I hand you a garden hose and a cup. Then imagine
that I ask you to fill that cup halfway full of water, but open the faucet's flow to its
full rate. How hard will it be for you to fill that cup halfway? Pretty hard.

Now, imagine I turn down the rate the water is coming out to a trickle. How hard will
it be then? Nowhere near as hard. If you need to fill the cup halfway, all you have to
do is keep the hose there longer.

Let's say you paint with your brush at 10% opacity. When you regulate your brush
using the Opacity setting, every brush stroke is at that opacity (10%). Any brush
stroke on top of the original brush stroke (releasing the mouse button between
strokes) would be an additional 10%.

If I keep the Opacity setting at 100% and reduce the Flow down to 8%, it is as if I
turned the hose down on how much color is coming out of the brush. This lets me
step into an effect a lot more smoothly. If I want to add more of the effect, I just continue to brush the effect onto the photo a little more (with the same brush stroke).

6   Now we'll use a layer mask to hide the blurring (smoothing) from everywhere *except* the skin. Since the goal is to hide the blur from the majority of the image, Alt-click/Option-click the circle-within-a-square icon at the bottom of the Layers panel to add a layer mask filled with black. This hides the blurring from the entire image—with layer masks, black conceals and white reveals.

7   Press B on your keyboard to grab the Brush tool, and in the options bar, click the Brush Preset Picker and choose a soft-edged brush. Set the Mode menu to Normal, and then set the brush's Opacity to 100% and Flow to 8%.

▶ **Tip:** If you would like to learn some of the best techniques in the world for restoration and retouching, *Adobe Photoshop Restoration & Retouching* (4th Edition), by Katrin Eismann, Wayne Palmer, and Dennis Dunbar, is my gold standard. You can learn more about the book at peachpit.com.

8 If your Foreground color isn't white already, press D on your keyboard to set your Foreground and Background colors to their layer mask default values of white and black. The Foreground color is the color the Brush tool uses. Since you want to reveal the skin smoothing, the Foreground color needs to be white.

9 Brush across your subject's skin to smooth it. Avoid blurring the eyes, lips, and any hair, including eyebrows, mustache, and beard. If you mess up and reveal the smoothing in an area you didn't mean to, press X to flip your Foreground and Background colors so that black is your Foreground color, and then brush back across that area. You can also use the Opacity setting on the layer to minimize the effect.

10 Save and close the file in Photoshop to return to Lightroom.

As you can see, this technique really helped even out the skin tones in this portrait, yet the skin texture is preserved. Below, you can see the before (left) and after (right).

Sculpting a portrait using Photoshop's Liquify filter

Bad posing, bulges in pockets, fabric wrinkles, and the occasional shifting of the subject's weight can all pose challenges in your photography. Photoshop's Liquify feature can be a valuable tool for moving pixels around to counteract these things, but it does require a softer touch for fear of getting out of hand.

● **Note:** Because the Liquify filter lets you move, bend, and warp pixels, make sure you're finished retouching the subject in Photoshop before using it.

Because of people's constant use of the Liquify filter to change features on their portrait subjects, Adobe added a series of tools to automate these kinds of transformations. In addition, you'll learn how the changes in the Liquify filter can help you with a landscape image in need of a push.

Pushing portions of a picture

In this exercise, you'll learn how to move around portions of a picture using the Forward Warp tool in the Liquify filter.

1 Select the rc2.dng portrait in Lightroom's Library module, and then send it to Photoshop by choosing Photo > Edit In > Edit In Adobe Photoshop CC or by pressing Ctrl+E/Command+E.

2 Choose Filter > Liquify to be taken to the Liquify workspace. At the upper left, choose the Forward Warp tool. This tool works similarly to any brush tool in Photoshop. The tool options for this brush are on the right side of the window.

In the photo here, you need to push in the area on my right side, where you see the brush, so the shirt doesn't stick out as much (I shouldn't have crossed my arms so high in this pose, but...it happens). Use the center of a soft brush to push that part in. Keep your movements small.

● **Note:** When using the Forward Warp tool, align the center of the brush with the edge of what you want to move, and use several small movements, rather than one large one.

The natural instinct in retouching is to pull in an image. That said, it might be a better idea to pull out this section to create the even look, rather than pushing it inward. Again, use the center of the brush.

You can use the same technique on the sleeve of my t-shirt above that area. Instead of pushing the fabric in, pull it out to even the drape of the sleeve.

Also do the same for the small wrinkles in the fabric on my opposite shoulder, using a smaller brush.

3   I purposely distorted the picture more than I should have to highlight the second tool in the Liquify tools, the Reconstruct tool. This tool also behaves like a brush with similar settings, but it paints back the original image that you brought into Liquify. So instead of having to undo all your steps for a specific fix, this tool brings back the original picture wherever you paint and lets you try again.

You can see how much better it looks in the before (left) and after (right) on the next page.

Face-Aware features in the Liquify filter

In previous versions of Photoshop, the tools directly below the warp tools were responsible for most facial feature manipulations. As Photoshop evolved, Adobe streamlined these manipulations, making them quicker and easier.

1   Photoshop scans the picture and looks for facial features. Once that's complete, it plots a series of points around the eyes, mouth, forehead, jawline, and so on. Select the Face tool (A), and as you point your cursor at different parts of the face, you'll see an overlay of what Photoshop detected. On the right is a series of sliders you can adjust. The technology is pretty amazing, and a little scary.

2   In the Face-Aware Liquify section, there are groups of sliders for each part of the face. Each of those components is broken down into smaller components. To adjust the eye size on the left, drag the left Eye Size slider. To adjust both eyes, click the link icon between the left and right sliders.

I made adjustments to Eye Distance (−15), left Eye Size (−17), Nose Height (13), Jawline (−30), and Face Width (−18), so you can see some changes in the photo.

3   Once you've made your changes, click OK. Save and close the image to get back to Lightroom.

▶ **Tip:** To really see how much the facial features can be transformed in the Liquify tool, you should consider downloading the accompanying video for this lesson. Refer to the "Getting Started" section at the beginning of the book for instructions.

Below is a before (right) and after (left) comparison. The goal was to be subtle and realistic. Taking it slow definitely helps.

Using the Liquify tool for landscape images

Earlier versions of Photoshop limited your brush size to either 600 or 1400. As Photoshop evolved, the brush size limits increased to a staggering 15,000. This took pixel pushing in a whole new direction, letting you transform entire landscapes.

1 Select the content-scale-1.dng photo in Lightroom's Library module, and then send it to Photoshop by choosing Photo > Edit In > Edit In Adobe Photoshop CC or by pressing Ctrl+E/Command+E.

2 Choose Filter > Liquify to open the photo in the Liquify filter workspace.

3 Using the Forward Warp tool, select an extremely large brush (I set it to 2223). Use the brush to straighten the butte (the center rock) in the picture so that it doesn't appear to lean left. As this brush is so large, you can really do some large-scale pushing in the picture. Just keep in mind that it's a good idea not to completely alter the look of the image. I tend to use this to mitigate any distortion I may have created by shooting the picture at an odd angle.

4 Once you have transformed the image to taste, save and close the file to return to Lightroom.

Review questions

1 How does the Healing Brush tool differ from the Spot Healing Brush tool?

2 How does the Clone Stamp tool differ from the healing brushes?

3 What is the major advantage to using the Content-Aware Fill workspace rather than the Content-Aware option in the Fill dialog box?

4 How do you keep Content-Aware Scale from stretching any people in your photo?

5 What is the easiest way to do facial retouching in the Liquify filter?

Review answers

1 The Healing Brush tool and the Spot Healing Brush tool sample pixels from a source area and use them to cover content in a destination area, blending them with the surrounding pixels. The main difference between these tools is that the Healing Brush tool allows you to choose the source area; the Spot Healing Brush tool doesn't.

2 The Clone Stamp tool copies and pastes pixels without automatically blending surrounding pixels, whereas the healing brushes do blend.

3 The Content-Aware Fill workspace's major advantage is that it lets you specify the portion of the image that you want Photoshop to use to cover your selected area. The Content-Aware option in the Fill dialog box also covers the content in your selected area, but Photoshop chooses which pixels to use.

4 To keep Content-Aware Scale from stretching people in your image, create and save a selection of the people, then choose that saved selection in the Protect menu in the options bar. You can also click the Protect Skin Tones icon to the right of the Protect menu.

5 The new Face tool, with its facial mapping, and the Face-Aware Liquify sliders based on individual facial features, are the easiest way to do facial retouching in the Liquify filter.

9 LIGHTROOM TO PHOTOSHOP FOR SPECIAL EFFECTS

Lesson overview

In previous lessons, you learned essential Photoshop skills for combining photos, selecting and masking, and retouching photos. This lesson covers using Photoshop to add special effects to your photos, including adding text. You'll be able to use several of the techniques covered in earlier lessons as you work through the projects covered here.

In this lesson, you'll learn how to use Photoshop to:

- Add an old Hollywood-style glamour glow effect to portraits.

- Turn a portrait into a painting.

- Turn a portrait into a colored pencil sketch.

- Accentuate a focal point with the Iris Blur filter.

- Create a tilt-shift blur effect.

- Add motion to your background and your subject.

- Combine photos and text into a social media cover photo.

 This lesson will take 2 to 2 1/2 hours to complete. Please log in to your account on peachpit.com to download the files for this lesson, or go to the "Getting Started" section at the beginning of this book and follow the instructions under "Accessing the lesson files and Web Edition." Store the files on your computer in a convenient location. Your Account page is also where you'll find any updates to the lessons or to the lesson files. Look on the Lesson & Update Files tab to access the most current content.

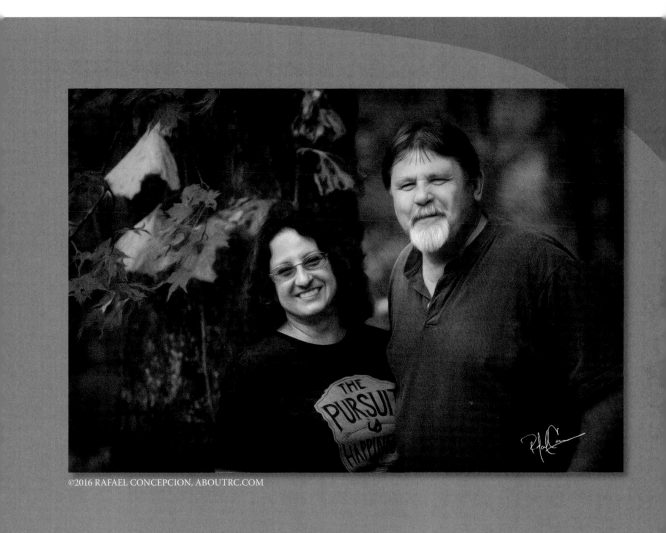

Photoshop provides great flexibility for creating special effects, such as this oil painting effect of my dear friends Kim and Denise Patti.

Preparing for this lesson

1 Follow the instructions in the "Getting Started" section at the beginning of this book for setting up an LPCIB folder on your computer, downloading the lesson files to that LPCIB folder, and creating an LPCIB catalog in Lightroom.

2 Download the Lesson 09 folder from your Account page at peachpit.com to *username*/Documents/LPCIB/Lessons.

3 Launch Lightroom, and open the LPCIB catalog you created in "Getting Started" by choosing File > Open Catalog and navigating to the LPCIB Catalog. Alternatively, you can choose File > Open Recent > LPCIB Catalog.

4 Add the Lesson 9 files to the LPCIB catalog using the steps in the Lesson 1 section "Importing photos from a hard drive."

5 In the Library module's Folders panel, select Lesson 09.

6 Create a collection called **Lesson 09 Images** and place the images from the Lesson 09 folder in the collection.

7 Set the Sort menu beneath the image preview to File Name.

The next section gets you started in the special effects realm by showing you how to add artistic treatments to some images.

Artistic portrait treatments

Lightroom is great for improving and enhancing your photos, and while you can create interpretations of your images that are very different from the original, the results remain firmly rooted in the photographic realm. Photoshop, on the other hand, lets you experiment more with your creative voice through a variety of filters and effects.

In this section, we'll start building your creative arsenal with effects and techiniques that add a soft glow to your photo, make a photo look like an oil painting, and turn a photo into a pencil sketch.

Adding a soft glamour glow

In the '80s, "glamour shots" were all the rage. While such images have largely fallen out of favor stylistically, adding a soft glow to an image can give it an ethereal feel. The glow can be used with portraits, as well as landscape images, when you're looking for a very airy mood.

In this exercise, you'll learn how to use one of Photoshop's oldest filters to quickly produce a soft and ethereal portrait effect that's sure to please brides, prom queens, expectant mothers, or your little princess.

1   Select the photo of the mom-to-be (mia-max.dng) in Lightroom's Library module, and then choose Photo > Edit In > Open As Smart Object in Photoshop.

2   In Photoshop, choose Image > Mode > 8 Bits/Channel. Many Photoshop filters refuse to work with 16-bit images, so if a filter's name is dimmed in the menu, that's likely the reason. Just convert the image to 8-bit, and you should be able to access any dimmed filters.

3   The filter you'll use for this technique uses the Background color swatch at the bottom of your Tools panel for the glow color. Set it to white by pressing D on your keyboard to reset the Foreground and Background colors to their default settings of black and white, respectively.

4   Choose Filter > Filter Gallery, and in the resulting dialog box, click the triangle next to Distort to expand that area and click Diffuse Glow (in older versions of Photoshop, you would choose Filter > Distort > Diffuse Glow). Use the zoom buttons at the lower left of the portrait preview to adjust the zoom level so you can see the model. On the right side of the dialog box, drag the Graininess slider all the way to the left. Set Glow Amount to around 5, and set Clear Amount to around 15.

● **Note:** You'll need to experiment with the Glow and Clear sliders when using your own photos, but these settings are a good starting point.

Click OK to close the Filter gallery and Photoshop adds a Smart Filter layer with a Filter Gallery sublayer to the Layers panel. To see a before version, click the Smart Filter's visibility icon; click again to see the after version. To reopen the filter and experiment with different settings, double-click *Filter Gallery*.

The white thumbnail with it is the filter's mask, which you'll use in a moment to hide the glow effect from the background and the subject's dress.

5 In the Layers panel, double-click the tiny icon to the right of the filter's name. When the Blending Options dialog box opens, click an important part of the image to see it in the dialog box's preview. Next, set the Mode menu to Luminosity. If you'd like, you can reduce the Opacity setting in this dialog box to tone down the strength of the filter (100% was used here to keep the results visible in this book). Click OK.

Filter mask   Double-click to open
                     filter blending options.

Changing the filter's blend mode to Luminosity keeps the photo's colors from shifting. If at any point you want to change the opacity of the filter, you can open this dialog again and adjust the Opacity setting.

6 Let's hide the glow from the background of the photo and from the model's dress. Click the white filter mask beneath the image layer in the Layers panel, and white brackets appear around its thumbnail. Press B to activate the regular Brush tool, and pick a soft-edged brush from the Brush Preset picker toward the left end of the options bar. Make sure the Mode menu is set to Normal, the Opacity is at 100%, and the Flow is set to a low amount. Because you want to hide the filter from the background, you need to paint with black, so if your Foreground color isn't already black, press X on your keyboard.

7 With a large, soft brush (say, 1000 pixels), paint across the background and brightest areas of her dress, dimming or hiding the glow.

If you hide too much of the glow, press X on your keyboard so that white is the Foreground color, and then brush across that area again.

8 Choose File > Save (or press Ctrl+S/Command+S) to save the file, and then choose File > Close (or press Ctrl+W/Command+W) to close the document in Photoshop.

As you can see in the before (left) and after (right) comparison here, this technique not only produces a soft, warm image but also smooths out portions of the picture.

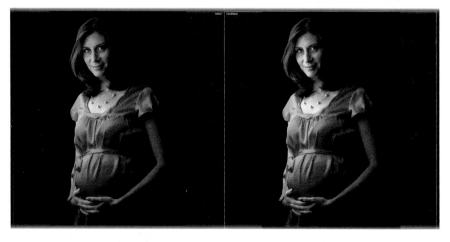

From portrait to painting

Note: Photoshop also includes a Mixer Brush tool that combines colors as a painter would mix colors on an easel. After using the Oil Paint filter, I like to use the Mixer Brush to smooth out details and give the "painting" my own personal touch.

One of the most frequently asked Photoshop questions is how to turn a photo into a painting. Unless you know how to paint digitally, it can be an overwhelming task. Thankfully, Photoshop brought back a favorite filter of mine, Oil Paint. It can give you an incredibly artistic feel that you can manipulate to create something of your own. Once you've adjusted tone and color in Lightroom, use the following exercise to create a realistic painting of my dear friends Kim and Denise.

1 Select the friends.dng photo in Lightroom's Library module, and then choose Photo > Edit In > Edit In Adobe Photoshop CC.

2 Press Ctrl+J/Command+J to duplicate the Background layer, and then choose Filter > Stylize > Oil Paint to bring up the Oil Paint dialog box.

Before we make any changes, let's talk about the sliders in the Oil Paint dialog box and how to use them.

The Stylization slider takes you through a series of stroke styles. Daubed strokes start at 0 and smooth strokes are found as you approach 10.

The Cleanliness slider adjusts the length of the strokes, ranging from short and choppy at 0 to long and fluid at 10.

The Scale slider affects the thickness of the paint in the picture, from a thin coat at 0 to a thick coat at 10 (a very Vincent van Gogh look).

Bristle Detail adjusts how much of the paintbrush-hair indentation is apparent, moving from soft indentation at 0 to strong grooves at 10.

The Angle setting in the Lighting section adjusts the incidence angle of the light hitting the object.

Finally, the Shine slider adjusts the brightness of the light source and the amount of bounce off the paint's surface.

3   I tend to go for a very soft and smooth look. For this image, set the Oil Paint filter sliders as follows: Stylization at 10, Cleanliness at 9.4, Scale at 0.6, Bristle Detail at 1.0, Angle at −60, and Shine at 1.9. Click OK when you're done.

Adding the Mixer Brush

Once you have created your basic oil painting effect, you'll finish it off with the powerful Mixer Brush tool.

For a long time, brushes in Photoshop did a good job of working with color, but did not do a great job at mixing color the way a painter would. If you used a brush and painted a stroke in red, then painted a stroke in blue above it, the blue color would simply go over the red, covering it without blending in. This frustrated many artists who wanted the colors in Photoshop to behave much in the same way paint colors on a canvas behave, mixing with any paint color below and being affected by the paint color on the brush.

Photoshop changed all of this with the introduction of the Mixer Brush. The Mixer Brush allows you to blend colors that are already on the canvas with colors that are

● **Note:** If you don't see the Mixer Brush tool in your Tools panel, click the ellipsis (three dots) icon near the bottom of the panel, and choose Edit Toolbar at the top of the menu. In the resulting dialog box, click Restore Defaults to add the extra tools back to the Tools panel, or drag the Mixer Brush tool from the right side to the Brush tool group on the left, and then click OK.

▶ **Tip:** If you want to see exactly how the Mixer Brush behaves, make sure you check out the accompanying videos for this lesson. Refer to the "Getting Started" section at the beginning of this book for how to access them.

loaded onto the brush. Like a traditional paint brush, the Mixer Brush remembers what color has been loaded onto it, and mixes that color with the colors on the canvas, giving your painted work a traditional art feel. We are going to use the Mixer Brush here to blend some of the oil painting effect that we created on the image of my friends to give it a unique feel.

1 Click the Brush tool in the Tools panel to access the Mixer Brush. Once it is selected, in the options bar, click the arrow next to the color swatch and choose Clean Brush, and then click the second icon to the right of that to make sure that the Mixer Brush will clean itself after every brush stroke. This will ensure that you are always blending only the colors that you are brushing over on the canvas. Then, Alt-click/ Option-click the canvas to load a color onto your brush.

2 Once you have the brush ready, go over any areas of the picture where you believe the detail is a little excessive, to smooth them out. Blend some of the brush strokes the Oil Paint filter created on the facial features, as they take away from the portrait.

When you are working with the Mixer Brush, you'll need to change your brush size to ensure that you are not creating large blobs of color on the picture and taking away from the oil painting effect.

Also, make sure you are using short brush strokes on the picture and try to create your brushstrokes in the same direction as the Oil Paint filter. This will ensure that you keep the style of the painting as much as possible.

3   Click the Create New Fill or Adjustment Layer icon (the black-and-white circle) at the bottom of the Layers panel, and select Curves from the menu. In the Curves options in the Properties panel, click the center of the Curve and drag downward to darken the entire image.

4   The Curves adjustment layer has a white mask, revealing all the darkening you've done to the picture. Switch to your Brush tool by clicking the Mixer Brush tool in the Tools panel and selecting the Brush tool from the menu. Press the letter D to set your Foreground and Background colors to white and black, respectively, and press the X key to swap them, so black is your Foreground

color. With an Opacity of 100% and a Flow of 18%, paint over Kim and Denise to hide the darkening of the layer and make them brighter.

At any point in time, if you want to change the darkening of the layer, you can double-click the Curves adjustment layer's icon (to the left of the layer mask) and reposition the dot at the center of the curve—drag it upward to make the image brighter and down to make it darker.

5   Save and close the file to return to Lightroom. You will see the PSD appear next to the original image. Shift-click the original image and the PSD file and press the N key to see both of the images in Survey mode. This will give you a good way to see the before (left) and after (right) of the Oil Painting effect.

From portrait to stylistic sketch

Although there are many ways to turn a photo into a stylistic sketch, this technique produces a great result and gives you the ability to stack a series of filters in Photoshop's Filter Gallery. The technique works best on subjects shot on a white or light-colored background, so you may want to shoot with that in mind.

1 Click the del.dng photo in Lightroom's Library module and choose Photo > Edit In > Edit In Adobe Photoshop CC or press Ctrl+E/Command+E.

2 Choose Image > Mode > 8 Bits/Channel.

3 Duplicate the Background layer by pressing Ctrl+J/Command+J.

4 Choose Filter > Filter Gallery. With the image now in 8-bit mode, we should be able to access a host of filters here. While you can access these filters individually in the Filter menu, it's better to use the Filter Gallery when you want to stack a series of filters.

The Filter Gallery is also a good place to start with filters when you cannot find a specific filter you are used to seeing. As Photoshop has evolved, Adobe has moved some filters out of the menu and into the Filter Gallery in an attempt to declutter the user experience. It can be frustrating if you are used to seeing a specific filter in the menu—they still exist, just in a new place.

5 Let's start by clicking Artistic to expand the category, and then clicking the Poster Edges thumbnail. In the Poster Edges options on the right, set all the sliders to 1.

6 In the lower-right corner of the Filter Gallery, click the New Effect Layer icon. This automatically adds the previously used filter to the list below the filter options (in this case, Poster Edges). In the Artistic category in the middle, click the Cutout thumbnail to make that the new filter.

The Cutout filter makes your picture look more like a stylized sketch. Manipulating its sliders is largely a matter of taste. For the look we want here, set Number of Levels to 6, Edge Simplicity to 4, and Edge Fidelity to 2. Click OK.

7 Once you are happy with the image, save and close the file and return to Lightroom. You can see the two images side by side by selecting them and pressing the letter N to go into Survey mode.

Adding creative blur effects

Lightroom has many ways to bring attention to part of a picture, but blurring is not one of them. Photoshop, on the other hand, includes an impressive array of filters for blurring your image, letting you really expand your creativity.

In the next few sections, you'll learn how to use the most practical of Photoshop's blur filters to change a photo's depth of field, add a tilt-shift effect to an image, and add motion to a vehicle that appears to be standing still.

Accentuating a focal point with the Iris Blur filter

When you make a photograph with a lens with a shallow depth of field, the out-of-focus blur makes the in-focus subject of the picture the center of attention. Unfortunately, this effect is limited to lenses with wide openings (apertures), but that doesn't mean that you can't attempt this effect inside Photoshop. Will it be the same as having a lens with an extremely shallow depth of field? Not quite, but it certainly is better than not having the tool at all.

● **Note:** You also can use the Iris Blur filter to add multiple points of focus, which produces an effect that can't quite be achieved in camera.

1   Click the iris.dng photo in Lightroom's Library module, and then right-click and choose Edit In > Edit In Adobe Photoshop CC.

● **Note:** All the filters in the Blur Gallery section of the Filter menu work on 16-bit images, so there's no need to reduce them to 8-bit.

2   Choose Filter > Blur Gallery > Iris Blur to open the Blur Gallery workspace.

Photoshop places a pin in the center of your image inside an elliptical blur with a white outline. The blur is fully applied outside the elliptical outline and decreases gradually in the transition area between that boundary and the four dots. The area inside the dots remains in focus.

▶ **Tip:** To view the image temporarily without the pin and the other elements of the Iris Blur overlay, hold down the H key on your keyboard.

3 Position the blur atop the large leaf- and moss-covered rock in the center of the foreground by dragging the pin. Change the size of the blur by dragging the four size handles (tiny dots on the blur outline). Position your cursor outside the blur outline near a handle, and your cursor turns into a curved arrow that you can use to rotate the blur. Adjust the blur shape by dragging the square handle to make it more round or square (circled here).

4 Adjust the transition width between blurry and in-focus pixels by dragging one of the larger four circles *inside* the blur outline inward toward the rock. When you drag one of these "feather handles," they all move; however, you can move them individually by Alt-dragging/Option-dragging instead.

5 Adjust blur strength by dragging the inner circle around the pin counterclockwise to decrease the amount of blur to taste.

Alternatively, mouse over to the Blur Tools panel on the right side of the workspace and drag the Blur slider to the left to decrease it.

6 To compare before and after views, select Preview in the options bar at the top of the workspace (or press P on your keyboard). When you're finished, click OK in the options bar to close the workspace.

7 Save and close the image in Photoshop to return to Lightroom. Select the original image and the PSD file and press N to view the before and after images in Survey mode.

Creating a tilt-shift blur effect

The Tilt-Shift filter has its origins in an effect created by the use of a tilt-shift lens. Below is a picture I took in Abu Dhabi, where I wish I'd had a tilt-shift lens.

For this picture, my camera was pointed at a very large building, the Grand Mosque. To capture the full height of the building, the camera had to be tilted upward to make a shot. So the sensor was tilted up, but the building was still straight. The result? The lines in the building look like they are falling backward. Add to that the fact that the camera may have rotated in one direction or another and the sensor plane may have shifted, resulting in the building being slanted to the left.

A tilt-shift lens moves in several directions to counteract that and is a tool used by architectual photographers to keep these lines straight. In the process of shifting the perspective of the lens, however, the depth of field is distorted, causing blurring above and below the point that's in focus. This blur on opposite sides of the focus area gives the illusion that elements in the photo are miniatures, and it has become a sought-after effffect.

Tilt-shift (also known as perspective control) lenses can be expensive, but you can re-create the effect in Photoshop with surprising success.

● **Note:** Be careful not to click the image, rather than the tilt-shift controls, as that will add another pin for a separate tilt-shift blur (unless, of course, you want another blur).

1 Select the tilt.jpg photo (showing the Flatiron Building in New York City) in Lightroom and choose Photo > Edit In >Edit In Adobe Photoshop CC. Select Edit A Copy With Lightroom Adjustments, and click Edit.

2 Choose Filter > Blur Gallery > Tilt-Shift to open the photo in the Blur Gallery workspace. Photoshop places a pin and blur ring in the middle of the photo, with a solid line and a dashed line on either side.

The area between each solid line and the dashed line on the same side is partially blurred; the area beyond the dashed lines is completely blurred.

▶ **Tip:** If there are specular highlights in your photo, experiment with adding bokeh using the controls in the Effects section of the Blur Gallery workspace. This trick works on any of the Blur Gallery filters.

3 Drag the blur by its center pin to change its location, and then drag up or down on any line to adjust that area's width.

You can rotate a tilt-shift blur as well. Point your cursor at one of two dots (above and below the pin), and drag diagonally (Photoshop displays the rotation's angle).

The Distortion slider in the Tilt-Shift panel on the right lets you change the shape of the lower blur zone; drag left for a circular blur or right for a zoom effect. Select Symmetric Distortion to distort the upper blur zone too.

To throw the area between the solid white lines slightly out of focus, decrease the Focus setting in the options bar.

4 Click OK in the options bar to close the workspace, and then save and close the Photoshop document.

Adding motion to skies

A great way to add the illusion of motion to skies is to capture them using a slow shutter speed. If the clouds are moving, they appear beautifully blurred. However, that can be a time-consuming and challenging project, and it requires a tripod. You can easily simulate the effect using Photoshop's Radial Blur filter.

1 Right-click the trees.jpg photo in Lightroom's Library module and choose Edit In > Edit In Adobe Photoshop CC. Select Edit A Copy With Lightroom Adjustments, and click Edit.

2 Make a duplicate copy of the layer by pressing Ctrl+J/Command+J.

Note: If your photo consists only of sky, there's no need to make a selection first.

3 Use the selection tool of your choice to select the area you want to blur. In this example, the area you want to blur is rectangular, so press M to select the Rectangular Marquee tool, and then click the upper-left corner of the photo and drag diagonally downward to draw a selection around the sky. Don't worry if you select some of the trees, as we'll fix that later.

▶ **Tip:** If you're working with a very large image, you may need to use an Amount higher than 40.

4 Choose Filter > Blur > Radial Blur. In the resulting dialog box, set Amount to between 10 and 40 (15 was used here)—the higher the amount, the blurrier the clouds get. Next, set Blur Method to Zoom and Quality to Best. Then, drag within the Blur Center preview to tell Photoshop where in the image the blur should emanate from. Press Ctrl+D/Command+D to deselect.

To make the clouds appear to be moving slightly rightward in this photo, drag the blur center to the left side of the preview, and to keep the clouds level, drag it upward so it's at about the same height as the clouds. You don't get a preview with this filter, so click OK to see the results.

Note: Whenever you're working inside a layer mask, remember this rhyme: "black conceals; white reveals."

5 We limited this effect to a selection on a duplicate layer to control how much blur spilled onto the trees. To remove it from them, click the Add Layer Mask icon at the bottom of the Layers panel, adding a mask to the blurred layer. Press B to select the Brush tool, make sure your Foreground color is set to black, raise the Flow, and choose a soft, round brush in the options bar's Brush Picker.

Paint over the trees to mask out the blur from them—it should look similar to what you see on the next page. Right along the tops of the trees, as you get to the clouds on the right, you may want to lower your Flow setting so you don't erase all of the effect from the clouds there. In short order, the Radial Blur filter added some interesting movement in the sky.

6 Save and close the document in Photoshop.

Adding motion to a subject

To add extra visual interest to a photo, use a blur filter to put your subject in motion. Even though your subject is stationary, the viewer's brain experiences the movement, which adds excitement. We are going to use some of Photoshop's newer blurs—Path Blur and Spin Blur—and combine them with the power of Adobe Sensei to quickly give us an outline of a stationary car and get it moving.

1 Select the car.dng photo in Lightroom's Library module and choose Photo > Edit In > Edit In Adobe Photoshop CC.

2 To keep things in order, make two duplicates of the Background layer by pressing Ctrl+J/Command+J twice, and then double-click each layer's name (one at a time) and rename them. For the top layer, type **Blurred Background** and press Enter/Return. For the middle layer, type **Wheels**. Finally, for the Background layer, type **Car**.

In an image like this, there are two different kinds of blur at play. First, there should be the dynamic movement of the car as it speeds along the track. That movement is linear in nature. Second, if the car is in motion, it would stand to reason that the wheels should be spinning. To create both in one image, you'll apply two different blur filters and use layer masks to isolate portions of them.

3 First, let's blur the background so it looks like the car is moving. Click the Blurred Background layer, and then choose Filter > Blur Gallery > Path Blur.

4 The Path Blur is pretty simple. An arrow appears on your image, letting you specify the direction of the path. Here, the blur should go from left to right, so click the circle at the left end of the arrow, and drag it upward and a bit more to the left. Then, circle next to the arrowhead and drag it to the right, angling it to better match the angle of the car and background. In the Blur Tools panel, adjust the intensity of the blur (I gave it a speed of 121%), and then click OK.

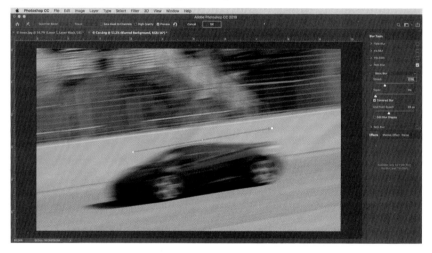

5 Temporarily hide the blur by clicking the Blurred Background layer's visibility icon. Drag this layer below the Wheels layer in the Layers panel for use later.

6 Select the Wheels layer and choose Filter > Blur Gallery > Spin Blur.

7 The Spin Blur behaves similarly to the Iris Blur we used earlier. Drag the blur so the center pin is over the center of the front wheel. Then, drag the white circle inward until it fits snugly around the wheel.

8 Move your cursor off the blur, and it becomes a pin. Click the center of the rear wheel to create a second blur. Resize this blur to fit the wheel, and adjust the Blur Angle in the Blur Tools panel to your liking.

Press Enter/Return to accept these changes and close the Blur Gallery workspace.

9 Now that the blurs are set, let's make a selection of the car and apply some layer masks to finish the project. Hide the Wheels layer and select the Car layer. Choose Select > Subject to make an initial selection of the car.

10 If you notice that some of the selection is missing (like the little bit of the shadow at the bottom of the car that was missing here), switch to the Lasso tool (L) and add it to the selection by holding down the Shift key and drawing a circle around it. Although the selection was not perfect, it certainly saved us a bit of time tracing the edges of the car.

11 With the selection active, select the Blurred Background layer and click where its visibility icon was. Then, click the Add Layer Mask icon at the bottom of the Layers panel while holding down the Alt/Option key. This creates a white mask with black inside the selection, which hides the path blur within the confines of the mask and leaves it on everything outside the car, making it look as if the camera was panning with the car.

12 Here's a great timesaver: instead of making another selection of the car, simply drag the mask onto the Wheels layer while holding down the Alt/Option key. A dimmed version of the mask moves with your cursor, letting you know you are dragging a copy of it. Click where the visibility icon was to turn on the Wheels layer again.

13 The only catch? The mask on the Wheels layer is the exact opposite of what you need. It is hiding all of the car on this layer, including the blurring of the wheels, and revealing everything outside the car on this layer, which hides the blurred background on the layer below. Not a problem. With the Wheels layer's mask selected (there are white lines around the corners), press Ctrl+I/Command+I to invert it, and the wheels will spin and there will be motion in the background.

14 Save and close the file to return to Lightroom. Select both of the images and press N to view them in Survey mode and see the before and after.

Creating a social media cover photo

Social media is essential for self-promotion. While many people use a photo of themselves as their profile picture (the thumbnail that appears next to your name), you can make far more impact by crafting a *cover photo*—the wide photo at the top of your social media page—that showcases your best photos and your URL. Sizes vary from site to site, but the process of creating one in Photoshop is the same.

In this exercise, you'll learn how to specify a crop size for a personal Facebook banner image, and send the image into Photoshop. Once you're there, you'll add a layer of type, which is not possible to do inside Lightroom.

1 Select the smokies-2.dng photo in Lightroom's Library module.

2 Press the D key to switch to the Develop module.

3 You'll need to crop the image so that it matches the dimensions of a Facebook banner on your page. Press the letter R to select the Crop Overlay tool. In the

▶ **Tip:** Before designing your own cover photo, do a quick online search to ensure that the dimensions haven't changed for that particular social media service. The size used here for the Facebook banner is current as of November 2018.

Crop Overlay tool options, click the menu to the right of Aspect Ratio and, near the bottom of the menu, choose Enter Custom to specify your own layout.

4   In the dialog box that opens, type in the current dimensions for a Facebook page header: **851** x **315**, and click OK. Resize the overlay to include the entire width of the photo, reposition it to your liking, and then press Enter/Return.

5   Let's add a Graduated Filter to the upper-left corner of the image. Click the Graduated Filter in the toolbar, reset the sliders in the tool options, and set the Exposure slider to –0.99. Click the photo near the rocks in the upper left and drag down and to the right to create your gradient. Drag the center pin to reposition it and drag the lines above and below the pin outward to expand the transition area. To change the angle of the gradient, move your cursor over the center line until it becomes a curved arrow, and then drag the direction you want it to go. Press Enter/Return twice to close the tool options.

6   We need to add text to the image. Photoshop's text features are incredibly powerful and creative, so right-click the image and choose Edit In > Edit In Adobe Photoshop CC. Set your Foreground color to the color you want for your text.

7   There several ways to add type using the Horizontal Type tool (T). The first is called *point type*, which is created by clicking and typing with the tool. Each line of point type is independent—the line expands or contracts as you edit it, but it doesn't wrap to the next line. The second is called *paragraph type*, which is created by dragging out a text box. The lines of paragraph type wrap to fit the dimensions of the bounding box, and you can enter multiple paragraphs and select a paragraph justification option.

With the Horizontal Type tool selected, drag out a rectangle over the lower-right corner of the photo to create a paragraph type text box.

8   Photoshop automatically populates the text box with some sample type, already selected for easy replacement. Type your business name, and then press Ctrl+A/Command+A to select it.

Now, this is one of my favorite tricks with the Type tool: Instead of choosing a font size from the menu in the options bar or typing in a font size there, move your cursor over the double-T icon and it turns into a hand with an arrow on either side, meaning this is a scrubby slider. Drag to the right to make the font size bigger; drag left to make it smaller.

9 To select your font, here's another favorite trick: Photoshop now lets you browse through your fonts in the font menu (in the options bar) by simply pointing your cursor over a font name rather than having to actually select the font.

▶ **Tip:** Typekit fonts are part of your Adobe Creative Cloud subscription. You can access them by clicking the font menu to open it, and then clicking the green icon that appears at the upper right.

I've selected Abadi Condensed here, but the fonts on your computer may be different. Select a font that is a little thick so that it is easy to read. Click the Right Align Text icon in the options bar to align it with the right side of the text box.

10 Double-click the open space to the right of the type layer's name in the Layers panel and the Layer Style dialog box appears. Layer styles are preset effects that you can apply to elements on a layer.

We could write an entire book just on the use of layer styles in Photoshop, but I want to add just one simple one to give the text a little more dimension. At the very bottom of the list on the left, click the words *Drop Shadow* to add the layer style and see its options. Adjust the Opacity, Distance, Size, and Angle of the drop shadow to your liking, and then click OK.

11 Press Ctrl+J/Command+J to make a duplicate copy of the type layer, then change the text to a phone number (this one is fake). Make the font size smaller than the company name and align it to the right side, as we did with the name.

● **Note:** As mentioned, there are other ways to add type in Photoshop, but for our purposes, we are covering only paragraph type. If you would like to learn more about the Type tool, make sure you check out *Photoshop CC Classroom in a Book*, by Andrew Faulkner and Conrad Chavez.

12 The last thing is to add a Curves adjustment layer. Select the Background layer, click the Create New Fill or Adjustment Layer icon, and choose Curves. In the Properties panel, drag the center of the curve downward to darken the image. Then, select the layer mask and press Ctrl+I/Command+I to invert it, hiding the adjustment. Get the Brush tool (B), choose a soft-edged brush, make sure your Foreground color is white, and brush in the lower-right corner. This reveals the darkening only in that area, making it easier to see your text.

13 Once your image is complete, save and close the document to return to Light-room, and press N to inspect the two images using Survey mode.

When it comes to adding text to an image, or layer styles onto text or elements of a picture, Photoshop is the gold standard program. That said, all of these images will need to be kept in order, so that you can find them when you need them. For that, there is no better program than Lightroom. Thankfully, both programs are good at working with each other to do the best of each.

Review questions

1   What Photoshop shortcut is an easy way to duplicate a layer?

2   How do you adjust a Smart Filter's settings?

3   How does the Mixer Brush tool differ from the Brush tool?

4   How do you hide a Smart Filter's effects from parts of your image?

5   What filters can you use to create motion in a photo?

6   What is the difference between point type and paragraph type in Photoshop?

Review answers

1   Ctrl+J/Command+J, which can also be found under Layer > New > Layer Via Copy.

2   You can adjust a Smart Filter's settings by double-clicking its name in the Layers panel.

3   The Brush tool simply paints one color over another. The Mixer Brush tool mixes the color on the brush with the color on the image as you paint.

4   You can hide the effects of any filter run as a Smart Filter by using the filter mask that comes with it.

5   Any of the blur filters.

6   Point type is independent and does not wrap the text. Paragraph type is created within a text box and wraps each line.

10 LIGHTROOM TO PHOTOSHOP FOR COMBINING PHOTOS

Lesson overview

One of the most rewarding image-editing techniques is combining photos in creative ways, whether adding texture or fading photos into a collage. Lightroom doesn't support layers, so you need Adobe Photoshop for these feats. Lightroom lets you merge multiple exposures into a high dynamic range (HDR) image or stitch several photos together into a panorama, though. It also has a few new tricks for merging photos of different exposures into an HDR panorama image.

In this lesson, you'll learn how to:

- Add texture to a photo using another photo and Photoshop's layer blend modes.

- Fade photos together using a soft brush and layer masks or Photoshop's shape tools.

- Combine photos into a collage.

- Merge photos into an HDR image and a panorama in Lightroom, and create HDR panoramas in one step.

 This lesson will take 2 to 2 1/2 hours to complete. Please log in to your account on peachpit.com to download the files for this lesson, or go to the "Getting Started" section at the beginning of this book and follow the instructions under "Accessing the lesson files and Web Edition." Store the files on your computer in a convenient location. Your Account page is also where you'll find any updates to the lessons or to the lesson files. Look on the Lesson & Update Files tab to access the most current content.

Unless you're merging multiple exposures into a high dynamic range image or a panorama, Photoshop is the place to go to combine photos.

Preparing for this lesson

1 Follow the instructions in the "Getting Started" section at the beginning of this book for setting up an LPCIB folder on your computer, downloading the lesson files to that LPCIB folder, and creating an LPCIB catalog in Lightroom.

2 Download the Lesson 10 folder from your Account page at peachpit.com to *username*/Documents/LPCIB/Lessons.

3 Launch Lightroom, and open the LPCIB catalog you created in "Getting Started" by choosing File > Open Catalog and navigating to the LPCIB Catalog. Alternatively, you can choose File > Open Recent > LPCIB Catalog.

4 Add the Lesson 10 files to the LPCIB catalog using the steps in the Lesson 1 section "Importing photos from a hard drive."

5 In the Library module's Folders panel, select Lesson 10.

6 Create a collection called **Lesson 10 Images** and place the images from the Lesson 10 folder in the collection.

7 Set the Sort menu beneath the image preview to File Name.

Now you're ready to learn how to combine images in Photoshop. You'll begin with a handy technique for adding texture to a photo, and then you'll progress to fading photos together.

Combining photos for texture and collage effects

You can use many methods for combining photos in Photoshop, though they all begin with placing each photo on its own layer inside a single Photoshop document. Lightroom's Open As Layers In Photoshop command does that in an instant, which saves you the step of having to do it manually.

Having each photo on a separate layer gives you a lot of editing flexibility because you can control the opacity, size, and position of each layer individually to produce the effect you want. You can also control the way color behaves between layers to produce interesting blending effects.

Before embarking on your first foray into combining images, be sure to adjust the tone and color of each photo. Save your finishing touches, such as adding an edge vignette, until after you've combined the photos in Photoshop.

The next section teaches you how to use one photo to add texture to another photo.

Adding texture to a photo using another photo

An easy way to add texture to a photo is to blend it with another photo. By experimenting with Photoshop's layer blend modes, you can change the way colors on each layer blend or cancel each other out. You can use nearly any photo for the texture, including shots of nature, a rusty piece of metal, concrete flooring, marble, wood, and so on.

In this exercise, you'll use a photo of an old, grungy wall blended with another picture to make it look older than it really is.

1   In the Collections panel in Lightroom's Library module, click the Lesson 07 Images collection and drag a copy of the DanielleP.dng photo into the Lesson 10 Images collection. Select the DanielleP.dng photo and Ctrl-click/Command-click to also select the Doortexture.jpg photo.

2   Choose Photo > Edit In > Open As Layers In Photoshop, or right-click one of the selected images and choose Edit In > Open As Layers In Photoshop from the menu that appears. Photoshop launches, if it isn't already running, and both images open in a new document on separate layers.

3   Since the portrait photo isn't as big as the texture photo, you need to enlarge it. In the Layers panel, make sure the portrait layer is active and press Ctrl+T/Command+T to go into Free Transform (alternatively, you can choose Edit > Free Transform). Photoshop surrounds the portrait with a frame with draggable resizing handles in the corners.

> ▶ **Tip:** If you don't see the Layers panel, choose Window > Layers to open it.

4 To resize the portrait proportionally from the center, Alt-drag/Option-drag one of the corner handles outward until the portrait is the same height as the texture. If you can't see the corner handles, press Ctrl+0/Command+0 or choose View > Fit On Screen to make Photoshop adjust the document zoom level. Press Enter/Return to accept the transformation.

5 In the Layers panel, drag the texture layer to the top of the layer stack. Release your mouse button when a blue line appears above the other layer.

6 Choose Soft Light from the blend mode menu at the upper left of the Layers panel. The texture blends into the image below, and in some areas, the image appears slightly tinted.

The blend mode you pick depends on the colors in your photos and the effect you're after. To produce a vintage look from these two photos, Soft Light works well (it decreases the brightness of colors darker than 50 percent gray and increases the brightness of colors lighter than 50 percent gray).

For more on blend modes, see the sidebar "Layer blend modes 101."

▶ **Tip:** When using your own imagery, experiment with other blend modes using keyboard shortcuts. To do that, activate the Move tool (V), hold down the Shift key on your keyboard, and then tap the plus icon (+) on your keyboard to go forward through the menu, or the minus icon (–) to go backward. As of the October 2018 release, you can click the blend mode menu and see a live preview as you scroll over each choice.

7 Lower the Opacity setting at the upper right of the Layers panel until the texture looks good to you. A value of 54% was used here.

8 If you're going for a tinted film look, you may want to desaturate the image slightly and add a color tint. To do that in Photoshop, click the half-white/half-black circle icon at the bottom of the Layers panel (the Create New Fill or Adjustment Layer icon, circled below) and choose Hue/Saturation.

9 In the Properties panel, drag the Saturation slider to the left to around −35.

10 In the Hue/Saturation properties, dragging the Hue slider shifts all the colors in the order they are on the color wheel (watch the two color ramps at the bottom of the panel). Instead, select Colorize first, and it tints the image with the color that you are pointing to in the Hue ramp. You can still adjust the Saturation and Lightness for that color to fine-tune the adjustment. Drag the Hue slider to 39, Saturation to 25, and Lightness to 0.

Note: If you decide to tweak the texture opacity or drop the saturation later, reopen the PSD by selecting it in Lightroom and choosing Photo > Edit In > Edit In Adobe Photoshop CC. In the resulting dialog, choose Edit Original, and the layered PSD opens in Photoshop.

11 To assess your work, click the texture layer's visibility icon (it looks like an eye) to turn it off; click the empty space where the visibility icon used to be to turn it back on. To hide both the texture layer and the Hue/Saturation adjustment layer, Alt-click/Option-click the portrait layer's visibility icon; Alt-click/Option-click it again to turn them back on.

12 Choose File > Save (or press Ctrl+S/Command+S) to save the file, and then choose File > Close (or press Ctrl+W/Command+W) to close the document in Photoshop.

The edited photo is saved back to the same folder as the original, and the PSD appears in Lightroom. Here you can see before and after versions.

Fading photos together using a soft brush and a layer mask

A wonderfully practical and flexible way to fade photos together is to paint on a layer mask with a large soft brush. A layer mask is like digital masking tape in Photoshop. You can use masks to hide layer content, which is a far more flexible approach than erasing (deleting) content.

In this exercise, you'll use Photoshop's Brush tool to paint on a layer mask and fade two landscape portraits together.

1 Select the top-1.dng picture in Lightroom's Library module, and then Ctrl-click/ Command-click to select bottom-1.dng.

2 Choose Photo > Edit In > Open As Layers In Photoshop.

The bottom-1 layer is smaller than the top-1 layer. We want to crop the image to the bottom layer, but don't want to lose any information from the top-1 layer.

3 Ctrl-click/Command-click the bottom-1.dng layer's thumbnail and a series of marching ants will appear around the contents of the layer. Once you have that selected, press C to access the Crop tool.

4 Because you had a selection active, the Crop tool starts at its boundaries. Make sure Delete Cropped Pixels is not selected, and then press Enter/Return twice. The first press sets the crop overlay, which we don't need to change, and the second press completes the crop.

5 Drag the top-1 layer to the top of the layer stack. This will serve as the top portion of the picture, but we will paint in only the part we need—the top of the sky. Hold down the Alt/Option key and click the Add Layer Mask icon at the bottom of the Layers panel to add a black layer mask, which hides the entire contents of the top-1 layer.

6 Grab the Brush tool (B), select a soft brush in the Brush Preset picker, and then press D to set your Foreground color to white. In the options bar, set a low Flow and an Opacity of 100%. With the mask active, paint over the top portion of

Layer blend modes 101

When you're experimenting with layer blend modes, it's helpful to think of the colors on your layers as being made up of three parts:

- Base. This is the color you start out with, the one that's already in your photo. Although layer stacking order doesn't matter with *most* blend modes, you can think of the base color as the color on the bottommost layer.

- Blend. This is the color you're *adding* to the base color, whether it's in a photo on another layer or a color you've added to another layer using one of Photoshop's painting tools.

- Result. This is the color you get after mixing the base and blend colors using a layer blend mode.

To illustrate this concept, you can draw yellow and blue circles on separate layers and then change the blend mode of the blue circle layer to Darken. This produces a third color (green) that doesn't exist in either layer. Another way to understand this concept is to put on a pair of sunglasses and then look around. The colors you see are a product of the actual colors plus the tint of your sunglasses' lenses.

Base color   Result color   Blend color

When you open Photoshop's layer blend mode menu, you'll notice that it's divided into several categories. The second, third, and fourth categories are the most useful for blending photos. The second category begins with Darken, as those modes darken or burn images. When you use one of these modes, Photoshop compares the base and blend colors and keeps the darkest colors, so you end up with a darker image than you started with. White, and other light colors, may disappear.

The third category begins with Lighten, as those modes lighten, or dodge, your image. Photoshop compares the base and blend color and keeps the lightest colors, so you end up with a lighter image than you started with. Black, and other dark colors, may disappear.

The fourth category begins with Overlay. You can think of these as contrast modes because they do a little darkening and a little lightening, and thus increase the contrast of your image.

the image to reveal the sky from the top-1.dng layer. Having the blue sky in this picture will greatly change its mood.

7   While the layer mask you created is automatically tied to the content of the layer it's on (it moves with the layer), you can change this. There is a link icon between the image thumbnail and the layer mask. Click this link icon to unlink the image and the mask, allowing you to move them independently.

Once the icon disappears, press Ctrl+T/Command+T to enter Free Transform and Alt-drag/Option-drag an upper corner handle to make the image larger and see more of the sky. Drag the image around to reveal (or hide) more of the sky, and the mask stays in place. Press Enter/Return to commit the transformation.

8 The lower right portion of the picture does not have any whitewater showing the flow. The water's darkness takes away from the effect of the long exposure. Let's use a copy of our two layers to paint in some visual interest in that area.

Merge a copy of both of the layers into a brand new layer by holding down the Alt/Option key and choosing Layer > Merge Visible.

9 Once the new layer appears at the top of the stack, press Ctrl+T/Command+T to enter Free Transform. Then, right-click the picture and, near the bottom of the menu that appears, choose Flip Horizontal. Press Enter/Return to complete the transformation.

10 Hold down the Alt/Option key and create a black mask on this layer. With the same soft white brush as before, paint back in some of the water in the lower right. If you paint too much, switch your Foreground color to black and paint it back out. Save and close the file to return to Lightroom.

11 In Lightroom, make sure your edited file is selected and press D to switch to the Develop module. Press M to get the Graduated Filter, and drag a gradient from the middle of the water to the top of the waterfall. In the tool options, drag the Temp slider to –32, the Exposure slider to –1.27, and the Saturation slider to –34.

Opening the images in Survey mode will give you a good look at how different the two images appear.

Fading photos together using a gradient mask

Another way to create a smooth fade between two photos is to use Photoshop's Gradient tool on a layer mask. This is handy when you don't need the mask to follow the contours of your subject.

The steps for fading two photos using a gradient are basically the same as those for the soft-brush method in the previous technique. However, instead of painting on the layer mask with a brush, you'll use a black-to-white gradient for a smooth and seamless fade from one photo to the other.

● **Note:** A gradient is a gradual, smooth transition from one color to another. A natural gradient occurs in the sky each day during sunrise and sunset (well, minus any clouds!).

1 Select the d1.dng picture in Lightroom's Library module, and then Ctrl-click/ Command-click to also select d2.dng.

2 Choose Photo > Edit In > Open As Layers In Photoshop. These two pictures were taken in Dubai, of the Burj al-Arab, about two hours apart. In a perfect world, I would have left the tripod in exactly the same spot to make sure the pictures aligned perfectly. They are a little off, but it still works.

3 With the d1 layer selected, hold down the Alt/Option key and click the Add Layer Mask icon at the bottom of the Layers panel. This adds a black mask to the layer, hiding it and revealing the bottom (d2) layer.

4 We know that painting with a white brush will reveal the contents of this d1 layer, but what if we used a gradient as a transition between the two layers? Press G to select the Gradient tool, and press D to make sure that your Foreground and Background colors are set to their defaults (white and black, when the layer mask is active). If they are inverted, press X to swap them.

5 Click the arrow next to the gradient thumbnail in the options bar to open the Gradient picker. Leave it set to the default Foreground to Background gradient (in the upper left), which paints the Foreground color (white, here) where you start dragging your gradient and ends

up with black at the end of the gradient. If we drag it on the mask, it reveals everything (white) at the start of the gradient, then slowly transitions to hiding everything (black).

6　Drag a gradient from the center of the building to the middle of the small cloud just to the right of the vertical center of the building, as shown in the image below. Keep in mind that the length and direction of the line make a difference when you create a gradient.

The shorter the line, the narrower the fade and the harsher the transition (it won't be a hard edge, but it'll be close); the longer the line, the wider the fade and the softer the transition. If you drag the line from the bottom of the picture upward, the dark part of the image will show at the bottom. Dragging from the top downward will reveal the night version of the picture at the top.

Finally, when you drag to the right, any part of the mask to the left of where you start dragging will contain the full strength of the Foreground color and any area of the mask from the point you stop dragging to the right will contain the full strength of the Background color. To have enough of the daytime and the nighttime images on either side of the building, you need to make sure that the start of the gradient is close to the middle of the picture.

7　Let's also get rid of some of the silhouettes of people that are cut off at the bottom of the picture. Some are in the bottom layer; others are in the top layer. Press Shift+Alt+Ctrl+E/Shift+Option+Command+E or hold down the Alt/ Option key while choosing Layer > Merge Visible to create a new merged layer at the top of the layer stack.

8 Press M to select the Rectangular Marquee tool and draw a rectangle around the couple on the right side of the picture (zoom in if you need to). Hold down the Shift key to add to your selection, and then draw two additional rectangles around the people and shadows on the left side of the photo.

9 Choose Edit > Fill, and in the Fill dialog box, select Content-Aware from the Contents menu. This should get rid of the silhouettes and replace them with some of the surrounding area, emptying the beach.

10 Choose File > Save (or press Ctrl+S/Command+S) to save the file, and then choose File > Close (or press Ctrl+W/Command+W) to close the document in Photoshop. Back in Lightroom, press D to go to the Develop module, and use the Basic panel to adjust the new base image. Change the Contrast to +43, the Highlights to −50, the Shadows to −36, the Whites to +10, and the Clarity to +31, in addition to cropping and rotating the picture.

While it's not necessary, I made a virtual copy of the Photoshop file before I added the finishing touches to the image. That gave me four images to compare in Survey view: the night image, the day image, the merged version of the two images, and the final merged and adjusted image. The concept is incredibly easy to get. Making it look amazing is the part you'll spend hours over.

Fading photos together using shape tools

You can also use Photoshop's shape tools to quickly fade photos together. The program includes all manner of shape tools that are handy for masking, including Rectangle, Rounded Rectangle, Ellipse, and Polygon tools, as well as a Custom Shape tool that you can use to access a plethora of built-in shapes (leaves, flowers, animals, and so on).

In this exercise, we'll go through three different shape options to get you creatively inspired to make a collage.

1   In Lightroom's Library module, click multiple-1.dng and then Shift-click multiple-4.dng to select them and the two images in between.

2   Choose Photo > Edit In > Open As Layers In Photoshop.

3   Drag the multiple-1 layer to the bottom of the layer stack and the multiple-4 layer to the top of the stack, and then Alt-click/Option-click the bottom layer's visibility icon (it looks like an eye) to turn off the other layers. We will be turning on each layer individually and experimenting with a different shape for each. Once we finish with one layer, we'll turn it off and proceed to the next one.

4   The multiple-1 photo (the bottom layer) is smaller than the document itself, so we'll start by resizing it. Press Ctrl+T/Command+T to go into Free Tansform, then grab the lower-right corner handle and drag it outward until it is slightly larger than the document. Press Enter/Return to lock in the transformation.

Note: As of this writing, there's no way to send photos from Lightroom to Photoshop as stacked layers that are automatically converted to individual Smart Objects.

▶ **Tip:** To cycle through all of Photoshop's shape tools, press Shift-U repeatedly.

5 Click the multiple-2 layer to activate it, and click where its visibility icon was to turn it back on again and reveal its contents.

6 We'll start with the simplest of the shape tools—the Rectangle tool. Press U to select it. In the options bar, set the menu near the left end to Path, and then drag out a rectangle around the girl and her goat. To reposition a shape as you create it, hold down the Spacebar while dragging. Release the Spacebar without releasing the mouse button, and you can continue to drag out the shape.

Note: Vectors are mathematical in nature; they're made by connecting points and paths. Since they're not made from pixels, you can resize them infinitely without losing quality around the edges.

The shape (a blue outline) is a vector path, which uses mathematical data instead of pixels to calculate the path. The benefit of working with a vector shape for this is that you can edit the path using a selection tool, or change the properties of the path using Photoshop's Properties panel.

7 Click Mask in the options bar to turn this path into a vector mask. If you press Ctrl+T/Command+T to go into Free Transform now, you will be transforming only the vector mask. Click the mask in the Layers panel to deselect it. Once it is deselected, you can press Ctrl+T/Command+T and drag a corner handle to resize the multiple-2 layer and move it over the upper right of the image. Press Enter/Return to lock in the transformation.

▶ **Tip:** To draw a perfect shape—say, a circle or a square— Shift-drag with that particular shape tool. To draw the shape from the center outward, Alt-drag/Option-drag. To draw a perfect shape from the center outward, Shift+Alt-drag/ Shift+Option-drag.

8 Next, let's hide the multiple-2 layer and experiment with the Rounded Rectangle tool. To do this, reveal the multiple-3 layer and click it to make it active.

9 Press Shift-U to cycle to the Rounded Rectangle tool, make sure Path is still chosen in the options bar, and draw a rounded rectangle around the second image.

10 Choose Window > Properties to show the Properties panel. In the bottom half of the panel, you can change the roundness of each corner individually or change all of them at once. Let's do the latter by clicking the link icon at the center of the corner settings, if necessary, and then entering **80 px** for one of them.

11 Select Mask in the options bar to turn this shape into a vector mask.

12 Make sure you click the multiple-3 layer's vector mask to deselect it, and then press Ctrl+T/Command+T to go to Free Transform and resize and position the image like we did the multiple-2 layer. Press Enter/Return.

Here, you changed the properties of the path by manipulating the corners of the rounded rectangle. You can also change the feathering of the path, giving you a semi-transparent mask that offers a little bit more creativity to your collage.

13 Hide this layer, reveal the remaining layer, and click it to make it active. Press Shift-U to cycle to the Ellipse tool, choose Path in the options bar menu, and draw an ellipse on the image (I dragged it off the bottom onto the canvas).

14 Click Mask in the options bar, and then click the vector mask in the Layers panel to deselect it. Go to Free Transform and resize and reposition the layer. This time, place it in the center right of the image.

15 The hard edge cuts off the goat's foot, so let's fix that. Select the vector mask again, and in the Masks options in the Properties panel, drag the Feather slider to the right. That makes the edges of the vector mask semi-transparent, giving you a soft fade on the mask and blending it into the image behind it.

16 Once it looks good, save and close the document in Photoshop to return to Lightroom.

As you can see, combining photos this way can stretch your creative vision. Experiment with this technique using other shape tools, as well.

The next section teaches you how to combine a series of photos using layer masks to create another compelling collage.

Combining photos into the perfect group shot

Let's face it—group photography can be difficult. It seems inevitable that someone is smiling in one photo and not in another, or that someone has their eyes closed in the photo where everyone is smiling. Thankfully, Photoshop makes it pretty easy to select subjects in a picture, make layer masks, and creatively place smaller groups into a larger group.

In this exercise, we'll fix a personal family picture emergency of mine. I took some family pictures of my mother and brother, and others of my wife, daughter, and myself. What I didn't take was one of all of us together!

◆ **Warning:** When performing this technique using your own images, save the step of cropping the images until after you're finished combining them in Photoshop. That way, you'll have maximum pixels to work with.

1 Select the familycomp-1 and familycomp-2 photos in Lightroom's Library module.

2 Choose Photo > Edit In > Open As Layers In Photoshop.

3 One of these pictures is in landscape (wide) format and the other is in portrait (tall) format. We will combine them to make a panoramic image of the five of us. To do this, we need to make selections of the people on each layer.

   With the familycomp-1 layer active, choose Select > Subject. Since they are on a white background, Photoshop makes selecting my brother and mother easy.

4 Once the selection appears, click the Add Layer Mask icon at the bottom of the Layers panel to hide the white background and leave them floating on a transparent pixel grid.

5 Click the visibility icon for the familycomp-1 layer to hide it, and then select the familycomp-2 layer and choose the same Select > Subject command. This time, go into the Select and Mask workspace by choosing Select > Select And Mask.

You will use this workspace to clean up the selection around my wife's and my hair. Click the View thumbnail at the top of the Properties panel and choose On Black to see the edges of the selection better. Using the Refine Edge Brush tool (R), paint with a small brush along the edges of our hair to remove the bits of background, soften the edges, and make it more realistic. At the bottom of the Properties panel, choose Layer Mask from the Output To menu, and click OK.

6   Next, you'll need to create the canvas for the panorama. Click where the visibility icon was on the familycomp-1 layer to show it and make the layer active. Ctrl-click/Command-click the familycomp-1 layer's thumbnail to select the whole layer. Press C to get the Crop tool, press Enter/Return to set your selection as the crop overlay, and drag the left edge of the overlay to the left, extending the canvas. Be sure that you do not have Delete Cropped Pixels selected, as you'll need the entire second layer to add to the group. Press Enter/Return again.

7 Select the familycomp-2 layer and press Ctrl+T/Command+T to use Free Transform to resize and reposition the layer, as you see below. Press Enter/Return when it looks good to you.

8 Let's add a new background before we go further. Click the Create New Fill or Adjustment Layer icon at the bottom of the Layers panel and choose Solid Color. In the Color Picker that appears, select white, although you can change this at any time. Drag the adjustment layer to the bottom of the layer stack.

9 Where my mother's arm overlaps my wife, you can see my brother's fingers. It looks awkward, so let's remove them using the layer mask already there. Select the familycomp-1 layer, click the layer mask, and zoom in a little. Grab the Brush tool (B) and choose a hard-edged brush from the Brush Preset picker. Set your Foreground color to black, the brush's Opacity to 100%, and the Flow to 15%. Paint over the fingers to mask them out and make the collage more believable.

10 The final adjustment is to create a new Curves adjustment layer to add a little more contrast. In the Properties panel, click the center of the curve and pull it slightly downward.

11 Click the adjument layer's mask to make it active, and then press Ctrl+I/ Command+I to invert the mask and hide the adjustment. With the Brush tool still active, select a soft-edged brush, switch your Foreground color to white, and slowly brush in the darker effect on my shirt, my hair, and my wife's hair to darken them a little.

12 Save and close the image to close Photoshop and return to Lightroom.

The family crisis has been averted, and the picture looks more creative as a panorama. You can see the final result on the next page.

Making HDR images

Very few images exploit the full range of possible brightness tones, from the lightest lights to the darkest darks. Often, you'll have more info on one end of the histogram than the other, meaning that either the highlights *or* the shadows are well exposed and full of detail, but not both. That's because digital cameras have a limited dynamic range; they can collect only so much data in a single shot. If you have a scene with both light and dark areas, you have to choose which area to expose correctly. In other words, you can't expose for both areas in the same photo.

To create photos that take advantage of the full range of tones from light to dark, you need to do one of the following:

- Shoot in raw format and tone map the photo in Lightroom. As long as you capture good detail in the highlights—check the histogram on the back of your camera to make sure you do—you may be able to pull out an incredible amount of detail using the sliders in the Basic panel.

- Shoot multiple versions of the same shot at different exposure values (EVs), and then merge them into a high dynamic range (HDR) image. You can do this manually by taking three to four photos with, say, a single f-stop difference between them, or you can have your camera do it automatically by turning on its bracketing feature.

Bracketing lets you tell the camera how many shots to take (use a minimum of three, though more is better) and how much of an exposure difference you want between each one (pick one or two EV stops if you have the choice). For example, for three shots, you'd have one at normal exposure, one that's one or two stops lighter than normal, and another that's one or two stops darker than normal.

Note: The term *tone mapping* means to take the existing tones in your image and alter them so they reflect a broader dynamic range.

Note: Even if you're shooting in raw, it's worth knowing how to quickly turn on your camera's bracketing feature. For example, you may want to capture multiple exposures of a poorly lit scene in case you can't achieve the results you want by tone mapping only one exposure. If the single exposure gets you where you want to go, then you can always delete the other exposures from your Lightroom catalog or hard drive.

In the last couple of releases, Lightroom has taken great leaps forward in the ease of creating HDR images. While both Lightroom and Photoshop can merge to HDR, it's easier to do it in Lightroom because you can quickly switch to the Basic panel to tone map the merged result.

Let's cover how to create an HDR image in Lightroom and how to speed up the process when we need to work with more than one set of images. You will be shocked to see how simple it actually is.

Merging to HDR in Lightroom

In this exercise, you'll use Lightroom to merge five exposures into a single image that you'll then tone map and add additional effects to.

1   Select hdr-1.dng through hdr-5.dng in the Library module by clicking the first image in the series and Shift-clicking the last image in the series.

2   Right-click one of the thumbnails and choose Photo Merge > HDR or press Ctrl+H/Control+H.

The first thing that is immediately apparent is the overall speed with which Lightroom creates an HDR preview of your images. I've merged really large image files to HDR and been amazed at how fast the preview renders.

3   The HDR Preview window gives you a quick series of options to help you along with the process:

•   Auto Align automatically corrects any movement in between the capture of the images—perhaps you moved the tripod slightly as you made the images.

•   Auto Settings applies Develop module settings you normally see in the Basic panel, so you get a good result out of the gate. It's okay to leave it on since you can always change any settings when the merge is complete.

- Deghosting compensates for anything inside the frame that moved. Imagine there was a strong wind and the trees moved when you made the picture, or people walked through the frame. Deghosting gives you a choice of intensities to remove the movement. Select this setting on a case-by-case basis.

- If you have selected a Deghosting amount, you can select the Deghosted Overlay option to see where changes will be made.

- Finally, you have the option to create a stack of all the component images and the resulting HDR. Stacks are outside the realm of this book, so let's leave this unselected.

Once you click Merge, the HDR processing happens in the background—another benefit of doing this in Lightroom. In older versions, merging HDR images in Lightroom meant that you were locked out of doing any work until the HDR image was complete. Now, you can go back into Lightroom and continue to work until the HDR is finished.

One of the other powerful features of HDR in Lightroom is that the resulting HDR file that is created is still a raw file (a DNG, specifically). This means that you can change temperature and tint, and perform Develop adjustments with much greater range than if the image was turned into pixel data. You can see on the previous page how much toning we can do to this image as a raw file.

Headless mode for HDR

Another great feature that has been added to HDR in Lightroom is headless mode. There are plenty of times when you do not need to see the HDR Merge Preview dialog box to make any decisions—you just want Lightroom to get to work. Hold down the Shift key when you choose Photo Merge > HDR, and Lightroom bypasses the preview dialog box and starts making your HDR file immediately.

Exaggerating edge contrast in Photoshop

Another way to simulate the look of an extended dynamic range is to exaggerate edge contrast in Photoshop using the High Pass filter. It works similarly to Lightroom's Clarity and Dehaze sliders, although you gain a bit more control.

Follow these steps to give it a spin.

1   Select the finished HDR image, and choose Photo > Edit In > Edit In Adobe Photoshop CC or press Ctrl+E/Command+E.

2   Duplicate the background layer by pressing Ctrl+J/Command+J.

3   Choose Filter > Other > High Pass.

    This filter exaggerates contrasting edge details and leaves the rest of the photo alone, which greatly accentuates your subject.

4   In the resulting dialog box, drag the Radius slider all the way to the left, and then drag it to the right until you see the outlines of the objects in your image,

Note: An HDR image can be tone mapped to look realistic or super-realistic. The realistic approach brings out detail but leaves the image looking natural. The superrealistic look emphasizes local contrast and detail, and is either very saturated or undersaturated (for a grungy style). There's no right or wrong here; it's purely subjective.

Tip: If you are interested in exploring how to make realistic and surrealistic HDR images. your author wrote a book on the subject. Go check out *The HDR Book*, second edition.

around 4 pixels in this example. Click OK, and your image will become gray, but we'll fix that in the next step.

5 In the Layers panel, set the layer's blend mode to Soft Light.

6 Keep in mind that although edge contrast looks good on textured details, it looks bad in softer areas, like skies and clouds. Click the Add Layer Mask icon at the bottom of the Layers panel and grab the Brush tool (B). Choose a soft brush in the Brush Preset picker, and set the Foreground color to black, the Opacity to 100%, and the Flow to 15%. Paint over the sky and clouds to mask out some of the effect.

7 Save and close the document in Photoshop to return to Lightroom.

Making panoramas

Panoramic images can give people a feeling of complete immersion into a picture. But, taking panoramic pictures used to require specialized lenses that were wide enough to fit the scene you wanted to capture. Lightroom and Photoshop have made such incredible strides in making panoramic images out of regular-sized images that it borders on magic. Simply take a series of pictures, and let Photoshop take care of the rest.

As with merging to HDR, both Lightroom and Photoshop can stitch multiple images into a panorama. And just as with making an HDR, it's easier to do it in Lightroom, for several reasons.

First and foremost, Lightroom includes a Boundary Warp slider that all but negates the need to crop the resulting panorama due to the spherical distortion necessary to align so many images. Previously, you had to rely on Photoshop to use Content-Aware Fill to avoid cropping, but now more of that can be done in Lightroom.

Second, the resulting file in Lightroom is also a raw file (specifically, a DNG), allowing you to work in the Develop module with a much greater range than you were able to previously. Third, the panorama merge also supports a headless mode.

Finally, the October 2018 release of Lightroom added another tool to its panorama arsenal: you can now make HDR panoramas, making the task of creating individual HDR files and then merging them into a panorama a thing of the past.

Merging to a panorama in Lightroom

In this exercise, you'll stitch four photos together to create a panorama. Happily, it doesn't matter what order the photos are in because Lightroom intelligently analyzes the photos to see how they logically fit together. You can wait to adjust tone and color until after you've merged the images.

▶ **Tip:** When capturing images for a panorama, try to overlap each shot with the preceding one by about 30 percent. Set your camera to manual focus and manual exposure so that those parameters don't change automatically as the camera moves from shot to shot. If possible, use a tripod.

1 Select pano-1.dng through pano-4.dng in the Library module by clicking the first image in the series and Shift-clicking the last image in the series.

2 Right-click one of the thumbnails and choose Photo Merge > Panorama or press Ctrl+M/Control+M.

As with HDR, one of the first things that is apparent is the speed at which the panorama is built. In recent versions of Lightroom, it uses the embedded JPEG images to create your preview. There's nothing more frustrating than waiting a while to see if the panorama is good, only to find out it's a bust.

3   The options in the Panorama Merge Preview dialog box control the layout method Lightroom uses to align the individual images. It's worth taking each method for a spin, although if your pano is really wide (and this example is), Adobe suggests using Cylindrical. If it's a 360-degree or multi-row pano (you took two rows of photos), try Spherical. If it has a lot of lines in it (say, an architectural shot), try Perspective.

In this case, Spherical works well; however, there are white areas all around the image that need to be cropped out or filled in.

4   Drag the Boundary Warp slider to the right until the white areas disappear and your image fills the preview area.

This slider corrects the distortion to such a level that you may never need to crop or fill in the edges of your panorama again. If you decide that you want to crop out the edges, select the Auto Crop option.

5   Click Merge to close the dialog box.

Lightroom merges all four images, and the result is a seamlessly blended panorama of New York City.

◆ **Warning:** If the panorama doesn't immediately appear in the Library module's Grid view or the Filmstrip panel, give it a few seconds. The same goes for merging to HDR.

6   Select the panorama in the Filmstrip (it has the word *pano* in its name), and then use the panels in the Develop module to produce the tone and color that

you want. The merged file is a DNG, so you have all of the tonal benefits of a raw file.

Headless mode for panoramas

Since panoramas take some time to perform their final merge, I tend to use headless mode to speed things up a bit. Hold down the Shift key as you select Photo Merge > Panorama, and the file will skip the Panorama Merge Preview dialog box and render the file in the background.

When the file appears in the Library module, you can select it and perform your finishing touches.

Creating HDR panoramas

With the October 2018 release of Lightroom, you can now create panoramas with a series of HDR images all at once. Previously, you had to merge each bracketed series of exposures into an individual HDR file, and then merge those files into a panorama. Lightroom has automated the entire process and still kept the resulting file as a DNG, letting you tone it with great detail.

Some time ago, I took a series of bracketed exposures (5 stops each) of an old saloon. Because the room was so small and I didn't have a super-wide lens, I took vertical images. We'll let Lightroom do the driving here and see how it does.

1   Select hdr-pano-1.dng through hdr-pano-15.dng in the Library module by clicking the first image in the series and Shift-clicking the last image.

2   Right-click one of the thumbnails and choose Photo Merge > HDR Panorama. With 15 images being merged to HDR and then merged as a panorama, you might expect it to take quite a while, but it's actually faster than you'd think.

In this instance, using the Boundary Warp slider would distort the image too much, so leave it at 0. In Lightroom, use the Develop module's Crop Overlay tool (R) to crop in to create a rectangular frame of the scene instead.

3   The final result is an extremely compelling HDR panorama that I can further tone and pull details from—and it was all done automatically.

Review questions

1 What is the Lightroom menu choice for handing off multiple files from Lightroom to Photoshop to create a multi-layered document in Photoshop?

2 What Photoshop feature would you use to blend textures with photographs?

3 In a layer mask, does black reveal or conceal?

4 What's the advantage of merging multiple exposures into an HDR in Lightroom instead of Photoshop?

5 What's the advantage of merging multiple images into a panorama in Lightroom instead of Photoshop?

6 Is it possible to merge bracketed images into individual HDR files and then merge those files into a panorama in one step?

Review answers

1   Photo > Edit In > Open As Layers In Photoshop hands off multiple files from Lightroom to Photoshop and creates a multi-layered document in Photoshop.

2   Layer blend modes are useful for blending textures with photographs.

3   In a layer mask, black conceals.

4   You have easier access to tone-mapping controls, and you don't end up with an extra PSD in your Lightroom catalog and on your hard drive.

5   You can use Lightroom's Boundary Warp feature to reduce the need to crop or fill in edges due to the distortion necessary for aligning multiple images. You also have easy access to tone-mapping controls, and you don't end up with an extra PSD.

6   Yes, using Photo Merge > HDR Panorama.

11 EXPORTING AND SHOWING OFF YOUR WORK

Lesson overview

When you're finished editing your pictures in Lightroom and Photoshop, it's time to show them off. This is where Lightroom really shines. It offers a variety of options for photos: emailing, exporting, sharing on social media, printing, or crafting them into a custom book, slideshow, or web gallery.

In this lesson, you'll learn how to:

- Set up an identity plate.

- Create a watermark and signature graphic to add to your photos.

- Email or export photos from your Lightroom catalog.

- Create drag-and-drop publish services for exporting and sharing photos on social media sites.

- Create a custom single-photo fine art–style print template.

- Calculate the maximum print size of a photo.

- Get started creating books, slideshows, and web galleries.

 This lesson will take 2 hours to complete. Please log in to your account on peachpit.com to download the files for this lesson, or go to the "Getting Started" section at the beginning of this book and follow the instructions under "Accessing the lesson files and Web Edition." Store the files on your computer in a convenient location. Your Account page is also where you'll find any updates to the lessons or to the lesson files. Look on the Lesson & Update Files tab to access the most current content.

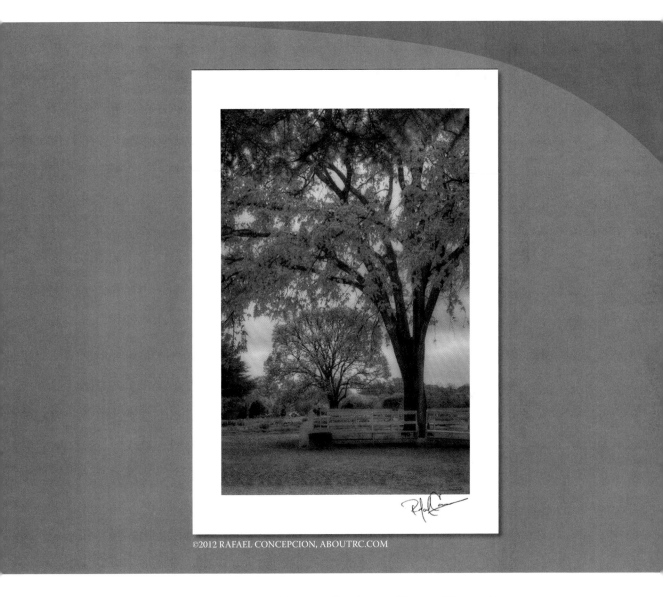

Lightroom excels at showing off your work in a variety of ways and complete with branding, such as the fine art–style print shown here.

Preparing for this lesson

1   Follow the instructions in the "Getting Started" section at the beginning of this book for setting up an LPCIB folder on your computer, downloading the lesson files to that LPCIB folder, and creating an LPCIB catalog in Lightroom.

2   Download the Lesson 11 folder from your Account page at peachpit.com to *username*/Documents/LPCIB/Lessons.

3   Launch Lightroom, and open the LPCIB catalog you created in "Getting Started" by choosing File > Open Catalog and navigating to the LPCIB Catalog. Alternatively, you can choose File > Open Recent > LPCIB Catalog.

4   Add the Lesson 11 files to the LPCIB catalog using the steps in the Lesson 1 section "Importing photos from a hard drive."

5   In the Library module's Folders panel, select Lesson 11.

6   Create a collection called **Lesson 11 Images** and place the images from the Lesson 11 folder in the collection.

7   Set the Sort menu beneath the image preview to File Name.

The next two sections walk you through setting up identity plates—a handy way to personalize or brand your copy of Lightroom and your projects—and watermarks, which you can use throughout the program to brand your images.

Setting up an identity plate

Adobe knows that some photographers use Lightroom in public—say, on a computer in a studio sales room or in a teaching situation. That's why you can personalize the Adobe branding at the upper left of the Lightroom window using its identity plate feature. You can use stylized text, a custom graphic you've made, or both. You can create as many custom identity plates as you want and save them as presets that are accessible in the Book, Slideshow, Print, and Web modules.

In this exercise, you'll create a text-based identity plate.

1 Choose Edit > Identity Plate Setup (Windows) or Lightroom > Identity Plate Setup (macOS). In the dialog box that opens, choose Personalized from the Identity Plate menu at the upper left.

2 Select Use A Styled Text Identity Plate, and enter your name, studio name, or URL into the black field beneath the radio button.

3 Format the text as you would in a word processing program: Highlight the text you want to change, and then use the font, style, and size menus beneath the text field. In this example, Helvetica Nueue Condensed Bold was used for the type. To change the color of all or a portion of the text, highlight it and then click the square gray button to the right of the size menu to open the color picker, and select a new color.

As you format the text, your changes appear in the upper-left corner of the Lightroom window in real time.

On the right side of the dialog box, you can change the font, style, size, and color of the module names to match your new text identity plate.

4 When you're finished, click the Custom menu and choose Save As. Enter a name into the resulting dialog box, and click Save.

From now on, your new identity plate preset will appear in that menu.

5 Click OK to close the Identity Plate Editor.

Now you can access your identity plate in Lightroom's other modules, where you can control its opacity, scale (size), and positioning.

▶ **Tip:** Some photographers prefer to use their signature as a graphical identity plate. The sidebar "Creating a graphic from your signature" explains how to do that.

If you want to go the graphic route instead, create the graphic in Photoshop first. Design it to be no more than 46 pixels (Windows) or 41 pixels (macOS) tall, and then save it in PNG format to preserve any transparency. In the Identity Plate Editor, select the Use A Graphical Identity Plate option and click the Locate File button that appears. Navigate to the file on your hard drive, select it, and click Choose.

In the next section, you'll learn how to create a custom watermark.

Creating a watermark

Note: Just as with identity plates, you can create as many text or graphical watermarks as you want, and they don't always have to be about branding. If you create a watermark that reads PROOF in a thick, bold font, you can use it in the Print module to indicate a photo's status.

One way to let people know who created an image online is to add a watermark—text or a graphic that's placed atop the image, usually at the lower left or right. Watermarking your photos serves not only as a deterrent for would-be thieves, but also as a branding opportunity; by including your URL in the watermark, anyone who sees the image online can easily find you and book a session.

In this exercise, you'll create a simple text-based watermark.

1 Choose Edit > Edit Watermarks (Windows) or Lightroom > Edit Watermarks (macOS). In the dialog box that appears, select Text at the upper right.

2 In the field beneath the image preview, enter your watermark text. You could enter your name or your URL. By default, you will start with a copyright symbol or the word *Copyright*, so place any other information to the right of it.

Tip: To create a copyright symbol in Windows, press Alt+0169. In macOS, press Option+G.

3 Use the settings in the Text Options panel on the right to format your text, and make sure Shadow is selected.

You don't have to highlight your text to format it in this dialog box, which also means you can't format portions of it in different ways. Leaving the shadow selected ensures that the watermark can be read even when it's placed atop a white background. Adjust its sliders until the shadow looks the way you want it.

Tip: To rotate your watermark, click the Rotate buttons to the right of the anchor icon.

4 In the Watermark Effects panel, set Opacity to around 70. Select Proportional in the Size section, and use the slider to set a size (10 was used here). Scoot the watermark away from the edges of the photo by entering **3** into the Horizontal and Vertical fields in the Inset section. Click the lower-right circle in the Anchor icon to position your watermark at the lower right.

The Proportional option instructs Lightroom to resize the watermark so that it looks the same no matter what pixels dimensions you export the photo at.

5 Click Save, and in the New Preset dialog box that appears, enter a descriptive name, such as **RC Watermark Helvetica Neue CB** and click Create.

Lightroom adds the watermark preset to the Custom menu at the upper left.

From this point forward, your watermark preset is available in several places throughout the program, including the Export dialog.

Emailing photos

Emailing photos from your Lightroom catalog is a snap, and you don't have to export them first. Lightroom handles all the resizing and, if necessary, the file format change (say, from raw to JPEG). Here's how to do it:

1   Select a few photos, and choose File > Email Photos.

2   In the resulting dialog box, enter the email address of your recipient(s) into the To field, and then enter something into the Subject field.

3   Use the From menu to pick your email program. If you use web-based email, choose Go To Email Account Manager from the same menu. In the dialog box that appears, click the Add button at the lower left.

Creating a graphic from your signature

Adding your own signature as a Lightroom identity plate or watermark is incredibly handy and fairly easy to do. If you add it as an identity plate, you can use it in other places in the program—to, say, autograph a fine art–style print, which you'll learn about later in this lesson.

Begin by signing a white piece of paper with a thin black marker. Scan or take a picture of your signature, and then open the graphic in Photoshop. In the Layers panel, click the padlock to unlock the layer, click the Add a Layer Style (fx) icon at the bottom of the panel, and choose Blending Options from the menu.

In the Blend If section of the dialog box that opens, drag the right triangle on the This Layer slider to the left until the signature's white background becomes transparent (as shown below).

Click OK, and save the file in Photoshop format (PSD) so you can edit it later if necessary.

To save a transparent version that you can use in Lightroom, choose File > Save As, and choose PNG as the format. Click OK in the PNG Options dialog box that appears. In Lightroom, use the Identity Plate Editor or Watermark Editor as described in the previous sections to add the graphic.

In the New Account dialog box, name your account preset and choose your service provider from that menu. If you are using one of the providers in the menu, your server settings will be added for you. If you choose Other, you will need to add your server settings. With all choices, you will need to provide your login information and click Validate, and then click Done.

You have to set this up only once. After that, it will show up in the From menu.

4   From the Preset menu at the lower left, pick a size, and then click Send.

Lightroom prepares the photos for emailing, opens your email program, and prepares a new message with the photos attached.

5   If your email program includes a resize option, choose Actual Size (or something similar), and then send the email on its way.

Exporting photos

When you're finished adjusting your photos and adding effects, you can free them from your Lightroom catalog using the Export command. This command generates a copy of the photo(s) with all your edits intact. The Export dialog also lets you rename, resize, change the file format of (say, from raw to JPEG), sharpen, and add a watermark to your photos en masse. Exporting is also a background operation, meaning you don't have to wait until Lightroom is finished exporting your photos to do something else, including triggering another export.

In this exercise, you'll export a batch of photos destined for online use at specific settings that you'll save as an export preset.

1   In the Collections panel of the Library module, make sure the Lesson 11 collection is highlighted and then, in Grid view, select several thumbnails—it doesn't

● **Note:** The Export command is available in all of Lightroom's modules. For example, to export from the Develop module, select one or more images in the Filmstrip and choose File > Export.

matter which ones you pick. Choose File > Export, or click the Export button at the bottom left of the Library module.

Lightroom opens the Export dialog box. The Preset column on the left includes some handy built-in combinations of Export settings, along with any export presets you create. There's no limit to the number of files you can export at one time.

2   Click the Export To menu at the top of the Export dialog, and choose Hard Drive.

3   Expand the Export Location area of the dialog box by clicking its title bar and choose Export To > Desktop at the top. Select Put In Subfolder, and enter **Final Images for Client** in the field to its right. Leave Add To This Catalog unselected. Ensure that the Existing Files menu is set to Ask What To Do.

When working with your own photos, you may want to set the destination to Specific Folder or Same Folder As Original Photo instead of Desktop, but you still may want to name the subfolder **Final Images for Client** or something else that makes sense in your workflow.

Selecting Add To This Catalog automatically imports the exported copy into your Lightroom catalog, which is unnecessary because the master file is already in your catalog, from which you can always output another copy.

4   Under File Naming, select Rename To and pick the filename convention you want to use from the menu to its right.

The Rename To menu lets you access the filenaming template system in Lightroom's External Editing preferences.

Note: Lightroom can't export a photo in PNG format, but Photoshop can. In fact, you learned how to do that in the Lesson 7 section, "Creating curved selections" and in the Lesson 8 section "Creating a social media cover photo."

If you upload the exported photos online, replace any spaces with an underscore. In this example, the Custom Name - Sequence template was chosen, with **rc_finals** entered for the Custom Text, and the Start Number set to **1**.

5   In the File Settings area, choose JPEG from the Image Format menu, set Quality to 80, and choose sRGB from the Color Space menu.

When working with your own photos, set the quality to 100 if you'll submit them to an online stock photography service or upload them to an online lab for printing, or if you're preparing final, print-worthy JPEGs to give to your client. Doing so produces a file at the highest possible quality, although it'll also be huge in file size. Dropping the quality to 80, which is fine for almost all uses that don't involve printing, cuts the size in half.

Tip: The Limit File Size To field is handy for limiting the resulting file size of your exported photo for, say, a website limitation. Select the option, and then enter your maximum size in kilobytes.

The Internet-standard color space is sRGB, and it's the one used by most online printing labs (check with the lab to determine which color space to use). Exporting with one of the other, larger color spaces can cause a photo to look dull when viewed online.

6 In the Image Sizing area, leave Resize To Fit unselected. If you are exporting these photos for use online, you'll use this to ensure your images fit and that the site you're uploading to won't do the resizing for you. In that case, you'll choose Long Edge from the menu to the right, set the measurement field menu to Pixels (the best choice for images bound for the web), and enter the maximum size you want your images to be on the longest edge, whether that's height or width. Leave the Resolution field at its current value.

If you're preparing photos for print, preserve the photo's pixel count by leaving Resize To Fit turned off. Enter the image resolution that's best for your printer—240 pixels per inch (ppi) is adequate for most desktop inkjet printers and online printing labs. If you're preparing photos for inclusion in *National Geographic* magazine, ask what resolution is best to use. When you're exporting images for online use, resolution doesn't matter, because resolution here refers to the number of pixels per printed inch.

7 Under Output Sharpening, leave Sharpen For unselected.

When you resize a photo, it becomes a little less sharp, so extra sharpening is a good thing. However, this is an *extra* round of sharpening that's added on top of any input or creative sharpening you've done in Lightroom (or Photoshop, for that matter).

If you are planning to use these photos online, choose Screen from the Sharpen For menu and set the Amount menu to Standard.

8 In the Metadata area, choose Copyright & Contact Info Only from the Include menu.

⬤ **Note:** Copyright information is embedded in the metadata of the exported file, but it does not appear across the face of the photo like a watermark does.

9 In the Watermarking area, select Watermark, and from the menu to its right, choose the watermark you made earlier in this lesson. Lightroom adds your watermark to the face of each photo you export.

When preparing images for a real client, you'll likely leave this section turned off.

10 Under Post-Processing, choose Do Nothing.

If you want Lightroom to open the location of the exported files in your operating system when the export is complete, choose Show in Explorer/Show in Finder instead.

11 Click Add at the bottom of the Preset column.

12 In the New Preset dialog box, enter a descriptive name, such as **JPEG 80 sRGB CC**, choose User Presets from the Folder menu, and click Create.

● **Note:** This excellent preset naming convention was suggested by Adobe's Principal Evangelist, Julieanne Kost (blogs.adobe.com/jkost).

This saves the combination of settings you made as a preset that you can use in the future. The preset's descriptive name lets you know at a glance what file format, quality, color space, and metadata (copyright contact) you used.

To export other photos using this preset, click the preset's name in the User Presets section of the Export dialog, or choose File > Export With Preset, and then pick the preset you want to use.

13 Click Export at the bottom of the Export dialog. In no time flat, Lightroom exports a JPEG copy of the photos to the destination you picked in step 3.

Lightroom remembers the export settings you last used even after you quit and relaunch the program. So if you forgot to include one or more photos in the export, you can quickly export them with the same settings by selecting the new files and choosing File> Export With Previous. You don't get a dialog box with this method; Lightroom immediately exports the photos and adds them to the same location you used last time.

Exporting and sharing using publish services

If you regularly prepare images for other destinations—to, say, send to a printer, feature on your website, or submit to a stock photography service—or if you regularly upload them to social media sites such as Flickr, you can automate the process using the Lightroom drag-and-drop export presets known as *publish services*. In the Publish Services panel in the Library module, you see that it already includes presets for Hard Drive, Adobe Stock, Facebook, and Flickr, although you can download more by clicking the Find More Services Online button.

To set up one of these presets, click the publish service button you want to use— Hard Drive, Adobe Stock, or Flickr (see the note here for more information about Facebook). In the dialog box that appears, you see the same Export settings you learned about in the previous section; however, the dialog box for Flickr includes an area for you to enter your account information.

Note: You can no longer upload photos to Facebook from Lightroom desktop apps— Lightroom CC (new), Lightroom Classic CC, and Lightroom CC 2015/ Lightroom 6—as of August 1, 2018. If you have images that are synced with Facebook currently, go to the following page to learn how to move them permanently to your personal repository: https://helpx.adobe. com/lightroom/kb/ facebook-publish- service-error.html

When you're finished entering all the settings, the new preset appears beneath the service button. Simply drag the photo(s) you want to export (or upload) atop the new preset, named Photostream here, which puts them into an export queue. When you've added all the photos you want to publish, click the preset in the Publish Services panel to see the photos it includes, and then click the Publish button beneath the Publish Services panel or the one that appears above and to the upper right of the thumbnails.

Lightroom publishes the photos at the settings you entered. If you then make changes to a published photo, Lightroom marks it as modified—click the preset to view its contents, and the photo you edited appears in a section named Modified. To publish the modified version, click Publish. If you don't want to update it, right-click it and choose Mark As Up-To-Date in the menu.

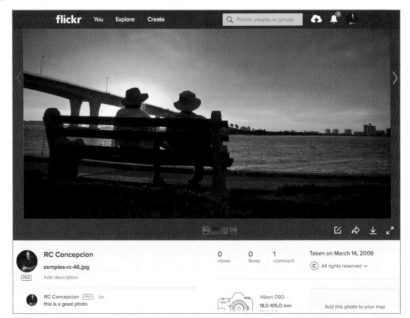

If the social media platform allows commenting by visitors, those comments appear in Lightroom too. Take a look at the Comments panel at the bottom right of the Library module (it's beneath the Metadata panel) to see them. To update it with the newest comments, click the Refresh Comments icon in the upper-left corner of the panel.

Creating prints

Lightroom's Print module is very powerful; you can use it to print a single photo per page or several per page. It also includes many useful template presets for printing your photos, although you can create your own. Lightroom also gives you the choice of sending a file to your own printer or saving the print as a JPEG that you can email to a local printer or upload to one online.

● **Note:** Saving a print as a JPEG is handy for posting online or emailing to a client. For example, you could create a multi-photo template that you use on social media or your blog. Although you could use this feature to make a social media cover photo, adding text is far easier in Photoshop, where you can also save the result as a PNG, which keeps text crisper than a JPEG.

In this exercise, you'll learn how to print a single photo and add your signature identity plate, for the look of a signed print.

1   Select a photo in the Library module, and then click the Print module button at the top of the workspace (or press Ctrl+P/Command+P).

    You're going to create your own print template, but there also is a Template Browser panel here with a number of common and creative layouts.

2   Click the Page Setup button at the lower left, and in the resulting dialog box, choose your printer and paper size. Click OK.

3 Back in Lightroom, locate the Layout Style panel at the upper right, and click Single Image/Contact Sheet to print one photo.

4 In the Image Settings panel, make sure all the options are unselected.

▶ **Tip:** You can also point your cursor at the edges of the photo—when it turns into a double-sided arrow, drag to adjust the margins.

5 In the Layout panel, leave the Margins and Page Grid settings at their default values. Use the Cell Size slider to adjust the size of the photo on the page, or simply enter the size you want in the fields to the right of the sliders. Depending on the photo you're working with, you may need to alter these dimensions.

If you use the Cell Size section to control photo size, Lightroom calculates the margins for you. Alternatively, you can adjust the margin sliders to create the size you want.

6 In the Page panel, select Identity Plate. Click within the

preview area beneath the checkbox, and from the menu that appears, choose the identity plate you want to use. The identity plate appears atop the photo.

7 Drag the identity plate into the desired position, and then use the Opacity and Scale sliders in the Page panel to make it look the way you want.

8 In the Print Job panel, choose Printer from the Print To menu. Deselect Draft Mode Printing (it's low quality), and then deselect Print Resolution. From the Print Sharpening menu, choose Standard, and choose Matte from the Media Type menu. If you're printing a raw format photo, turn on 16 Bit Output (macOS only).

As mentioned, you can send a print to your printer or save it as a JPEG file. When you deselect Printer Resolution, Lightroom calculates the resolution based on the printer you chose, the photo's original size, and the desired size of your print.

9 In the Color Management area, choose Other from the Profile menu. In the dialog box that appears, select the profile that matches the paper you chose in step 2, and then click OK.

10 Click Print, and your printer springs into action.

If you click the Printer button instead, you open your printer's print dialog again.

Note: A print profile is a mathematical description of a device's color space. For more on color spaces, see the Lesson 6 sidebar "Choosing a color space."

11 Save these settings as a preset by clicking the plus icon (+) at the upper right of the Template Browser panel on the left side of the workspace. In the dialog box that opens, enter a descriptive name such as **15.75 x 11 in print on 13 x 19 paper**, and click Create.

The new template appears in the User Templates section at the bottom of the Template Browser panel.

If you want to use this template again with the same photo, click the Create Saved Print button at the upper right of the print preview.

● **Note:** Make sure you check out the accompanying videos for this lesson, where I cover printer profiles and show you the entire print process from start to finish. You can access those lessons by following the instructions in the "Gettting Started" section at the beginning of this book.

That's all there is to printing one photo per page. If you want to print a contact sheet, where multiple thumbnails are arranged in a grid, select a slew of images and, in the Print module, choose Single Image/Contact Sheet, and then use the Page Grid section of the Layout panel to add more rows and columns.

When you have time, use the exercise files to experiment with other templates in the Template Browser. Be aware that if you pick a template that includes the word *custom* in its name—meaning its layout style is Custom Package, as noted in the Layout panel—you can drag and drop photos from the Filmstrip into the black-outlined photo slots in the layout preview.

Calculating maximum print size

Before you make a print, it's a good idea to calculate the maximum print size that you can make from the photo. For example, you may not have enough pixels to create, say, a 13 × 19-inch print. If you go forth without calculating your maximum print size first, you may not be satisfied with the results.

The first step in calculating your maximum print size is to find the photo's pixel dimensions and jot them down. In Lightroom, the dimensions are visible in the Library module in the Metadata panel.

Next, grab a calculator and divide the longest edge of your image (measured in pixels) by the longest edge of your desired print size (measured in inches). For example, if an image measures 3840 × 5760 pixels and you want an 8 × 10 print, take the longest edge in pixels and divide it by the longest edge in inches of the target print size: 5760 pixels divided by 10 inches = 576 ppi. That's more than enough resolution to produce an awesome print; remember that you need a *minimum* of 240 ppi, though it really depends on the printer (resolution determines pixel density and thus pixel size when the image is printed). However, if you want to make a 30 × 20-inch poster out of that image, you'd have a resolution of 192 ppi (5760 ÷ 30), which isn't high enough to print well.

Since big prints aren't cheap, you'll wisely decide on a smaller size and you'll be more satisfied with the results. And if you typically shoot with the same camera, you only have to do this calculation once to know how big you can go.

The benefits of soft proofing

Wouldn't it be great if you could see what a photo will look like before you print it on a certain kind of paper or post it online? As it turns out, Lightroom can simulate the result through *soft proofing*. Doing so gives you the opportunity to adjust the photo's tone and color for the particular profile you're using.

1 Open the photo in the Develop module, and click the down-pointing triangle to the right of the toolbar beneath the image preview (if you don't see the toolbar, press T on your keyboard).

2 From the menu that appears, choose Soft Proofing, and then select Soft Proofing in the toolbar.

3 In the Soft Proofing panel that appears at the upper right of the workspace, click the menu to the right of the word Profile. If you're posting the photo online, choose sRGB. Otherwise, choose Other.

4 In the dialog that appears, select the appropriate profile for the printer and paper you're using and click OK. (If you're sending a photo to an online lab for printing, they often have profiles you can download for this use.)

5 To the right of Intent in the panel, click Perceptual, and then, if you're printing the photo, select Simulate Paper & Ink (this option isn't available for all profiles).

6 To see if your photo includes colors that are outside your monitor's or printer's gamut (range of colors), click the tiny icons at the upper left and upper right of the histogram in the Soft Proofing panel. When you do, colors outside your monitor's gamut appear in blue, and those outside your printer's gamut appear in red; colors outside both appear in pink.

7 To edit a photo specifically for the destination profile, either to make it look better or to clear the gamut warnings, click Create Proof Copy, and Lightroom makes a virtual copy (shortcut/alias) of the photo. If you start editing the photo without clicking that button, Lightroom politely asks if you'd like it to make a copy for you.

To populate other template styles, such as Single Image/Contact Sheet or Picture Package, activate photos in the Filmstrip to make them appear in the layout preview—otherwise, it'll be empty. For example, if a template has three slots, select three photos in the Filmstrip by Ctrl-clicking/Command-clicking or Shift-clicking them. If you deactivate a photo in the Filmstrip, Lightroom empties that slot in the layout preview.

To rearrange the order of photos in the layout preview, you must drag to rearrange them in the Filmstrip. This may feel a little strange at first, but you'll get the hang of it soon enough. (Alternatively, you can have Lightroom automatically fill template slots by choosing All Filmstrip Photos from the Use menu beneath the layout preview.) You can also add pick flags to the photos in the selected collection that you want to print, and then choose Flagged Photos from the Use menu.

Books, slideshows, and web galleries

Alas, detailed information on creating books, slideshows, and web galleries is beyond the scope of this book. But this section still has useful tips for you.

Book, slideshow, and web gallery projects should start in the same way: Create a collection for the purpose of the project (you can use the finals collection you made at the beginning of this lesson to practice). Use the collection to drag the photos into the order in which you want them to appear in the project, and then consider whether you want to add text (think captions) to those projects. If the answer is yes, use the Metadata panel in the Library module to add text to the Title or Caption fields before you jump into one of Lightroom's project modules.

When you're finished, click the collection in the Collections panel to select all the photos it contains (there will be white borders around all the thumbnails), and then click the button—Book, Slideshow, Web—for the module you want to work in.

▶ **Tip:** If you're in the Library or Develop module, you can trigger a full-screen, impromptu slideshow of the photos you're viewing without using the Slideshow module. To do that, click the down-pointing triangle to the far right of the toolbar below the image preview (press T on your keyboard to show the toolbar if it's hidden). In the menu that appears, choose Slideshow, and a play button appears in the toolbar.

Lightroom creates the project and autofills the default template, which you can change. In the Slideshow and Web modules, you can choose a different template to start with in the Template Browser panel on the left. In all three modules, use the panels on the right to format the project to your liking.

If you took the time to add captions or titles in the Library module, you need to know how to access them. In the Book module, select a page in your project, and in the Text panel on the right, select Photo Text and choose Caption or Title from the Custom Text menu. In the Slideshow module, select Text Overlays at the bottom of the Overlays panel, and then click the ABC button in the toolbar (press T if you don't see the toolbar). From the Custom Text menu that appears, choose Caption or Title. In the Web module, select Caption in the Image Info panel, and choose Caption or Title from the menu to its right.

The identity plates or watermarks you created earlier in this lesson are available in the Slideshow module's Overlays panel and the Web module's Site Info and Output Settings panels.

To add a graphical logo to the book, import it into your Lightroom catalog and drag it into the same collection as your book. Then, treat it like any other photo: Drag it from the Filmstrip onto the page you want to use it on, and use the panels on the right to control size and opacity.

Books can be ordered through Blurb.com from inside Lightroom; the price calculates as you build the book. Books can also be saved as a PDF or a series of JPEGs. Slideshows can be exported as a video or a PDF. Web galleries can be exported to your hard drive or uploaded directly to your web server.

To save any project with a certain set of photos that you can work on later, click the Create Saved Book, Create Saved Slideshow, or Create Saved Web Gallery button that appears at the upper right of the workspace.

Next steps

Now that you know how Lightroom and Photoshop work together, and when you should use one program over the other, you can apply everything you've learned in this book to your own workflow. Practice on the exercise files until you're comfortable with the techniques presented in this book—each technique was chosen very carefully in order to give you a practical and firm foundation in both programs.

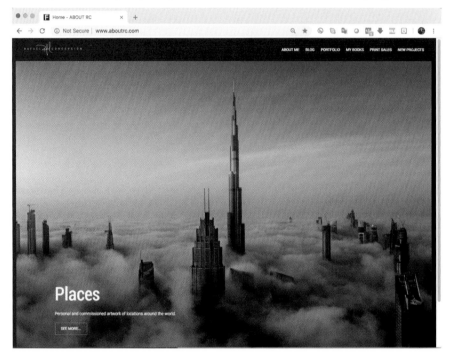

If you have any questions, please feel free to email me at rc@aboutrc.com or connect with me at Facebook.com/aboutrc.

When you are ready to learn more or want to dig deeper, please check out the other books in the Adobe Classroom in a Book series, including my upcoming book *Adobe Photoshop Lightroom Classic CC Classroom in a Book, 2019 release*.

Finally, if you find yourself by Syracuse University, please feel free to stop by Newhouse College. I'd be happy to take you on a tour to show how our future creatives are using Lightroom and Photoshop to share their unique world view.

Thanks for learning with me. I can't wait to see what you make next!

Review questions

1 How is an identity plate used?

2 Do you have to wait until the export process is finished before doing other things in Lightroom?

3 Can you add your signature to a print made in Lightroom?

4 How do you add captions to photos in book, slideshow, print, and web projects?

Review answers

1 It can be used to add your name or logo to the Lightroom workspace, as well as to add your name, logo, signature, or other text to slideshows, prints, and websites created in Lightroom.

2 No. The export process happens in the background, so you can keep working.

3 Yes. To do that, digitize your signature and save it as a custom identity plate, which you can access in the Print module.

4 The easiest way to add captions that you can access in other modules is to enter text into the Title or Caption field in the Metadata panel in the Library module.

INDEX

marquee tools, cycling between, 175

mask overlay colors, cycling through, 132. *See also* colors

Masking slider, Detail panel, 82

masks. *See also* gradient masks; Select And Mask workspace; vector masks
    dragging to layers, 260
    inverting, 291
    tightening, 194

matting and fringing, 194

Maximize Compatibility preference, Photoshop, 150–151

memory cards, importing photos, 21–23

merging layers, 228, 281

Metadata
    menu, 27
    panel, 34, 322

Minimal and Embedded & Sidecar options, 29

Minimum filter, 194

Mixer Brush tool, 245–248

motion
    adding to skies, 255–257
    adding to subjects, 257–261

N

Navigator panel, Library module, 31

.NEF files, 153, 163

negative Clarity adjustments, 113

Neutral color profile, 70

Noise Reduction, 83–84

O

objects
    removing and repositioning, 11
    removing from photos, 111
    removing with Patch tool, 210–215

Oil Paint filter, 246

online posts, saving JPEGs for, 317

opacity
    changing, 274
    changing for adjustments, 131
    vs. flow, 230
    reducing, 198

output sharpening, 83

outputting images, 10

Overlay view, Select And Mask workspace, 195

P

Panel switch, 100

panels
    collapsing and expanding, 30
    hiding, 35–36

Information, 33–35

resetting locations, 221

Solo mode, 37, 67

Source, 31–33

toggling adjustments, 68

panorama stitching, Lightroom, 9

panoramas, making, 297–301

panoramic image, creating canvas, 289

Paste Special command, 176, 180

Patch tool, Photoshop, 210–215

Path Blur, 257–261

paths
    creating, 182
    loading as selections, 180
    moving, 179

Pen tool, 178–185

perspective corrections, 87

Photo > Edit In menu, accessing, 154

photo adjustments, making globally, 9

photo books, Lightroom, 10

photo management, Lightroom, 7

photos. *See also* documents; fading photos together; files; images; pictures
    accessing in Develop module, 67
    combining, 10–11, 287–292
    emailing, 309, 311
    exporting, 311–315
    importing from hard drive, 26–30
    importing into catalogs, 20–30
    opening, 175
    processing, 10
    removing from selections, 40
    renaming, 40–41
    reordering in layout preview, 321
    resizing, 176, 187
    Select All, 41
    sending as Smart Objects, 163–168
    sending to Lightroom, 155–156
    syncing changes, 90–92

Photoshop. *See also* Lightroom–Photoshop integration
    applying filters, 165
    body sculpting, 225–226, 228
    Clone Stamp tool, 208–210
    color settings, 149–150
    Content-Aware Fill, 215–221
    Content-Aware Scale command, 222–225
    Content-Aware technologies, 12
    defaults for tools, 186
    desaturating images, 273
    exaggerating edge contrast, 295–296
    Healing Brush tool, 205–208
    High Pass filter, 228–232
    installing, 4

Contributors

Rafael "RC" Concepcion is an award-winning photographer, podcast host, and educator, and the author of six best-selling books on photography, Photoshop, Lightroom, and HDR. He is digital post-production specialist and adjunct professor at the S.I. Newhouse School for Visual Communications at Syracuse University.

He is an Adobe Certified Instructor in Photoshop, Illustrator, and Lightroom, and worked with Adobe to write the Adobe Certified Expert exam for Photoshop CS6, Lightroom 4, and Lightroom 5. RC has more than 20 years of experience producing content in the creative, IT, and e-commerce industries. He has presented at seminars and workshops around the world. RC's production company, First Shot School, creates educational content and video productions for clients such as Intel, Dell, Epson, Nikon, Canon, Samsung, Nokia, Sandisk, Western Digital, G-Technology, Google, and Creative Live.

Production notes

Adobe® Photoshop® CC and Lightroom® CC for Photographers Classroom in a Book®, Second Edition was created electronically using Adobe InDesign CC. Art was produced using Adobe InDesign, Adobe Illustrator, and Adobe Photoshop. The Myriad Pro and Warnock Pro OpenType families of typefaces were used throughout this book. For information about OpenType and Adobe fonts, visit www.adobe.com/type/opentype/.

References to company names in the lessons are for demonstration purposes only and are not intended to refer to any actual organization or person.

Images

Photographic images and illustrations are intended for use with the tutorials.

Typefaces used

Adobe Myriad Pro and Adobe Warnock Pro are used throughout this book. For more information about OpenType and Adobe fonts, visit www.adobe.com/type/opentype/.

Team credits

The following individuals contributed to the development of this edition of the *Adobe Photoshop CC and Lightroom CC for Photographers Classroom in a Book, Second Edition:*

Writer: Rafael "RC" Concepcion

Compositor: Cindy Snyder

Copyeditor and Technical Editor: Cindy Snyder

Proofreader: Scout Festa

Indexer: Valerie Haynes Perry

Keystroker: Megan Ahearn

Cover design: Eddie Yuen

Interior design: Mimi Heft

Adobe Press Executive Editor: Laura Norman

Adobe Press Production Editor: Tracey Croom

Special Thanks

This book would not have been possible without the help, guidance, and support of some truly amazing people: Cristela, Jennifer, and Sabine Concepcion, Latanya and Linwood Henry, Alvaro Misericordia, Ken and Elyse Falk, Kim and Denise Patti, Cindy Snyder, Meredith Payne Stotzner at Adobe Systems, Albert J. Fudger, Ladislav and Monika Soukup, and Karyn and Michael Allard. To my team at the S.I. Newhouse School of Public Communications at Syracuse University: Bruce and Claudia Strong, Dean Lorraine Branham, Dean Amy Falkner, Michael Davis, Hal Silverman, David Sutherland, Renée Stevens, Sherri Taylor, Seth Gitner, Ken Harper, Soo Yeon Hong, OIivia Stomski, Stanley Bondy, Donna Till, and Christi MacClurg. Thank you for all of your help and support.

This book is dedicated to Gregory Heisler. Gregory started as an inspiration, a legendary photographer, became a mentor, and finally—my most cherished moment—became my friend.

The fastest, easiest, most comprehensive way to learn
Adobe Creative Cloud

Classroom in a Book®, the best-selling series of hands-on software training books, helps you learn the features of Adobe software quickly and easily.

The **Classroom in a Book** series offers what no other book or training program does—an official training series from Adobe Systems, developed with the support of Adobe product experts.

To see a complete list of our Classroom in a Book titles covering the 2019 release of Adobe Creative Cloud go to: www.adobepress.com/cc2019

Adobe Photoshop CC Classroom in a Book (2019 release)
ISBN: 9780135261781

Adobe Illustrator CC Classroom in a Book (2019 release)
ISBN: 9780135262160

Adobe InDesign CC Classroom in a Book (2019 release)
ISBN: 9780135262153

Adobe Dreamweaver CC Classroom in a Book (2019 release)
ISBN: 9780135262146

Adobe Premiere Pro CC Classroom in a Book (2019 release)
ISBN: 9780135298893

Adobe Dimension CC Classroom in a Book (2019 release)
ISBN: 9780134863542

Adobe Audition CC Classroom in a Book, Second edition
ISBN: 9780135228326

Adobe After Effects CC Classroom in a Book (2019 release)
ISBN: 9780135298640

Adobe Animate CC Classroom in a Book (2019 release)
ISBN: 9780135298886

Adobe Lightroom CC Classroom in a Book (2019 release)
ISBN: 9780135298657

Adobe Photoshop Elements Classroom in a Book (2019 release)
ISBN: 9780135298657

Adobe**Press**